Sources of
World Societies

VOLUME I: TO 1715

D0953909

Sources of
World Societies

VOLUME I: TO 1715

Walter D. Ward
GEORGIA STATE UNIVERSITY

Carol L. White
GEORGIA STATE UNIVERSITY

BEDFORD/ST. MARTIN'S   BOSTON ◆ NEW YORK

For Bedford/St. Martin's

Publisher for History: Mary Dougherty
Director of Development for History: Jane Knetzger
Executive Editor for History: Traci Mueller
Associate Editor for History: Lynn Sternberger
Assistant Production Manager: Joe Ford
Production Supervisor: Samuel Jones
Executive Marketing Manager: Jenna Bookin Barry
Project Management: DeMasi Design and Publishing Service
Cover Design: Sara Gates
Cover Art: *Portrait of Yintang, Prince Yi, Looking through a Window*. China, Qing dynasty, 18th century. Hanging scroll. Ink and color on silk. Arthur M. Sackler Gallery, Smithsonian Institution, Washington, D.C. Purchase from Smithsonian Collections Acquisition Program, and partial gift of Richard G. Pritzlaff, S1991.64. *Islamic Scholar*, late 17th century C.E. Indian miniature, 10.6 cm × 6.7 cm. Inv. 4601, fol. 37. Museum fuer Islamisce Kunst, Staatliche Museen zu Berlin, Berlin, Germany/Bildarchiv Preussischer Kulturbesitz/Art Resource, NY.
Composition: Jeff Miller Book Design
Printing and Binding: RR Donnelley & Sons Company

President: Joan E. Feinberg
Editorial Director: Denise B. Wydra
Director of Marketing: Karen R. Soeltz
Director of Editing, Design, and Production: Marcia Cohen
Assistant Director of Editing, Design, and Production: Elise S. Kaiser
Manager, Publishing Services: Emily Berleth

Manufactured in the United States of America.

4 3 2 1 0 9
f e d c b a

For information, write: Bedford/St. Martin's, 75 Arlington Street, Boston, MA 02116 (617-399-4000)

ISBN-10: 0-312-68857-1
ISBN-13: 978-0-312-68857-8

Acknowledgments
Acknowledgments and copyrights are continued at the back of the book on pages 253–256, which constitute an extension of the copyright page.

Sources of World Societies is a compilation of primary sources recorded by those who shaped and experienced the cultural evolutions and interactions that comprise the world's history from ancient times to the present — among them rulers and subjects alike, men and women, philosophers, revolutionaries, economists, and laborers. With a parallel chapter structure and documents hand-picked to further illustrate elements of the text, this reader is designed to complement *A History of World Societies*, eighth edition. *Sources of World Societies* aspires to animate the past for students, providing resonant accounts of the people and events that changed the face of world history, from myths of creation to tallies of the spoils and fatalities of war.

While a good textbook creates a clear framework of major historical figures and movements, *Sources* evokes the experiences of historical moments as they were lived and creates a dynamic connection for students that bridges the events of the past with their own understandings of power and its abuses, of the ripple effects of human agency, and of the material conditions of life. For example, Chapter 15 of the textbook provides a personal history of Zheng He, commander of the Chinese Emperor Yongle's massive treasure fleet, and describes the political and commercial impact of his seven voyages. In *Sources*, Zheng He's own words convey the majesty of his expeditions as no other narrative can. Of the fleet and its missions he inscribes, "We have traversed more than one hundred thousand li of immense water spaces and have beheld in the ocean huge waves like mountains rising sky-high . . . traversing those savage waves as if we were treading a public thoroughfare."

With input from the textbook authors, as well as from current instructors of the world history survey course, we have compiled these documents with one goal foremost in mind: to make history's most classic and compelling voices accessible to students, from the most well-known thinkers and documentarians of their times to the galvanized or introspective commoners. In Chapter 28, for example, official government documents, newspaper editorials, and a personal letter depict in sharp relief numerous nationalist movements fermenting in Asia in the early twentieth century. Students can follow the evolutionary course of the British government's 1917 Balfour Declaration supporting the creation of a Jewish homeland, then contrast their conception of British imperial power with feminist nationalist Sarojini Naidu's outrage over the violence of British troops in India just two years later.

We have stepped back from drawing conclusions and instead provide just enough background to enable students' own analysis of the sources at hand. Chapter-opening paragraphs briefly review the major events of the time and place the documents that follow within the framework of the corresponding textbook chapter. A concise headnote for each document provides context about the author and the circumstances surrounding the document's creation, while gloss notes supply clarification to aid comprehension of unfamiliar terms and references. Each document is followed by Reading and Discussion Questions that spur deep student analysis of the material, while chapter-concluding Comparative Questions encourage students to contemplate the harmony and discord among the sources within and, when called for, between the chapters. The excerpts range widely in length to allow for a variety of class assignments.

ACKNOWLEDGMENTS

For their availability and insight, many thanks to *History of World Societies* authors John P. McKay, John Buckler, Clare Crowston, Patricia Ebrey, and Roger Beck, who went above and beyond to help us select and gather these sources despite full teaching and research schedules. Editor Shannon Hunt gave her time and expertise throughout, and this book would not have reached fruition without her hard work. Thanks to Lynn Sternberger for her wonderful insights and razor-sharp editor's pencil, and to Jane Knetzger and Heidi Hood for their support and encouragement. Sara Wise shepherded this project along from its very early stages. Emily Berleth of Bedford St. Martin's and Linda DeMasi of DeMasi Design made production of this book possible with remarkable finesse. Thanks also to C. Melissa Anderson for her thoughtful comments on wording and content.

CONTENTS

10 Civilizations of the Americas

11 Central and Southern Asia to 1400   153

12 East Asia ca. 800–1400   165

13 Europe in the Middle Ages 850–1400   183

Sources of
World Societies

VOLUME I: TO 1715

CHAPTER 1

Early Civilization in Afroeurasia

to 450 B.C.E.

With the development of agriculture and animal husbandry in the Neolithic period (ca. 7000–3000 B.C.E.), humans began to construct more complex societies that required systems of organization and communication. Around 3000 B.C.E., the Sumerians in Mesopotamia invented writing for administrative purposes. Early writing was cumbersome and limited to an elite group of scribes, but as writing became less complex, more people learned to read and write. Although literacy was still restricted to the priests and elite members of society, this larger audience prompted the recording of cultural, political, and religious documents such as myths, laws, scriptures, imperial propaganda, poems, and personal letters. Ancient Egyptians developed writing soon after the Sumerians, possibly after seeing how it was used in Mesopotamia. All successive civilizations in the Near East, such as the Hebrews, Assyrians, and Phoenicians, followed with written forms of their own languages.

DOCUMENT 1-1

From The Epic of Gilgamesh

ca. 2700–2500 B.C.E.

The exact composition date of The Epic of Gilgamesh *is unknown, but the legendary king Gilgamesh probably ruled the city of Uruk around 2700 B.C.E. While the core of the poem had been written by 2000 B.C.E., each successive culture in Mesopotamia added to or altered elements of the story to incorporate their own myths. The epic recounts the friendship of Gilgamesh and the warrior Enkidu and their various adventures in Mesopotamia and*

The Epic of Gilgamesh, 3d ed., trans. N. K. Sanders, Penguin Classics (Baltimore: Penguin, 1972). Copyright © N. K. Sanders, 1960, 1964, 1972.

the Near East. A fire in the seventh century B.C.E. destroyed the library of Nineveh in ancient Assyria but clay tablets bearing the standard text of the Epic survived and they were later excavated from the library's ruins.

As Enkidu slept alone in his sickness, in bitterness of spirit he poured out his heart to his friend. "It was I who cut down the cedar,[1] I who leveled the forest, I who slew Humbaba[2] and now see what has become of me. Listen, my friend, this is the dream I dreamed last night. The heavens roared, and earth rumbled back an answer; between them stood I before an awful being, the somber-faced manbird; he had directed on me his purpose. His was a vampire face, his foot was a lion's foot, his hand was an eagle's talon. He fell on me and his claws were in my hair, he held me fast and I smothered; then he transformed me so that my arms became wings covered with feathers. He turned his stare towards me, and he led me away to the palace of Irkalla, the Queen of Darkness [Goddess of the underworld], to the house from which none who enters ever returns, down the road from which there is no coming back.

"There is the house whose people sit in darkness; dust is their food and clay their meat. They are clothed like birds with wings for covering, they see no light, they sit in darkness. I entered the house of dust and I saw the kings of the earth, their crowns put away forever; rulers and princes, all those who once wore kingly crowns and ruled the world in the days of old. They who had stood in the place of the gods like Anu [King of the gods] and Enlil,[3] stood now like servants to fetch baked meats in the house of dust, to carry cooked meat and cold water from the waterskin. In the house of dust which I entered were high priests and acolytes, priests of the incantation and of ecstasy; there were servers of the temple, and there was Etana, that king of Kish[4] whom the eagle carried to Heaven in the days of old. There was Ereshkigal the Queen of the Underworld; and Belit-Sheri squatted in front of her, she who is recorder of the gods and keeps the book of death. She held a tablet from which she read. She raised her head, she saw me and spoke: 'Who has brought this one here?' Then I awoke like a

---

[1] **cedar**: He refers to a journey to Lebanon during which Gilgamesh and Enkidu cut down the cedar forest that Humbaba was appointed to guard.

[2] **Humbaba**: A giant from Lebanon whom Gilgamesh and Enkidu killed.

[3] **Enlil**: God of the sky who guided human affairs.

[4] **Kish**: A Sumerian city. Etana wanted to obtain a magical plant from heaven that would allow him to father a son.

man drained of blood who wanders alone in a waste of rushes; like one whom the bailiff has seized and his heart pounds with terror."

[After Enkidu dies Gilgamesh realizes that fame is no substitute for life. Facing his own imminent death, he begins a desperate search for immortality. He travels to the end of the Earth where he meets Siduri, a female tavern keeper, who offers the following advice:]

"Gilgamesh, where are you hurrying to? You will never find that life for which you are looking. When the gods created man they allotted to him death, but life they retained in their own keeping. As for you, Gilgamesh, fill your belly with good things; day and night, night and day, dance and be merry, feast and rejoice. Let your clothes be fresh, bathe yourself in water, cherish the little child that holds your hand, and make your wife happy in your embrace; for this too is the lot of man."

[Gilgamesh refuses to be deterred. After many harrowing experiences he finally reaches Utnapishtim, a former mortal whom the gods had sent to eternal paradise, and addresses him.]

"Oh, father Utnapishtim, you who have entered the assembly of the gods, I wish to question you concerning the living and the dead, how shall I find the life for which I am searching?"

Utnapishtim said, "There is no permanence. Do we build a house to stand forever, do we seal a contract to hold for all time? Do brothers divide an inheritance to keep forever, does the flood-time of rivers endure? It is only the nymph of the dragon-fly who sheds her larva and sees the sun in his glory. From the days of old there is no permanence. The sleeping and the dead, how alike they are, they are like a painted death. What is there between the master and the servant when both have fulfilled their doom? When the Anunnaki [gods], the judges, come together, and Mammetun the mother of destinies, together they decree the fates of men. Life and death they allot but the day of death they do not disclose."

Then Gilgamesh said to Utnapishtim the Faraway, "I look at you now, Utnapishtim, and your appearance is no different from mine; there is nothing strange in your features. I thought I should find you like a hero prepared for battle, but you lie here taking your ease on your back. Tell me truly, how was it that you came to enter the company of the gods and to possess everlasting life?" Utnapishtim said to Gilgamesh, "I will reveal to you a mystery, I will tell you a secret of the gods."

"You know the city Shurrupak [a Sumerian city] it stands on the banks of Euphrates? That city grew old and the gods that were in it were old. There was Anu, lord of the firmament, their father, and warrior Enlil their counselor, Ninurta the helper, and Ennugi watcher over canals; and with them also was Ea [God of water]. In those days the world teemed, the people multiplied, the world bellowed like a wild bull, and the great god was aroused by the clamor. Enlil heard the clamor and he said to the gods in council, 'The uproar of mankind is intolerable and sleep is no longer possible by reason of the babel.' So the gods agreed to exterminate mankind. Enlil did this, but Ea because of his oath [to protect mankind] warned me in a dream. He whispered their words to my house of reeds, 'Reed-house, reed-house! Wall, O wall, hearken reed-house, wall reflect; O man of Shurrupak, son of Ubara-Tutu; tear down your house and build a boat, abandon possessions and look for life, despise worldly goods and save your soul alive. Tear down your house, I say, and build a boat. . . . Then take up into the boat the seed of all living creatures.'

"When I had understood I said to my lord, 'Behold, what you have commanded I will honor and perform, but how shall I answer the people, the city, the elders?' Then Ea opened his mouth and said to me, his servant, 'Tell them this: I have learnt that Enlil is wrathful against me, I dare no longer walk in his land nor live in his city; I will go down to the Gulf to dwell with Ea my lord. But on you he will rain down abundance, rare fish and shy wildfowl, a rich harvest-tide. In the evening the rider of the storm will bring you wheat in torrents.' . . .

"On the seventh day the boat was complete. . . .

"I loaded into her all that I had of gold and of living things, my family, my kin, the beast of the field both wild and tame, and all the craftsmen. I sent them on board. . . . The time was fulfilled, the evening came, the rider of the storm sent down the rain. I looked out at the weather and it was terrible, so I too boarded the boat and battened her down. . . .

"For six days and six nights the winds blew, torrent and tempest and flood overwhelmed the world, tempest and flood raged together like warring hosts. When the seventh day dawned the storm from the south subsided, the sea grew calm, the flood was stilled; I looked at the face of the world and there was silence, all mankind was turned to clay. The surface of the sea stretched as flat as a roof-top; I opened a hatch and the light fell on my face. Then I bowed low, I sat down and I wept, the tears streamed down my face, for on every side was the waste of water. I looked for land in vain, but fourteen leagues distant there appeared a mountain, and there the boat grounded; on the mountain of Nisir the boat held fast, she held fast and did not budge. . . . When the seventh day dawned I loosed a dove and let her go. She flew away, but finding no resting-place she returned. Then I loosed a swallow, and she flew away but finding no resting-place she returned. I loosed a raven, she saw that the waters had retreated, she ate, she flew around, she cawed, and she did not come back. Then I threw everything open to the four winds, I made a sacrifice and poured out a liba-tion [liquid offering] on the mountain top. Seven and again seven caul-drons I set up on their stands, I heaped up wood and cane and cedar and myrtle. When the gods smelled the sweet savor, they gathered like flies over the sacrifice.[5] Then, at last, Ishtar [Goddess of love and war] also came, she lifted her necklace with the jewels of Heaven [rainbow] that once Anu had made to please her. 'O you gods here present, by the lapis lazuli[6] round my neck I shall remember these days as I remember the jewels of my throat; these last days I shall not forget. Let all the gods gather round the sacrifice, except Enlil. He shall not approach this offer-ing, for without reflection he brought the flood; he consigned my people to destruction.'

"When Enlil had come, when he saw the boat, he was wrath and swelled with anger at the gods, the host of Heaven, 'Has any of these mortals escaped? Not one was to have survived the destruction.' Then the god of the wells and canals Ninurta opened his mouth and said to the warrior Enlil, 'Who is there of the gods that can devise without Ea? It is Ea alone who knows all things.' Then Ea opened his mouth and spoke to warrior Enlil, 'Wisest of gods, hero Enlil, how could you so senselessly bring down the flood?' . . . It was not that I revealed the secret of the gods; the wise man learned it in a dream. Now take your counsel what shall be done with him.

"Then Enlil went up into the boat, he took me by the hand and my wife and made us enter the boat and kneel down on either side, he stand-ing between us. He touched our foreheads to bless us saying, 'In time past Utnapishtim was a mortal man; henceforth he and his wife shall live in the distance at the mouth of the rivers.' Thus it was that the gods took me and placed me here to live in the distance, at the mouth of the rivers."

Utnapishtim said, "As for you, Gilgamesh, who will assemble the gods for your sake, so that you may find that life for which you are searching?"

[After telling his story, Utnapishtim challenges Gilgamesh to resist sleep for six days and seven nights. When Gilgamesh fails the test, Utnapishtim points out how preposterous it is to search for immortality when one can-not even resist sleep. Out of kindness, Utnapishtim does tell Gilgamesh where he can find a submarine plant that will at least rejuvenate him.

---

[5] **like flies over the sacrifice**: The gods were thought to consume the smoke of incense and animal offerings.

[6] **lapis lazuli**: A gemstone with a deep blue color often used in Egyptian jewelry.

Consequently, the hero dives to the bottom of the sea and plucks it. However, humanity is to be denied even the blessing of forestalling old age and decrepitude, because the plant is stolen from Gilgamesh by a serpent. His mission a failure, Gilgamesh returns to Uruk.]

The destiny was fulfilled which the father of the gods, Enlil of the mountain, had decreed for Gilgamesh: "In nether-earth the darkness will show him a light: of mankind, all that are known, none will leave a monument for generations to come to compare with his. The heroes, the wise men, like the new moon have their waxing and waning. Men will say, 'Who has ever ruled with might and with power like him?' As in the dark month, the month of shadows, so without him there is no light. O Gilgamesh, this was the meaning of your dream. You were given the kingship, such was your destiny, everlasting life was not your destiny. Because of this do not be sad at heart, do not be grieved or oppressed; he has given you power to bind and to loose, to be the darkness and the light of mankind. He has given unexampled supremacy over the people, victory in battle from which no fugitive returns, in forays and assaults from which there is no going back. But do not abuse this power, deal justly with your servants in the palace, deal justly before the face of the Sun." . . .

Gilgamesh, the son of Ninsun, lies in the tomb. At the place of offerings he weighed the bread-offering, at the place of libation he poured out the wine. In those days the lord Gilgamesh departed, the son of Ninsun, the king, peerless, without an equal among men, who did not neglect Enlil his master. O Gilgamesh, lord of Kullab [in Uruk], great is thy praise.

READING AND DISCUSSION QUESTIONS

1. How does this passage describe the afterlife?
2. How are the gods characterized in this passage? What is the gods' attitude toward mortals?
3. Would you describe *The Epic of Gilgamesh* as pessimistic or optimistic? Why?

DOCUMENT 1-2

The Egyptian Book of the Dead:
The Declaration of Innocence

ca. 2100–1800 B.C.E.

The Egyptian Book of the Dead consists of spells, prayers, and rituals that were necessary for a successful transition to the afterlife. Illustrated quotations from the book discovered inside ornate tombs were placed so that the dead could consult important passages during their trying ordeal. Many other examples have been discovered written on papyrus with the dead person's name inserted into the text. The following passage from the Book of the Dead contains the formula that an Egyptian must recite in order to enter the afterlife.

To be said on reaching the Hall of the Two Truths [Hall of Judgment]
    so as to purge [name][7] of any sins committed and to see the face of
    every god:
Hail to you, great God, Lord of the Two Truths![8]
I have come to you, my Lord,
I was brought to see your beauty.
I know you, I know the names of the forty-two gods[9]
Who are with you in the Hall of the Two Truths,
Who live by warding off evildoers,
Who drink of their blood,
On that day of judging characters before Wennofer.[10]
Lo, your name is "He-of-Two-Daughters,"
(And) "He-of-Maat's[11]-Two-Eyes."

Miriam Lichtheim, trans. and ed., *Ancient Egyptian Literature* (Berkeley: University of California Press, 1973).

[7] **[name]**: This is where the dead would have inserted their name in the formula.
[8] **Lord of the Two Truths**: Thoth, the Egyptian god of wisdom, who weighed the souls of the dead (thought to live in the heart) against the feather of the goddess Ma'at. Those with hearts as light as the feather were permitted to go on to the afterlife; hearts made heavy by sin were devoured by a demon.
[9] **I know . . . the forty-two gods**: The dead had to recite the names and descriptions of the forty-two gods.
[10] **Wennofer**: Osiris, god of the underworld.
[11] **Maat**: The goddess who symbolized divine order, truth, and justice.

Lo, I come before you,
Bringing Maat to you,
Having repelled evil for you.
I have not done crimes against people,
I have not mistreated cattle,
I have not sinned in the Place of Truth,[12]
I have not known what should not be known,
I have not done any harm.
I did not begin a day by exacting more than my due,
My name did not reach the bark of the mighty ruler.
I have not blasphemed a god,
I have not robbed the poor.
I have not done what the god abhors,
I have not maligned a servant to his master.
I have not caused pain,
I have not caused tears.
I have not killed,
I have not ordered to kill,
I have not made anyone suffer.
I have not damaged the offerings in the temples,
I have not depleted the loaves of the gods,
I have not stolen the cakes of the dead.
I have not copulated nor defiled myself.
I have not increased nor reduced the measure,
I have not diminished the arura.[13]
I have not cheated in the fields.
I have not added to the weight of the balance,
I have not falsified the plummet of the scales.
I have not taken milk from the mouth of children,
I have not deprived cattle of their pasture.
I have not snared birds in the reeds of the gods,
I have not caught fish in their ponds.
I have not held back water in its season,
I have not dammed a flowing stream,
I have not quenched a needed fire.
I have not neglected the days of meat offerings,

---

[12] **the Place of Truth**: The Valley of the Kings in which the pharaohs were buried.
[13] **arura**: Unit of land measurement equal to the amount of land an ox could plow in one day.

I have not detained cattle belonging to the god,
I have not stopped a god in his procession.
I am pure, I am pure, I am pure, I am pure! . . .

READING AND DISCUSSION QUESTIONS

1. What actions could prevent someone from entering the afterlife? What does this imply about how people should live their lives?

2. A number of the prohibitions mention the Egyptian gods. What role did the gods play in mortals' lives? How were mortals supposed to treat them?

3. What information about agricultural life in ancient Egypt can be found in this passage?

DOCUMENT 1-3

HAMMURABI

Hammurabi's Code: The State Regulates Health Care

ca. 1800 B.C.E.

Among Hammurabi of Babylon's many accomplishments were the unification of Mesopotamia under Babylonian rule, the establishment of the supremacy of the Babylonian god Marduk, and the composition of a law code. Although Hammurabi's code is not the first known law code, it is the earliest one to survive largely intact. The code deals with the family, commercial activities, and agricultural life, providing valuable insight into Babylonian society. The following selections, which deal with medical practices, are typical of the laws in the code and exemplify the brutal nature of Babylonian justice often characterized by the phrase "an eye for an eye."

215. If a physician performed a major operation on a freeman with a bronze lancet and has saved the freeman's life, or he opened up the

James B. Pritchard, eds., *Ancient Near Eastern Texts Relating to the Old Testament*, 3d ed. with supplement (Princeton, N.J.: Princeton University Press, 1969), 175.

eye-socket of a freeman with a bronze lancet and has saved the free-man's eye, he shall receive ten shekels [coins] of silver.

216. If it was a commoner, he shall receive five shekels of silver.

217. If it was a freeman's slave, the owner of the slave shall give two shekels of silver to the physician.

218. If a physician performed a major operation on a freeman with a bronze lancet and has caused the freeman's death, or he opened up the eye-socket of a freeman and has destroyed the freeman's eye, they shall cut off his hand.

219. If a physician performed a major operation on a commoner's slave with a bronze lancet and has caused his death, he shall make good slave for slave.

220. If he opened up [the slave's] eye-socket with a bronze lancet and has destroyed his eye, he shall pay half his value in silver.

READING AND DISCUSSION QUESTIONS

1. What different social classes does this passage define? How does jus-tice differ for these various classes?

2. Do you think these laws would encourage the growth of the medical profession? Why or why not?

DOCUMENT 1-4

NEBMARE-NAKHT

Advice to Ambitious Young Egyptians from a Royal Scribe

ca. 1350–1200 B.C.E.

The Egyptians used the fiber of a plant from the Nile to make sheets of papyrus, on which they recorded both important religious and official texts and personal letters. Egypt's dry climate prevented the disintegration of

Miriam Lichtheim, trans. and ed., *Ancient Egyptian Literature* (Berkeley: University of California Press, 1973), 3:168–172.

*papyri and preserved a great deal of information about everyday life. The fol-
lowing passage was originally written to encourage a young scribe to continue working at his profession. The surviving examples of this text are likely
exercises copied by students as they contain frequent spelling and grammatical mistakes. The errors might indicate the difficulty of the training, and
why the young scribe in this passage was ignoring his studies.*

1. TITLE

[Beginning of the instruction in letter-writing made by the royal scribe and
chief overseer of the cattle of Amen-Re, King of Gods, Nebmare-nakht] for
his apprentice, the scribe Wenemdiamun.

2. PRAISE OF THE SCRIBE' S PROFESSION

[The royal scribe] and chief overseer of the cattle of Amen-[Re, King of
Gods, Nebmare-nakht speaks to the scribe Wenemdiamun]. [Apply yourself to this] noble profession. "Follower of Thoth" [God of wisdom] is the
good name of him who exercises it. —. He makes friends with those
greater than he. Joyful —. Write with your hand, read with your mouth.
Act according to my words. —, my heart is not disgusted. —. — to my
instructing you. You will find it useful. — [with bread and] beer. You
will be advanced by your superiors. You will be sent on a mission —. Love
writing, shun dancing; then you become a worthy official. Do not long
for the marsh ticket. Turn your back on throw stick and chase. By day
write with your fingers; recite by night. Befriend the scroll, the palette. It
pleases more than wine. Writing for him who knows it is better than all
other professions. It pleases more than bread and beer, more than clothing
and ointment. It is worth more than an inheritance in Egypt, than a tomb
in the west.

3. ADVICE TO THE UNWILLING PUPIL

Young fellow, how conceited you are! You do not listen when I speak. Your
heart is denser than a great obelisk, a hundred cubits[14] high, ten cubits
thick. When it is finished and ready for loading, many work gangs draw it.
It hears the words of men; it is loaded on a barge. Departing from Yebu [in
Upper Egypt] it is conveyed, until it comes to rest on its place in Thebes
[the capital of Egypt].

---

[14] **a hundred cubits**: A cubit was a unit of measurement equal to the length of a
forearm.

So also a cow is bought this year, and it plows the following year. It learns to listen to the herdsman; it only lacks words. Horses brought from the field, they forget their mothers. Yoked they go up and down on all his majesty's errands. They become like those that bore them, that stand in the stable. They do their utmost for fear of a beating.

But though I beat you with every kind of stick, you do not listen. If I knew another way of doing it, I would do it for you, that you might listen. You are a person fit for writing, though you have not yet known a woman. Your heart discerns, your fingers are skilled, your mouth is apt for reciting.

Writing is more enjoyable than enjoying a basket of — and beans; more enjoyable than a mother's giving birth, when her heart knows no distaste. She is constant in nursing her son; her breast is in his mouth every day. Happy is the heart (of) him who writes; he is young each day. . . .

5. ALL OCCUPATIONS ARE BAD EXCEPT THAT OF THE SCRIBE

See for yourself with your own eye. The occupations lie before you.

The washerman's day is going up, going down. All his limbs are weak, (from) whitening his neighbors' clothes every day, from washing their linen.

The maker of pots is smeared with soil, like one whose relations have died. His hands, his feet are full of clay; he is like one who lives in the bog.

The cobbler mingles with vats. His odor is penetrating. His hands are red with madder, like one who is smeared with blood. He looks behind him for the kite, like one whose flesh is exposed.

The watchman prepares garlands and polishes vasestands. He spends a night of toil just as one on whom the sun shines.

The merchants travel downstream and upstream. They are as busy as can be, carrying goods from one town to another. They supply him who has wants. But the tax collectors carry off the gold, that most precious of metals.

The ships' crews from every house (of commerce), they receive their loads. They depart from Egypt for Syria, and each man's god is with him. (But) not one of them says: "We shall see Egypt again!"

The carpenter who is in the shipyard carries the timber and stacks it. If he gives today the output of yesterday, woe to his limbs! The shipwright stands behind him to tell him evil things.

His outworker who is in the fields, his is the toughest of all the jobs. He spends the day loaded with his tools, tied to his tool-box. When he returns home at night, he is loaded with the tool-box and the timbers, his drinking mug, and his whetstones.

The scribe, he alone, records the output of all of them. Take note of it!

6. The Misfortunes of the Peasant

Let me also expound to you the situation of the peasant, that other tough occupation. [Comes] the inundation and soaks him —, he attends to his equipment. By day he cuts his farming tools; by night he twists rope. Even his midday hour he spends on farm labor. He equips himself to go to the field as if he were a warrior. The dried field lies before him; he goes out to get his team. When he has been after the herdsman for many days, he gets his team and comes back with it. He makes for it a place in the field. Comes dawn, he goes to make a start and does not find it in its place. He spends three days searching for it; he finds it in the bog. He finds no hides on them; the jackals have chewed them. He comes out, his garment in his hand, to beg for himself a team.

When he reaches his field he finds (it) [broken up]. He spends time cultivating, and the snake is after him. It finishes off the seed as it is cast to the ground. He does not see a green blade. He does three plowings with borrowed grain. His wife has gone down to the merchants and found nothing for [barter.] Now the scribe lands on the shore. He surveys the harvests. Attendants are behind him with staffs, Nubians with clubs. One says (to him): "Give grain." "There is none." He is beaten savagely. He is bound, thrown in the well, submerged head down. His wife is bound in his presence. His children are in fetters. His neighbors abandon them and flee. When it's over, there's no grain.

If you have any sense, be a scribe. If you have learned about the peasant, you will not be able to be one. Take note of it! . . .

8. The Scribe Does Not Suffer Like the Soldier

Furthermore. Look, I instruct you to make you sound; to make you hold the palette freely. To make you become one whom the king trusts; to make you gain entrance to treasury and granary. To make you receive the shipload at the gate of the granary. To make you issue the offerings on feast days. You are dressed in fine clothes; you own horses. Your boat is on the river; you are supplied with attendants. You stride about inspecting. A mansion is built in your town. You have a powerful office, given you by the king. Male and female slaves are about you. Those who are in the fields grasp your hand, on plots that you have made. Look, I make you into a staff of life! Put the writings in your heart, and you will be protected from all kinds of toil. You will become a worthy official.

Do you not recall the (fate of) the unskilled man? His name is not known. He is ever burdened (like an ass carrying) in front of the scribe who knows what he is about.

Come, (let me tell) you the woes of the soldier, and how many are his superiors: the general, the troop commander, the officer who leads, the standard-bearer, the lieutenant, the scribe, the commander of fifty, and the garrison-captain. They go in and out in the halls of the palace, saying: "Get laborers!" He is awakened at any hour. One is after him as (after) a donkey. He toils until the Aten [sun] sets in his darkness of night. He is hungry, his belly hurts; he is dead while yet alive. When he receives the grain-ration, having been released from duty, it is not good for grinding.

He is called up for Syria.[15] He may not rest. There are no clothes, no sandals. The weapons of war are assembled at the fortress of Sile. His march is uphill through mountains. He drinks water every third day; it is smelly and tastes of salt. His body is ravaged by illness. The enemy comes, surrounds him with missiles, and life recedes from him. He is told: "Quick, forward, valiant soldier! Win for yourself a good name!" He does not know what he is about. His body is weak, his legs fail him. When victory is won, the captives are handed over to his majesty, to be taken to Egypt. The foreign woman faints on the march; she hangs herself (on) the soldier's neck. His knapsack drops, another grabs it while he is burdened with the woman. His wife and children are in their village; he dies and does not reach it. If he comes out alive, he is worn out from marching. Be he at large, be he detained, the soldier suffers. If he leaps and joins the deserters, all his people are imprisoned. He dies on the edge of the desert, and there is none to perpetuate his name. He suffers in death as in life. A big sack is brought for him; he does not know his resting place.

Be a scribe, and be spared from soldiering! You call and one says: "Here I am." You are safe from torments. Every man seeks to raise himself up. Take note of it!

READING AND DISCUSSION QUESTIONS

1. What were the benefits of being a scribe?

2. According to the passage, why were other occupations worse than being a scribe? What does this imply about the social status of laborers, craftsmen, peasants, and scribes?

3. Describe the problems with military life. What would motivate someone to become a soldier?

---

[15] **Syria**: During the New Kingdom (1570–1075 B.C.E.), Egyptian power extended into the Near East.

4.   Although the passage implies that being a scribe was better than other occupations, the teacher still had to encourage his pupil. Why might the life of a scribe be unattractive?

DOCUMENT 1-5

Hymn to the Nile

ca. 1350–1100 B.C.E.

Ancient Egypt, unlike Mesopotamia, shared a unified political structure, religious beliefs, and culture for most of its history. Around 3100 B.C.E., King Narmer-Menes unified the two separate kingdoms of Egypt: Lower Egypt, the delta land where the Nile emptied into the Mediterranean, and Upper Egypt, a narrow strip of land that the Nile watered as it ran north through the desert. The economy of the ancient Egyptians depended entirely on the success of crops and trade along the river and they worshipped the river as a god. As this hymn extols the river's virtues, it becomes a catalogue of daily life in Egypt.

WORSHIP OF THE NILE

Hail to thee, O Nile, that issues from the earth and comes to keep Egypt alive! Hidden in his form of appearance, a darkness by day, to whom minstrels have sung. He that waters the meadows which Re created, in order to keep every kid alive. He that makes to drink the desert and the place distant from water: that is his dew coming down (from) heaven. The beloved of Geb [God of the earth], the one who controls Nepri [God of grain], and the one who makes the craftsmanship of Ptah[16] to flourish.

The lord of fishes, he who makes the marsh-birds to go upstream. There are no birds which come down because of the hot winds. He who makes barley and brings emmer [wheat] into being, that he may make the temples festive. If he is sluggish, . . . the nostrils are stopped up, and everybody is poor. If there be (thus) a cutting down in the food-offerings of the

---

James B. Pritchard, eds., *Ancient Near Eastern Texts Relating to the Old Testament*, 3d ed. with supplement (Princeton, N.J.: Princeton University Press, 1969), 372–373.

[16] **Ptah**: God of creation who was associated with inundated fields.

gods, then a million men perish among mortals, covetousness is practiced, the entire land is in a fury, and great and small are on the execution-block. (But) people are different when he approaches. Khnum[17] constructed him. When he rises, then the land is in jubilation, then every belly is in joy, every backbone takes on laughter, and every tooth is exposed.

The bringer of food, rich in provisions, creator of all good, lord of majesty, sweet of fragrance. What is in him is satisfaction. He who brings grass into being for the cattle and (thus) gives . . . sacrifice to every god, whether he be in the underworld, heaven, or earth, him who is under his authority. He who takes in possession the Two Lands [Upper and Lower Egypt], fills the magazines,[18] makes the granaries wide, and gives things (to) the poor.

He who makes every beloved tree to grow, without lack of them. He who brings a ship into being by his strength, without hewing in stone. The enduring image with the White Crown.[19] He cannot be seen; (he has) no taxes; he has no levies; no one can read of the mystery; no one knows the place where he is; he cannot be found by the power of writing. (He has) no shrines; he has no portion. He has no service of (his) desire. (But) generations of thy children jubilate for thee, and men give thee greeting as a king, stable of laws, coming forth (at) his season and filling Upper and Lower Egypt. . . . (Whenever) water is drunk, every eye is in him, who gives an excess of his good.

He who was sorrowful is come forth gay. . . . Vomiting forth and making the field to drink. Anointing the whole land. Making one man rich and laying another, (but) there is no coming to trial with him, who makes satisfaction without being thwarted, for whom no boundaries are made.

A maker of light when issuing from darkness, a fat for his cattle. His limits are all that is created. There is no district which can live without him. Men are clothed . . . with flax from his meadows, for (he) made Hedj-hotep [Goddess of weaving] for his service. (He) made anointing with his unguents, being the associate of Ptah in his nature, bringing into being all service in him, all writings and divine words, his responsibility in Lower Egypt.

Entering into the underworld and coming forth above, loving to come forth as a mystery. If thou art (too) heavy (to rise), the people are few, and one begs for the water of the year. (Then) the rich man looks like him who

---

[17] **Khnum**: God who was both the source of the Nile and creator of human bodies.

[18] **magazines**: Stores for military equipment.

[19] **White Crown**: The symbol of Upper Egypt worn by the pharaohs.

is worried, and every man is seen (to be) carrying his weapons. This is no companion backing up a companion. There are no garments for clothing; there are no ornaments for the children of nobles. There is no listening at night, that one may answer with coolness. There is no anointing for anybody.

He who establishes truth in the heart of men, for it is said: "Deceit comes after poverty." If one compares thee with the great green sea, which does not . . . control the Grain-God, whom all the gods praise, there are no birds coming down from his desert. His hand does not beat with gold, with making ingots of silver. No one can eat genuine lapis lazuli. (But) barley is foremost and lasting.

Men began to sing to thee with the harp, and men sing to thee with the hand. The generations of thy children jubilate for thee. Men equip messengers for thee, who come (back) bearing treasures (to) ornament this land. He who makes a ship to prosper before mankind; he who sustains hearts in pregnant women; he who loves a multitude of all (kinds of) his cattle.

When thou risest in the city of the ruler, then men are satisfied with the goodly produce of the meadows. . . . Oh for the little lotus-blossoms, everything that pours forth upon earth, all (kinds of) herbs in the hands of children! They have (even) forgotten how to eat. Good things are strewn about the houses. The land comes down frolicking.

When the Nile floods, offering is made to thee, oxen are sacrificed to thee, great oblations are made to thee, birds are fattened for thee, lions are hunted for thee in the desert, fire is provided for thee. And offering is made to every (other) god, as is done for the Nile, with prime incense, oxen, cattle, birds, and flame. The Nile has made his cavern in Thebes, and his name is no (longer) known in the underworld. Not a god will come forth in his form, if the plan is ignored.

O all men who uphold the Ennead, . . . fear ye the majesty which his son, the All-Lord, has made, (by) making verdant the two banks. So it is "Verdant art thou!" So it is "Verdant art thou!" So it is "O Nile, verdant art thou, who makest man and cattle to live!"

It has come to a good and successful end.

READING AND DISCUSSION QUESTIONS

1. In what ways did ancient Egyptians worship and describe the Nile?

2. What does the Nile provide for Egypt? What harm can the Nile cause?

3. Why did the gods honor the Nile? How does this affect your conception of the Egyptian deities?

4. What details about daily life in Egypt can you find in this passage?

DOCUMENT 1-6

Book of Exodus: Moses Descends Mount Sinai with the Ten Commandments

ca. 950–450 B.C.E.

The book of Exodus, the second book of the Hebrew Torah and the Christian Old Testament, recounts the escape of the Hebrew people from captivity in Egypt and their forty-year journey through the desert to the "promised land," modern-day Israel and Palestine. Although Moses, who led the Hebrew people, is traditionally thought to have written the Torah, modern scholars argue that the work was composed over many centuries. The following passage recounts the climactic event of the Exodus, when Moses received the Covenant from God. It establishes monotheism, the worship of only one God, as a tenet of the Hebrew religion.

And it came to pass on the third day in the morning, that there were thunders and lightnings, and a thick cloud upon the mount, and the voice of the trumpet exceeding loud; so that all the people that was in the camp trembled. And Moses brought forth the people out of the camp to meet with God; and they stood at the nether part of the mount. And mount Sinai was altogether on a smoke, because the Lord descended upon it in fire: and the smoke thereof ascended as the smoke of a furnace, and the whole mount quaked greatly. And when the voice of the trumpet sounded long, and waxed louder and louder, Moses spake, and God answered him by a voice. And the Lord came down upon mount Sinai, on the top of the mount: and the Lord called Moses up to the top of the mount; and Moses went up. And the Lord said unto Moses, Go down, charge the people, lest they break through unto the Lord to gaze, and many of them perish. And

---

Exodus 19:16–25; 20:1–21.

let the priests also, which come near to the Lord, sanctify themselves, lest the Lord break forth upon them. And Moses said unto the Lord, The people cannot come up to mount Sinai: for thou chargedst us, saying, Set bounds about the mount, and sanctify it. And the Lord said unto him, Away, get thee down, and thou shalt come up, thou, and Aaron with thee: but let not the priests and the people break through to come up unto the Lord, lest he break forth upon them. So Moses, went down unto the people, and spake unto them.

And God spake all these words, saying, I am the Lord thy God, which have brought thee out of the land of Egypt, out of the house of bondage. Thou shalt have no other gods before me. Thou shalt not make unto thee any graven image, or any likeness of any thing that is in heaven above, or that is in the earth beneath, or that is in the water under the earth: Thou shalt not bow down thyself to them, nor serve them: for I the Lord thy God am a jealous God, visiting the iniquity of the fathers upon the children unto the third and fourth generation of them that hate me; And shewing mercy unto thousands of them that love me, and keep my commandments. Thou shalt not take the name of the Lord thy God in vain; for the Lord will not hold him guiltless that taketh his name in vain. Remember the sabbath day, to keep it holy. Six days shalt thou labor, and do all thy work: But the seventh day is the sabbath of the Lord thy God: in it thou shalt not do any work, thou, nor thy son, nor thy daughter, thy manservant, nor thy maidservant, nor thy cattle, nor thy stranger that is within thy gates: For in six days the Lord made heaven and earth, the sea, and all that in them is, and rested the seventh day: wherefore the Lord blessed the sabbath day, and hallowed it.

Honor thy father and thy mother: that thy days may be long upon the land which the Lord thy God giveth thee. Thou shalt not kill. Thou shalt not commit adultery. Thou shalt not steal. Thou shalt not bear false witness against thy neighbor. Thou shalt not covet thy neighbor's house, thou shalt not covet thy neighbor's wife, nor his manservant, nor his maidservant, nor his ox, nor his ass, nor any thing that is thy neighbor's.

And all the people saw the thunderings, and the lightnings, and the noise of the trumpet, and the mountain smoking: and when the people saw it, they removed, and stood afar off. And they said unto Moses, Speak thou with us, and we will hear: but let not God speak with us, lest we die. And Moses said unto the people, Fear not: for God is come to prove you, and that his fear may be before your faces, that ye sin not. And the people stood afar off, and Moses drew near unto the thick darkness where God was.

READING AND DISCUSSION QUESTIONS

1. How should the followers of the Hebrew God live their lives in a way that is acceptable to Him? What actions are specifically prohibited?

2. What role does the Hebrew God play for His people? How should the Hebrew people act toward their God?

DOCUMENT 1-7

ASHUR-NASIR-PAL II

An Assyrian Emperor's Resumé

ca. 875 B.C.E.

Ashur-Nasir-Pal II (r. 883–859 B.C.E.) was responsible for expanding the emerging Neo-Assyrian Empire west from northern Mesopotamia to the Mediterranean. His account of the expansion describes excessively bloody and violent conquests and the use of terror as a common tactic to control conquered regions. Ashur-Nasir-Pal II most likely began the Assyrian habit of deporting people from their homelands and spreading them throughout the empire in order to prevent rebellions. The following selection is an official account of Ashur-Nasir-Pal II's campaigns in Mesopotamia.

YEAR 4: A THIRD CAMPAIGN AGAINST ZAMUA

In the eponymy of Limutti-adur,[20] while I was staying in Nineveh, men brought me word that Ameka and Arashtua [Mesopotamian cities] had withheld the tribute and forced labor due unto Assur,[21] my lord. At the word of Assur, the great lord, my lord, and of Nergal [God of war and the sun], my leader, on the first day of the month of *Simanu*[22] I ordered a call

---

D. D. Luckenbill, ed., *Ancient Records of Assyria and Babylonia* (Chicago: University of Chicago Press, 1926), 1:151–154.

[20] **eponymy of Limutti-adur**: In the Assyrian calendar the names of an elected official called "limmu" were used to name the year. The name Limutti-adur does not survive in any of the Assyrian lists, but this year probably corresponds to 879 B.C.E.

[21] **Assur**: Chief god of the Assyrians.

[22] *Simanu*: May or June in the modern calendar.

to arms for the third time against the land of Zamua. I did not wait for my chariots and hosts; I departed from the city of Kakzi, the Lower Zab I crossed. I entered the pass of Babite, I crossed the Radanu, drawing nearer every day to the foot of Mount Simaki. Cattle, sheep and wine, the tribute of the land of Dagara, I received. The — chariots and picked cavalry (men) I took with me, and all the night, until the dawn, I marched from (along) the foot of the mountain of Simaki. I crossed the Turnat, and with all haste to the city of Ammali, the stronghold of Arashtu, I drew near. With battle and assault I stormed the city, I took (it). 800 of their fighting men I struck down with the sword, with their corpses I filled the streets of their city, with their blood I dyed their houses. Many men I captured alive with my hand, and I carried off great spoil from them; the city I destroyed, I devastated, I burned with fire.

The city of Hudun and twenty cities of its neighborhood I captured; I slew the inhabitants thereof, their spoil, their cattle, and their sheep I carried off; their cities I destroyed, I devastated, I burned with fire; their young men and their maidens I burned in the flames. The city of Kisirtu, their stronghold, ruled by Sabini, together with ten cities of its neighborhood, I captured, I slew their inhabitants, their spoil I carried away. The cities of the Bareans, which were ruled by Kirtiara, and those of the men of Dera and of Bunisa, as far as the pass of Hashmar, I destroyed, I devastated, I burned with fire, I turned them into mounds and ruins. I departed from the cities of Arashtua, I entered the pass between the steep mountains of Lara and Bidirgi, which for the passage of chariots and hosts was not suited to Zamri, the royal city of Ameka of the land of Zamua, I drew near.

Ameka became afraid before my mighty weapons and my fierce battle array, and occupied a steep mountain. The goods of his palace and his chariot I carried away; from the city of Zamri I departed. I crossed the Lalle and marched to Mount Etini, a difficult region, which was not suited for the passage of chariots and armies, and unto which none among the kings, my fathers, had come nigh. The king, together with his armies, climbed up into Mount Etini. His goods and his possessions, many copper utensils, a copper wild-ox, vessels of copper, bowls of copper, cups of copper, the wealth of his palace, his heaped-up treasures, I carried out of the mountain, returned to my camp and spent the night. With the help of Assur and Shamash [God of justice], the gods, my helpers, I departed from that camp, and I set out after him. I crossed the Edir River and in the midst of the mighty mountains of Su and Elaniu I slew multitudes of them. His goods and his possessions, a copper wild-ox, vessels of copper, bowls of copper, dishes of copper; many copper utensils, tables which were overlaid with gold, their cattle and their flocks, their possessions, their heavy spoil, from the foot of Mount Elaniu I carried off. I took his horse from him. Ameka, to save his life, climbed up into Mount Sabua.

The cities of Zamru, Arasitku, Ammaru, Parsindu, Iritu, and Suritu, his strongholds, together with 150 cities which lay round about, I destroyed, I devastated, I burned with fire, into mounds and ruin heaps I turned them. While I was staying before the city of Parsindi, I placed in reserve the cavalry and pioneers.[23] Fifty of Ameka's warriors I slew in the field, I cut off their heads and bound them to the tree trunks within his palace court. Twenty men I captured alive and I immured them in the wall of his palace. From the city of Zamri I took with me the cavalry and pioneers, and marched against the cities of Ata, of Arzizu, unto which none among the kings my fathers had come nigh. The cities of Arzizu and Arsindu, his strongholds, together with ten cities which lay round about on the steep mountain of Nispi, I captured. I slew the inhabitants thereof; the cities I destroyed, I devastated, I burned with fire, and returned to my camp.

At that time I received copper, *tabbili* of copper, and rings of copper, and many *shariate* from the land of Sipirmena who(se inhabitants) speak like women.

From the city of Zamri I departed and into the difficult mountain of Lara, which was not suited for the passage of chariots and armies, with hatchets of iron I cut and with axes of bronze I hewed (a way), and I brought over the chariots and troops and came down to the city of Tukulti-Assur-asbat, which the men of the land of Lullu call Arakdi. All the kings of the land of Zamua were affrighted before the fury of my arms and the terror of my dominion, and embraced my feet. Tribute and tax, — silver, gold, lead, copper, vessels of copper, garments of brightly colored wool, horses, cattle, sheep, and wine I laid upon them (in greater measure) than before and used their forced laborers in the city of Calah. While I was staying in the land of Zamua, the men of the cities Huduni, Hartishi, Hubushkia and Gilzani were overwhelmed with the terrifying splendors of Assur, my lord, and they brought me tribute and tax, — silver, gold, horses, garments of brightly colored wool, cattle, flocks, and wine. The people, such as had fled from before my arms, climbed up into the mountains. I pursued them. Between the mountains of Aziru and Simaki they had settled themselves, and had made the city of Mesu their stronghold. Mount Aziru I destroyed, I devastated, and from the midst of Mount

---

[23] **pioneers**: Soldiers trained in siege warfare.

Simaki as far as the river Turnat I strewed their corpses. 500 of their warriors I slew and carried off their heavy spoil, the cities I burned with fire.

At that time, in the land of Zamua, the city of Atlila, which for the scepter of the king of Karduniash they had seized, had decayed and had become a mound and ruin heap. Assur-Nasir-Pal restored it. I surrounded it with a wall, and I erected therein a palace for my royal dwelling, I adorned it and made it glorious and greater than it was before. Grain and straw from the whole land I heaped up within it, and I called its name Der-Assur.

READING AND DISCUSSION QUESTIONS

1. How does Ashur-Nasir-Pal II describe his victories? What aspects of the story might he have exaggerated to make them seem more impressive?

2. Why would Ashur-Nasir-Pal II want to publicize his conquests? What does this say about him as a leader?

COMPARATIVE QUESTIONS

1. How are the prohibitions contained within the Egyptian Book of the Dead similar to or different from those in the Hebrew book of Exodus?

2. The passages in this chapter illustrate various ways in which humans relate to their gods. How do the Sumerian, Egyptian, and Hebrew people differ in this respect?

3. How does the life of a soldier described by Nebmare-nakht compare to the account of war by Ashur-Nasir-Pal II?

4. What differences can you discern between the everyday life and religious beliefs of Mesopotamians and those of Egyptians? What might account for those differences?

CHAPTER 2

The Foundation of Indian Society

to 300 C.E.

The earliest society in South Asia was the Harappan civilization (ca. 2500–2000 B.C.E.) based in the Indus River valley. They left written records, but their script remains undeciphered. With the Harappans' decline, a group who called themselves Aryans came to dominate North India. Around 1500 B.C.E., the Aryans began to compose oral poetry in Sanskrit, an Indo-European language closely related to ancient Persian and Hittite. According to the *Rigveda*, the earliest record of this sacred poetry, the Aryan religion initially focused on ritual sacrifices conducted by the priestly caste (Brahmans), who sought material benefits. Later religious movements in India, such as Buddhism, instead sought to fill spiritual needs and ignored the Aryans' strict caste system. In reaction to Buddhism, the Brahmans rejected ritual sacrifices and helped spread the worship of gods, such as Krishna, to all levels of society.

DOCUMENT 2-1

From Rigveda

ca. 600 B.C.E.

The Rigveda *is the oldest and most important Aryan scripture. Originally composed and transmitted in oral form between 1500 and 1000 B.C.E., it was only written down in Sanskrit around 800–500 B.C.E. because the Brahmans had long resisted losing control of the text to the lower castes. The* Rigveda *contains many different types of texts, such as hymns to gods, creation*

The Rig Veda, trans. Wendy Doniger O'Flaherty (New York: Penguin Books, 1981), 160–162.

stories, and instructions for religious rituals. The first two hymns below are dedicated to the warrior god Indra; the third concerns the myth of the sacrifice of Purusha, which created the world.

VICTORY OVER VRITRA[1]

I will declare the manly deeds of Indra, the first that he achieved, the thunder-wielder.

He slew the dragon, then disclosed the waters, and cleft the channels of the mountain torrents.

He slew the dragon lying on the mountain: his heavenly bolt of thunder Twashtar[2] fashioned.

Like lowing cows in rapid flow descending, the waters glided downward to the ocean.

Impetuous as a bull, he chose the Soma,[3] and quaffed in threefold sacrifice the juices.

Maghavan grasped the thunder for his weapon, and smote to death this firstborn of the dragons.

When, Indra, you had slain the dragon's firstborn, and overcome the charms of the enchanters.

Then, giving life to sun and dawn and heaven, you found not one foe to stand against you.

Indra with his own great and deadly thunder smote into pieces Vritra worst of Vritras.

As trunks of trees, what time the axe has felled them, low on the earth so lies the prostrate dragon.

He, like a mad weak warrior, challenged Indra, the great impetuous many-slaying hero.

He, brooking not the clashing of the weapons, crushed — Indra's foe — the shattered forts in falling.

Footless and handless still[4] he challenged Indra, who smote him with his bolt between the shoulders.

Emasculated yet claiming manly vigor, thus Vritra lay with scattered limbs dissevered. . . .

---

[1] **Vritra**: A three-headed dragon, the most powerful of the dragons.
[2] **Twashtar**: A creator god who was a blacksmith.
[3] **Soma**: A psychedelic drink extracted from an unknown plant that was imbibed by the gods and the writers of the Vedas.
[4] **Footless and handless still**: Vritra was more like a snake than the Western concept of a dragon.

Nothing availed him. Lightning, nothing, nor thunder, hailstorm or mist which he had spread around him.

When Indra and the dragon strove in battle, Maghavan [Indra] gained the victory for ever. . . .

Indra is king of all that moves and moves not, of creatures tame and horned, the thunder-wielder.

Over all living men he rules as sovereign, containing all as spokes within a rim.

WHO IS INDRA?

The god who had insight the moment he was born, the first who protected the gods with his power of thought, before whose hot breath the two world-halves [Heaven and Earth] tremble at the greatness of his manly powers — he, my people, is Indra.

He who made fast the tottering earth, who made still the quaking mountains, who measured out and extended the expanse of the air, who propped up the sky — he, my people, is Indra.

He who killed the serpent and loosed the seven rivers, who drove out the cows that had been pent up by Vala [a demon], who gave birth to fire between two stones, the winner of booty in combats — he, my people, is Indra.

He by whom all these changes were rung, who drove the race of Dasas[5] down into obscurity, who took away the flourishing wealth of the enemy as a winning gambler takes the stake — he, my people, is Indra.

He about whom they ask, "Where is he?" or they say of him, the terrible one, "He does not exist," he who diminishes the flourishing wealth of the enemy as a gambler does — believe in him! He, my people, is Indra.

He who encourages the weary and the sick, and the poor priest who is in need, who helps the man who harnesses the stones to press Soma, he who has lips fine for drinking — he, my people, is Indra.

He under whose command are horses and cows and villages and all chariots, who gave birth to the sun and the dawn and led out the waters, he, my people, is Indra.

He who is invoked by both of two armies, enemies locked in combat, on this side and that side, he who is even invoked separately by each of two men standing on the very same chariot, he, my people, is Indra.

---

[5] **Dasas**: The indigenous inhabitants of India before the coming of the Aryans; also used to mean "slaves."

He without whom people do not conquer, he whom they call on for help when they are fighting, who became the image of everything, who shakes the unshakeable — he, my people, is Indra.

He who killed with his weapon all those who had committed a great sin, even when they did not know it, he who does not pardon the arrogant man for his arrogance, who is the slayer of the Dasyus [Dasas], he, my people, is Indra.

He who in the fortieth autumn discovered Sambara [a demon] living in the mountains, who killed the violent serpent, the Danu [Vritra], as he lay there, he, my people, is Indra.

He, the mighty bull who with his seven reins let loose the seven rivers to flow, who with his thunderbolt in his hand hurled down Rauhina [another demon] as he was climbing up to the sky, he, my people, is Indra.

Even the sky and the earth bow low before him, and the mountains are terrified of his hot breath; he who is known as the Soma-drinker, with his thunderbolt in his hand, with the thunderbolt in his palm, he, my people, is Indra.

He who helps with his favor the one who presses and the one who cooks, the praiser and the preparer, he for whom prayer is nourishment, for whom Soma is the special gift, he, my people, is Indra.

You [Indra] who furiously grasp the prize for the one who presses and the one who cooks, you are truly real. Let us be dear to you, Indra, all our days, and let us speak as men of power in the sacrificial gathering.

To Purusha

A thousand heads had Purusha,[6] a thousand eyes, a thousand feet.
He covered earth on every side, and spread ten fingers' breadth beyond.
This Purusha is all that yet has been and all that is to be;
The lord of immortality which waxes greater still by food.
So mighty is his greatness; yea, greater than this is Purusha.
All creatures are one-fourth of him, three-fourths eternal life in heaven.
With three-fourths Purusha went up: one-fourth of him again was here.
Thence he strode out to every side over what eats not and what eats.
From him Viraj [masculinity] was born; again Purusha from Viraj was born.
As soon as he was born he spread eastward and westward o'er the earth.

---

[6]**Purusha**: The cosmic being who is both the sacrifice and the one performing the sacrifice.

When gods prepared the sacrifice with Purusha as their offering,

Its oil was spring, the holy gift was autumn; summer was the wood.

They balmed as victim on the grass Purusha born in earliest time.

With him the deities and all Sadhyas [lesser gods] and Rishis [sages] sacrificed.

From that great general sacrifice the dripping fat was gathered up.[7]

He formed the creatures of the air, and animals both wild and tame.

From that great general sacrifice Richas and Samahymns [elements of the *Rig Veda*] were born:

Therefrom the meters[8] were produced, the Yajus had its birth from it.

From it were horses born, from it all creatures with two rows of teeth:

From it were generated cows, from it the goats and sheep were born.

When they divided Purusha how many portions did they make?

What do they call his mouth, his arms? What do they call his thighs and feet?

The Brahmin [priest caste] was his mouth, of both his arms was the Rajanya [warrior caste] made.

His thighs became the Vaisya [merchant and artisan caste, including herders and farmers], from his feet the Sudra [laborer caste] was produced.

The Moon was gendered from his mind, and from his eye the Sun had birth;

Indra and Agni [God of sacrifice and fire] from his mouth were born, and Vayu [the wind] from his breath.

Forth from his navel came mid-air; the sky was fashioned from his head;

Earth from his feet, and from his ear the regions. Thus they formed the worlds.

Seven fencing-logs had he, thrice seven layers of fuel were prepared [for a sacrifice],

When the gods, offering sacrifice, bound, as their victim, Purusha.

Gods, sacrificing, sacrificed the victim: these were the earliest holy ordinances.

The mighty ones attained the height of heaven, there where the Sadhyas, gods of old, are dwelling.

---

[7] **From that great general sacrifice . . . up**: Vedic rituals involved the cooking of animal flesh.

[8] **the meters**: The *Sama Veda*, another sacred text of the Aryans.

READING AND DISCUSSION QUESTIONS

1. What distinctive qualities does Indra possess? Which of these qualities would have been particularly appealing to the nomadic Indo-
Europeans?

2. How was the world created? What elements of Vedic society were justified by this creation?

DOCUMENT 2-2

THE BUDDHA

Setting in Motion the Wheel of Law

ca. 530 B.C.E.

The Buddha was born into a kshatriya *(warrior caste) family near the
Himalaya mountains around 563* B.C.E. *At the age of twenty-nine, he had
four visions that made him question the value of his sheltered and comfort-
able life. He envisioned an old man, a sick person, a dead person, and a
monk. Following in the path of the monk, he experimented with extreme
forms of asceticism before developing the "Middle Path," which he describes
below in his first sermon to his followers. Through meditation he obtained
Enlightenment, or the freedom from reincarnation and desire that results
from understanding the reality of life, which Buddha taught was based on
suffering. He spent the rest of his life promoting his ideas throughout the
Ganges Valley.*

And the Blessed One thus addressed the five Bhikkhus [ascetics, the Buddha's companions]. "There are two extremes, O Bhikkhus, which he who
has given up the world ought to avoid. What are these two extremes? A life
given to pleasures, devoted to pleasures and lusts: this is degrading, sensual,
vulgar, ignoble, and profitless; and a life given to mortifications: this is

T. W. Rhys Davids and Hermann Oldenberg, trans., *Vinaya Texts*, in F. Max Mueller,
ed., *The Sacred Books of the East*, 50 vols. (Oxford: Clarendon Press, 1879–1910),
13:94–97, 100–102. Henry C. Warrant, ed. and trans., *Buddhism in Translations*
(Cambridge, Mass.: Harvard University Press, 1896), 117–122.

painful, ignoble, and profitless. By avoiding these two extremes, O Bhikkhus, the Tathagata [Buddha] has gained the knowledge of the Middle Path which leads to insight, which leads to wisdom, which conduces to calm, to knowledge, to the Sambodhi [Enlightenment], to Nirvana.[9]

"Which, O Bhikkhus, is this Middle Path the knowledge of which the Tathagata has gained, which leads to insight, which leads to wisdom, which conduces to calm, to knowledge, to the Sambodhi, to Nirvana? It is the Holy Eightfold Path, namely, Right Belief,[10] Right Aspiration,[11] Right Speech,[12] Right Conduct,[13] Right Means of Livelihood,[14] Right Endeavor,[15] Right Memory,[16] Right Meditation.[17] This, O Bhikkhus, is the Middle Path the knowledge of which the Tathagata has gained, which leads to insight, which leads to wisdom, which conduces to calm, to knowledge, to the Sambodhi, to Nirvana.

"This, O Bhikkhus, is the Noble Truth of Suffering: Birth is suffering; decay is suffering; illness is suffering; death is suffering. Presence of objects we hate, is suffering; Separation from objects we love, is suffering; not to obtain what we desire, is suffering. Briefly, . . . clinging to existence is suffering.

"This, O Bhikkhus, is the Noble Truth of the Cause of suffering: Thirst [i.e., desire], that leads to rebirth, accompanied by pleasure and lust, finding its delight here and there. This thirst is threefold, namely, thirst for pleasure, thirst for existence, thirst for prosperity.

"This, O Bhikkhus, is the Noble Truth of the Cessation of suffering: it ceases with the complete cessation of this thirst, — a cessation which consists in the absence of every passion — with the abandoning of this thirst,

---

[9] **Nirvana**: The state of both being and nonbeing when one is no longer subject to reincarnation or karma.

[10] **Right Belief**: Knowing the Four Noble Truths.

[11] **Right Aspiration**: Desiring to follow the path to Enlightenment and opening the mind.

[12] **Right Speech**: Only speaking the truth and not gossiping or using language that harms others.

[13] **Right Conduct**: Not committing evil acts. There are five important prohibitions: killing, stealing, committing sexual misconduct, telling lies, and using intoxicants.

[14] **Right Means of Livelihood**: Performing work that does not result in evil or violates the five prohibitions.

[15] **Right Endeavor**: Abstaining from unwholesome acts.

[16] **Right Memory**: Being aware of every moment and focusing on the nature of living, dying, and suffering.

[17] **Right Meditation**: Quieting the mind and body.

with the doing away with it, with the deliverance from it, with the destruction of desire.

"This, O Bhikkhus, is the Noble Truth of the Path which leads to the cessation of suffering: that Holy Eightfold Path, that is to say, Right Belief, Right Aspiration, Right Speech, Right Conduct, Right Means of Livelihood, Right Endeavor, Right Memory, Right Meditation. . . .

"As long, O Bhikkhus, as I did not possess with perfect purity this true knowledge and insight into these four Noble Truths . . . so long, O Bhikkhus, I knew that I had not yet obtained the highest, absolute Sambodhi in the world of men and gods. . . .

"But since I possessed, O Bhikkhus, with perfect purity this true knowledge and insight into these four Noble Truths . . . then I knew, O Bhikkhus, that I had obtained the highest, universal Sambodhi. . . .

"And this knowledge and insight arose in my mind: The emancipation of my mind cannot be lost; this is my last birth; hence I shall not be born again!"

READING AND DISCUSSION QUESTIONS

1. What are the Four Noble Truths?
2. How does one achieve Enlightenment and Nirvana?
3. Do you agree that life is nothing but suffering? Why or why not?

DOCUMENT 2-3

From Mahabharata: *An Account of the Gods and the Creation of the World*

200 B.C.E.–200 C.E.

The following passage is from the Mahabharata, *one of the most famous epics of Indian literature. It features incarnations of the god Vishnu and represents a transition from Brahmanic rituals to a religion based more on*

The Mahabharata, trans. J. A. B. van Buitenen (Chicago: University of Chicago Press, 1973).

devotion to the gods. Although the primary narrative of the Mahabharata *concerns a conflict between the five Pandavas and their cousins, the Kauravas, it contains many sections that deal with the actions of deities and* dharma *("the way").*

The seers said:

Tell us that ancient Lore that was related by the eminent sage Dvaipāyana, which the Gods and brahmin seers honored when they heard it! That divine language of the sublime Histories, in all the varieties of words and books, the sacred Account of the Bhāratas,[18] that language of complex word and meaning, ruled by refinement and reinforced by all sciences, which Vaiśaṃpāyana,[19] at Dvaipāyana's bidding, repeated truthfully to the satisfaction of King Janamejaya at the king's sacrifice. We wish to hear that Grand Collection [the Mahabharata], now joined to the Collections of the Four Vedas, which Vyāsa the miracle-monger compiled, replete with the Law and dispelling all danger of evil!

The Bard said:

I bow to the Primeval Person the Lord, widely invoked and lauded, who is the True, the One-Syllabled Brahman, manifest and unmanifest, everlasting, at once the existent and the nonexistent, Creator of things high and low. I bow to him who is the Ancient One, supreme, imperishable, blissful and blessing, the most desirable Viṣṇu, faultless and resplendent, who is Kṛṣṇa Hṛṣikeśa, the preceptor of all creatures, those that move and those that move not; the God Hari.

I shall speak the entire thought of that great seer and saint who is venerated in all the world, Vyāsa of limitless brilliance. Poets have told it before, poets are telling it now, other poets shall tell this history on earth in the future. It is indeed a great storehouse of knowledge, rooted in the three worlds, which the twiceborn retain in all its parts and summaries. Fine words adorn it, and usages human and divine; many meters scan it; it is the delight of the learned.

When all this was without light and unillumined, and on all its sides covered by darkness, there arose one large Egg, the inexhaustible seed of all creatures. They say that this was the great divine cause, in the beginning of the Eon;[20] and that on which it rests is revealed as the true Light,

---

[18] **the Bharatas**: A tribe of Aryans who are the focus of the Mahabharata.

[19] **Vaisampayana**: A sage and character in the Mahabharata.

[20] **the Eon**: One day in the life of the god Brahma, which equals 4.32 billion Earth years.

the everlasting Brahman. Wondrous it was and beyond imagining, in perfect balance in all its parts, this unmanifest subtle cause that is that which is and that which is not.

From it was born the Grandfather, the Sole Lord Prajāpati, who is known as Brahmā, as the Preceptor of the Gods, as Sthāṇu, Manu, Ka, and Parameṣṭhin. From him sprang Dakṣa, son of Pracetas, and thence the seven sons of Dakṣa, and from them came forth the twenty-one Lords of Creation. And the Person of immeasurable soul, the One whom the seers know as the universe; and the Viśve Devas,[21] and the Ādityas [lunar gods] as well as the Vasus [nature gods] and the two Aśvins [twin gods of healing]. Yakṣas [nature spirits], Sādhyas,[22] Piśācas,[23] Guhyakas,[24] and the Ancestors[25] were born from it, and the wise and impeccable Seers. So also the many royal seers, endowed with every virtue. Water, Heaven and Earth, Wind, Atmosphere, and Space, the year, the seasons, the months, the fortnights, and days and nights in turn, and whatever else, has all come forth as witnessed by the world. Whatever is found to exist, moving and unmoving, it is all again thrown together, all this world, when the destruction of the Eon has struck. Just as with the change of the season all the various signs of the season appear, so also these beings at the beginning of each Eon. Thus, without beginning and without end, rolls the wheel of existence around in this world, causing origin and destruction, beginningless and endless.

There are thirty-three thousand, thirty-three hundred, and thirty-three Gods — this is the summing-up of creation.

The great Sun is the son of the sky and the soul of the eye, the Resplendent One who is also Savitar, Rcīka, Arka, Āśāvaha, the Bringer-of-Hope, and Ravi. Of all the sons of the Sun Vivasvant, the last one was Mahya, who had a son that shone like a God, who is hence known as Subhrāj — the Well-Shining One. Subhrāj had three sons of much fame who had abundant offspring, Daśajyoti, Śatajyoti, and the self-possessed Shasrajyoti. The great-spirited Daśajyoti had ten thousands sons, Śatajyoti ten times that number, and Sahasrajyoti again ten times that. From them arose the lineage of the Kurus,[26] those of the Yadus[27] and of Bhararta

---

[21] **Viśve Devas**: The Vedic gods.

[22] **Sādhyas**: Minor gods who personify the rituals and prayers found in the Vedas.

[23] **Piśācas**: Disembodied forms of dead souls often associated with evil.

[24] **Guhyakas**: Ghosts created by the Yakṣas.

[25] **the Ancestors**: The original mortals.

[26] **Kurus**: An Aryan tribe who created the kingdom of Kuru.

[27] **Yadus**: An Aryan tribe mentioned in the Vedas.

[Bharata], the lines of Yayāti and Ikṣvāku[28] and of the royal seers in general — many dynasties arose and creations of creatures in their abundant varieties.

All are abodes of being. And there is a triple mystery — Veda,[29] Yoga,[30] and science — Law, Profit, and Pleasure. The seer saw the manifold sciences of Law, Profit, and Pleasure, and the rule that emerged for the conduct of worldly affairs. And the ancient histories with their commentaries, and the various revelations — *everything has been entered here*, and this describes this Book.

READING AND DISCUSSION QUESTIONS

1. According to this passage, how was the world created? Where did the gods come from?

2. How do humans know the story of the world's creation? What does this passage imply about the role of humans in the universe?

DOCUMENT 2-4

From The Laws of Manu

ca. 100 B.C.E.–200 C.E.

The Laws of Manu *were likely compiled by more than one person and later edited and expanded by others. In Indian mythology Manu was the sole survivor of a flood, much like Utnapishtim from* The Epic of Gilgamesh

---

B. Guehler, trans., *The Laws of Manu,* in F. Max Mueller, ed., *The Sacred Books of the East,* 50 vols. (Oxford: Clarendon Press, 1879–1910), 25:24, 69, 84–85, 195–197, 260–326, 329–330, 343–344, 370–371, 402–404, 413–416, 420, 423.

[28] **lines of Yayāti and Ikṣvāku**: Yayati was a prominent king of the Chandravansa (lunar line) and Iksvaku a king of the Suryavansa (solar line); they were the two most prominent families of the Kshatriya caste.

[29] **Veda**: A sacred text (for an example see the *Rigveda*, Document 2-1).

[30] **Yoga**: "To join." Included in the word Yoga are a number of different techniques for obtaining freedom from reincarnation, such as meditation, philosophical contemplation, and devotion.

(Document 1-1). In many ways, The Laws of Manu *are less a legal code than an instruction manual, explaining how different social classes by birth* (varna) *and occupation* (jati) *should fulfill their duty* (dharma). *Ascribing the laws to Manu suggests that they were given divine sanction and had universal meaning.*

VARNA[31]

The Brahmin, the Kshatriya, and the Vaisya castes are the twice-born ones,[32] but the fourth, the Sudra, has one birth only; there is no fifth caste.[33] . . .

To Brahmins he [Brahman, the creator god] assigned teaching and studying the Vedas, sacrificing for their own benefit and for others, giving and accepting of alms.

The Kshatriya he commanded to protect the people, to bestow gifts, to offer sacrifices, to study the Vedas, and to abstain from attaching himself to sensual pleasures;

The Vaisya to tend cattle, to bestow gifts, to offer sacrifices, to study the Vedas, to trade, to lend money, and to cultivate land.

One occupation only the lord prescribed to the Sudra, to serve meekly . . . these other three castes.

JATIS[34]

From a male Sudra are born an Ayogava, a Kshattri, and a Kandala, the lowest of men, by Vaisya, Kshatriya, and Brahmin females respectively, sons who owe their origin to a confusion of the castes.[35] . . .

Killing fish to Nishadas; carpenters' work to the Ayogava; to Medas, Andhras, Kunkus, and Madgus, the slaughter of wild animals. . . .

But the dwellings of Kandalas . . . shall be outside the village. . . .

---

[31] **varna:** The technical term for the castes, originally meaning "color." Some scholars believe that the caste system was originally based on skin color, with the lighter-skinned Aryans supplanting the darker-skinned Dasas.

[32] **the twice-born ones:** Those castes who could read the Vedas. They participated in a ceremony known as Upanayana in which they learned about the nature of the universe and so became born again.

[33] **fifth caste:** The untouchables would later rank below the Sudra.

[34] **jatis:** Occupations or subcastes.

[35] **sons . . . confusion of the castes:** These jatis were occupied by children whose parents belonged to different castes; the child of a male Sudra and female Brahmin occupied the lowest jati.

Their dress shall be the garments of the dead, they shall eat their food from broken dishes, black iron shall be their ornaments, and they must always wander from place to place.

A man who fulfills a religious duty, shall not seek intercourse with them; their [Kandala] transactions shall be among themselves, and their marriages with their equals. . . .

At night they shall not walk about in villages and in towns.

By day they may go about for the purpose of their work, distinguished by marks at the king's command, and they shall carry out the corpses of persons who have no relatives; that is a settled rule.

By the king's order they shall always execute the criminals, in accordance with the law, and they shall take for themselves the clothes, the beds, and the ornaments of such criminals.

DHARMA[36]

A king who knows the sacred law must inquire into the laws of castes [jatis], of districts, of guilds, and of families, and settle the peculiar law of each. . . .

Among the several occupations the most commendable are, teaching the Vedas for a Brahmin, protecting the people for a Kshatriya, and trade for a Vaisya.

But a Brahmin, unable to subsist by his peculiar occupations just mentioned, may live according to the law applicable to Kshatriyas; for the latter is next to him in rank. . . .

A man of low caste [varna] who through covetousness lives by the occupations of a higher one, the king shall deprive of his property and banish.

It is better to discharge one's own duty incompletely than to perform completely that of another; for he who lives according to the law of another caste is instantly excluded from his own.

A Vaisya who is unable to subsist by his own duties, may even maintain himself by a Sudra's mode of life, avoiding however acts forbidden to him, and he should give it up, when he is able to do so. . . .

Abstention from injuring creatures, veracity, abstention from unlawfully appropriating the goods of others, purity, and control of the organs,[37] Manu has declared to be the summary of the law for the four castes.

---

[36] dharma: The duties of each caste.

[37] control of the organs: Especially sexual organs.

THE NATURE OF WOMEN

It is the nature of women to seduce men in this world; for that reason the wise are never unguarded in the company of females. . . .

For women no rite is performed with sacred texts, thus the law is settled; women who are destitute of strength and destitute of the knowledge of Vedic texts are as impure as falsehood itself; that is a fixed rule.

HONORING WOMEN

Where women are honored, there the gods are pleased; but where they are not honored, no sacred rite yields rewards.

Where the female relations live in grief, the family soon wholly perishes; but that family where they are not unhappy ever prospers.

FEMALE PROPERTY RIGHTS

A wife, a son, and a slave, these three are declared to have no property; the wealth which they earn is acquired for him to whom they belong. . . .

What was given before the nuptial fire, what was given on the bridal procession, what was given in token of love, and what was received from her brother, mother, or father, that is called the six-fold property of a woman.

Such property, as well as a gift subsequent and what was given to her by her affectionate husband, shall go to her offspring, even if she dies in the lifetime of her husband. . . .

But when the mother has died, all the uterine [biological] brothers and the uterine sisters shall equally divide the mother's estate.

A WOMAN'S DEPENDENCE

In childhood a female must be subject to her father, in youth to her husband, when her lord is dead to her sons; a woman must never be independent.

She must not seek to separate herself from her father, husband, or sons; by leaving them she would make both her own and her husband's families contemptible. . . .

Him to whom her father may give her, or her brother with the father's permission, she shall obey as long as he lives, and when he is dead, she must not insult his memory.

BETROTHAL

No father who knows the law must take even the smallest gratuity for his daughter; for a man who, through avarice, takes a gratuity, is a seller of his offspring. . . .

Three years let a damsel wait, though she be marriageable,[38] but after that time let her choose for herself a bridegroom of equal caste and rank. If, being not given in marriage, she herself seeks a husband, she incurs no guilt, nor does he whom she weds.

MARRIAGE AND ITS DUTIES

To be mothers were women created, and to be fathers men; religious rites, therefore, are ordained in the Vedas to be performed by the husband together with the wife. . . .

No sacrifice, no vow, no fast must be performed by women apart from their husbands; if a wife obeys her husband, she will for that reason alone be exalted in heaven. . . .

By violating her duty towards her husband, a wife is disgraced in this world, after death she enters the womb of a jackal, and is tormented by diseases as punishment for her sin. . . .

Let the husband employ his wife in the collection and expenditure of his wealth, in keeping everything clean, in the fulfillment of religious duties, in the preparation of his food, and in looking after the household utensils. . . .

Drinking spirituous liquor, associating with wicked people, separation from the husband, rambling abroad, sleeping at unseasonable hours, and dwelling in other men's houses, are the six causes of the ruin of women. . . .

Offspring, religious rites, faithful service, highest conjugal happiness and heavenly bliss for the ancestors and oneself, depend on one's wife alone. . . .

"Let mutual fidelity continue until death" . . . may be considered as the summary of the highest law for husband and wife.

Let man and woman, united in marriage, constantly exert themselves, that they may not be disunited and may not violate their mutual fidelity.

DIVORCE

For one year let a husband bear with a wife who hates him; but after a year let him deprive her of her property and cease to cohabit with her. . . .

But she who shows aversion towards a mad or outcaste[39] husband, a eunuch,[40] one destitute of manly strength, or one afflicted with such

---

[38] **marriageable**: Girls were often married beginning at age 12.

[39] **outcaste**: Someone literally removed from their caste.

[40] **eunuch**: A castrated male. Here, eunuch may mean an impotent man.

diseases as punish crimes,[41] shall neither be cast off nor be deprived of her property. . . .

A barren wife may be superseded [replaced] in the eighth year, she whose children all die in the tenth, she who bears only daughters in the eleventh, but she who is quarrelsome without delay.

But a sick wife who is kind to her husband and virtuous in her conduct, may be superseded only with her own consent and must never be disgraced.

READING AND DISCUSSION QUESTIONS

1. Describe the social structure advocated in this passage. What is expected from the various levels of society?

2. What is the status and role of women in Indian society?

COMPARATIVE QUESTIONS

1. How is inequality in Indian society justified? Use evidence from the *Rigveda* and *The Laws of Manu* to justify your answer.

2. What aspects of Hinduism does Buddhism reject? What aspects of Hindu tradition does it retain?

3. Compare the way that the *Rigveda* and the *Mahabharata* explain the creation of the world. How might these different explanations reflect changes in Indian religion?

4. What are the differences between ancient Indian religion and the religions practiced in the ancient Near East (see Chapter 1)?

---

[41] **such diseases as punish crimes**: Illness caused by evil karmic actions.

CHAPTER 3

China's Classical Age

to 256 B.C.E.

The Shang Dynasty (ca. 1500–1050 B.C.E.) was the first Chinese dynasty to leave behind evidence of its culture, including written texts and bronze weapons. Following its collapse, China shifted between periods of unified empire and civil war, which often ushered in new dynasties. The Zhou Dynasty (ca. 1050–500 B.C.E.) helped establish this pattern by ascribing the fall of the Shang to the "Mandate of Heaven," which argued that dynasties lose Heaven's blessing when they become corrupt and can be overthrown. After a long period of rule, even the Zhou Dynasty lost control of China, leading to a period of civil war known as the Warring States Period (500–221 B.C.E.). The political chaos of this time inspired a series of important political philosophies, such as Confucianism, Daoism, and Legalism, on which later Chinese culture would be built.

DOCUMENT 3-1

From Book of Documents

ca. 900–100 B.C.E.

The Book of Documents *is one of the five texts traditionally ascribed to Confucius (551–479 B.C.E.) and studied as the basis of Confucianism. It was compiled in its original form by 300 B.C.E.; however, it had to be reconstructed by Chinese scholars after the Qin Dynasty (221–206 B.C.E.) attempted to destroy all Confucian texts. The* Book of Documents *claims to draw from the most ancient periods of Chinese history, but many of the texts are forgeries or fakes. The following advice given to the heir of Zheng Tang,*

James Legge, trans., *The Sacred Books of China: The Texts of Confucianism*, in F. Max Mueller, ed., *The Sacred Books of the East*, 50 vols. (Oxford: Clarendon Press, 1879–1910), 3:92–95.

*the first Shang king, by Zheng Tang's chief minister supposedly dates to the
early Shang Dynasty (1500–1050 B.C.E.), but its references to the Mandate
of Heaven suggest it was written much later.*

In the twelfth month of the first year . . . Yi Yin sacrificed to the former
king [Zheng Tang], and presented the heir-king reverently before the
shrine of his grandfather. All the princes from the domain of the nobles
and the royal domain were present; all the officers also, each continuing to
discharge his particular duties, were there to receive the orders of the chief
minister. Yi Yin then clearly described the complete virtue of the Meritorious Ancestor [Zheng Tang] for the instruction of the young king.

He said, "Oh! of old the former kings of Xia[1] cultivated earnestly their
virtue, and then there were no calamities from Heaven.[2] The spirits of the
hills and rivers likewise were all in tranquility; and the birds and beasts, the
fishes and tortoises, all enjoyed their existence according to their nature.
But their descendant did not follow their example, and great Heaven sent
down calamities, employing the agency of our ruler [Zheng Tang] who
was in possession of its favoring appointment. The attack on Xia may
be traced to the orgies in Ming Tiao [where Jie, the last Xia ruler, was
defeated]. . . . Our king of Shang brilliantly displayed his sagely prowess;
for oppression he substituted his generous gentleness; and the millions of
the people gave him their hearts. Now your Majesty is entering on the
inheritance of his virtue; — all depends on how you commence your
reign. To set up love, it is for you to love your relations; to set up respect, it
is for you to respect your elders. The commencement is in the family and
the state. . . .

"Oh! the former king began with careful attention to the bonds that
hold men together. He listened to expostulation, and did not seek to resist
it; he conformed to the wisdom of the ancients; occupying the highest
position, he displayed intelligence; occupying an inferior position, he displayed his loyalty; he allowed the good qualities of the men whom he
employed and did not seek that they should have every talent. . . .

"He extensively sought out wise men, who should be helpful to you,
his descendant and heir. He laid down the punishments for officers, and

---

[1] **Xia**: Traditionally defined as the first dynasty in China.
[2] **no calamities from Heaven**: This seems to refer to the later concept of the Mandate
of Heaven developed by the Zhou Dynasty and used to justify the overthrow of the
Shang.

warned those who were in authority, saying, 'If you dare to have constant dancing in your palaces, and drunken singing in your chambers, — that is called the fashion of sorcerers; if you dare to set your hearts on wealth and women, and abandon yourselves to wandering about or to the chase, — that is called the fashion of extravagance; if you dare to despise sage words, to resist the loyal and upright, to put far from you the aged and virtuous, and to seek the company of . . . youths, — that is called the fashion of disorder. Now if a high noble or officer be addicted to one of these three fashions with their ten evil ways, his family will surely come to ruin; if the prince of a country be so addicted, his state will surely come to ruin. The minister who does not try to correct such vices in the sovereign shall be punished with branding.' . . .

"Oh! do you, who now succeed to the throne, revere these warnings in your person. Think of them! — sacred counsels of vast importance, admirable words forcibly set forth! The ways of Heaven are not invariable: — on the good-doer it sends down all blessings, and on the evil-doer it sends down all miseries. Do you but be virtuous, be it in small things or in large, and the myriad regions will have cause for rejoicing. If you not be virtuous, be it in large things or in small, it will bring the ruin of your ancestral temple."

READING AND DISCUSSION QUESTIONS

1. What Shang religious rituals does this passage describe?

2. How does Yi Yin tell his son how he should rule? What are the qualities of a good ruler?

3. What actions are considered evil according to Zheng Tang? What are the consequences of living an evil life?

4. How does this text justify the Shang rebellion against the Xia Dynasty?

From Book of Songs

ca. 600 B.C.E.

The work known as the Book of Songs, *like the* Book of Documents, *was thought to have been compiled by Confucius and became one of the five classic books of China. The majority of the poems in the* Book of Songs *appear to have been written between 1000 and 700 B.C.E., but it is possible that some date as early as 1700 B.C.E. The following two poems describe the experiences of women, giving a rare glimpse into the often-hidden world of the ancient family. In the first, a divorced woman returns to the family into which she was born. In the second, a widow mourns the loss of her husband.*

The mulberry leaves have fallen
All yellow and seared.
Since I came to you,
Three years I have eaten poverty.
The waters of the Ch'i were in flood;
They wetted the curtains of the carriage.
It was not I who was at fault;
It is you who have altered your ways,
It is you who are unfaithful,
Whose favours are cast this way and that.

Three years I was your wife.
I never neglected my work.
I rose early and went to bed late;
Never did I idle.
First you took to finding fault with me,
Then you became rough with me.
My brothers disowned me;
"Ho, ho," they laughed.
And when I think calmly over it,
I see that it was I who brought all this upon myself.

A. Wayley, trans. *The Book of Songs* (Boston: Houghton Mifflin Company, 1937).

I swore to grow old along with you;
I am old, and have got nothing from you but trouble.
The Ch'i has its banks,
The swamp has its sides;
With hair looped and ribboned
How gaily you talked and laughed,
And how solemnly you swore to be true,
So that I never thought there could be a change.
No, of a change I never thought;
and that *this* should be the end!

[The next poem is the lament of a widow who has lost her husband in war.]

The cloth-plant grew till it covered the thorn bush;
The bindweed spread over the wilds.
My lovely one is here no more.
With whom? No, I sit alone.

The cloth-plant grew till it covered the brambles;
The bindweed spread across the borders of the field.
My lovely one is here no more.
With whom? No, I lie down alone.

The horn pillow[3] so beautiful,
The worked coverlet so bright!
My lovely one is here no more.
With whom? No, alone I watch till dawn.

Summer days, winter nights —
Year after year of them must pass.
Till I go to him where he dwells.
Winter nights, summer days —
Year after year of them must pass
Till I go to his home.

---

[3] **horn pillow:** A wooden pillow.

READING AND DISCUSSION QUESTIONS

1. How is the woman in the first document treated by her brothers? Why would they have acted this way?

2. In both passages, the women have lost their husbands, but under entirely different circumstances. Compare the way in which each woman speaks about her husband.

3. What role do plant analogies play in these passages? What might this suggest about the Chinese people's relationship to nature?

DOCUMENT 3-3

LAOZI

From Dao De Jing:
Administering the Empire

ca. 500–400 B.C.E.

According to tradition, the Dao De Jing (The Book of the Way) *was written by the sage Laozi, an official of the Zhou court. It was eventually adopted as the basis of the Chinese philosophy of Daoism, which teaches that action should be spontaneous, not purposeful, and that the universe works through the dual forces of yin and yang. The text of the* Dao De Jing *contains many short passages: some are speculative, some philosophical, and some, like those printed here, give advice to the rulers of China.*

LXII

The way is the refuge for the myriad creatures.
It is that by which the good man protects,
And that by which the bad is protected.
Beautiful words when offered will win high rank in return;
Beautiful deeds can raise a man above others.
Even if a man is not good, why should he be abandoned?

Lao-Tzu, *Tao Te Ching*, trans. D. C. Lau (London: Penguin Books, 1963).

Hence when the emperor is set up and the three ducal ministers [highest-ranking advisors] are appointed, he who makes a present of the way without stirring from his seat is preferable to one who offers presents of jade disks followed by a team of four horses. Why was this way valued of old? Was it not said that by means of it one got what one wanted and escaped the consequences when one transgressed?

Therefore it is valued by the empire.

LXIII

Do that which consists in taking no action; pursue that which is not meddlesome; savor that which has no flavor.

Make the small big and few many; do good to him who has done you an injury.

Lay plans for the accomplishment of the difficult before it becomes difficult; make something big by starting with it when small.

Difficult things in the world must needs have their beginnings in the easy; big things must needs have their beginnings in the small.

Therefore it is because the sage never attempts to be great that he succeeds in becoming great.

One who makes promises rashly rarely keeps good faith; one who is in the habit of considering things easy meets with frequent difficulties.

Therefore even the sage treats some things as difficult. That is why in the end no difficulties can get the better of him.

LXIV

It is easy to maintain a situation while it is still secure;
It is easy to deal with a situation before symptoms develop;
It is easy to break a thing when it is yet brittle;
It is easy to dissolve a thing when it is yet minute.
Deal with a thing while it is still nothing;
Keep a thing in order before disorder sets in.
A tree that can fill the span of a man's arms
Grows from a downy tip;
A terrace nine storeys high
Rises from hodfuls of earth;
A journey of a thousand miles
Starts from beneath one's feet.
Whoever does anything to it will ruin it; whoever lays hold of it will lose it.

Therefore the sage, because he does nothing never ruins anything; and, because he does not lay hold of anything, loses nothing.
In their enterprises the people
Always ruin them when on the verge of success.
Be as careful at the end as at the beginning
And there will be no ruined enterprises.
Therefore the sage desires not to desire
And does not value goods which are hard to come by;
Learns to be without learning
And makes good the mistakes of the multitude
In order to help the myriad creatures to be natural and to refrain from daring to act.

LXV

Of old those excelled in the pursuit of the way did not use it to enlighten the people but to hoodwink them. The reason why the people are difficult to govern is that they are too clever.
Hence to rule a state by cleverness
Will be to the detriment of the state;
Not to rule a state by cleverness
Will be a boon to the state.
These two are models.
Always to know the models
Is known as mysterious virtue.
Mysterious virtue is profound and far-reaching,
But when things turn back it turns back with them.
Only then is complete conformity [to the way] realized.

READING AND DISCUSSION QUESTIONS

1. What advice does Laozi give to the rulers of China? Is this advice practical? Could an empire be run using Laozi's suggestions?

2. What role do opposites play in these verses?

3. Do these passages depict humans as good or evil? How do they depict government?

DOCUMENT 3-4

Anecdotes from the Warring States Period

ca. 206–1 B.C.E.

When the Zhou Dynasty took control over China (ca. 1050 B.C.E.) they appointed officials to govern outlying lands. Over time, the officials passed the positions to their sons, who asserted more independence from the Zhou government. In 771 B.C.E., one of these officials revolted and killed the emperor. Although the Zhou defeated this uprising, they lost control of China by 500 B.C.E. Many states battled for supremacy, resulting in the Warring States Period (500–221 B.C.E.), during which traditional Chinese values broke down. The following passages, compiled during the later Han Dynasty (206 B.C.E.–220 C.E.) from a number of sources, provide a glimpse into the Warring States Period and the transformation of morality and values.

LORD MU OF LU ASKED ZISI

Lord Mu of Lu asked Zisi, "Of what sort is he who can be called a loyal minister?"

Zisi said, "One who constantly cites his lord's weaknesses can be called a loyal minister."

Displeased, the lord had [Zisi] bow and retire. In an audience with Chengsun Ge, the lord said, "Before, I asked Zisi about loyal ministers, and Zisi said, 'One who constantly cites his lord's weaknesses can be called a loyal minister.' I was confused by this and did not comprehend."

Chengsun Ge said, "Oh, well spoken (by Zisi)! There have been those who have killed themselves for the sake of their lord. But there has never been one who constantly cites his lord's weaknesses. One who would kill himself for the sake of his lord is one who is committed to rank and emolument; one who constantly cites his lord's weaknesses keeps rank and emolument at a distance. Practicing righteousness while keeping rank and emolument [profit from ministerial office] at a distance — other than Zisi, I have never heard of anyone (who does this)."

From *Hawai'i Reader in Traditional Chinese Culture*, eds. Victor H. Mair, Nancy S. Steinhardt, and Paul R. Goldin (Hawai'i: University of Hawai'i Press, 2005), 143–146.

Mr. He [From *Han Fei Zi*. Excerpt]

One Mr. He of Chu obtained a jade gem from within Mount Chu; he took it and presented it to King Li. King Li had a jeweler examine it; the jeweler said, "It is (a mere) stone." The king thought (Mr.) He was a cozener [con artist], so he cut off his left foot.

When King Li died, King Wu assumed the throne, and He took his gem once again to present it to King Wu. King Wu had a jeweler examine it; the jeweler said, "It is (a mere) stone." Once again, the king thought (Mr.) He was a cozener [con artist], so he cut off his right foot.

When King Wu died, King Wen assumed the throne. The (Mr.) He wrapped his arms around his gem and wept beneath Mount Chu. After three days and three nights, his tears were exhausted, so he continued by weeping blood. The king heard of this, and sent someone to ask (He's) reason, saying, "There are many people who have had their feet cut off; why do you weep so tragically?"

He said, "I am not weeping for my feet. I am weeping because a precious jade is labeled a stone, and an honest man-of-service is dubbed a cozener. That is what I consider tragic." Then the king had his jeweler polish the gem, and this revealed how precious it was. Consequently it was named "Mr. He's jade-disk."

From *Outer Commentary to the Han Odes*

Mencius's wife was sitting by herself in a squatting position. Mencius came in through the door and saw her. He announced to his mother, "My wife is without ritual. I entreat you to expel her."

His mother said, "Why?"

He said, "She was squatting."

His mother said, "How do you know that?"

Mencius said, "I saw her."

His mother said, "Then *you* are without ritual, not your wife. Do the *Rites* [Confucius's *Book of Rites*] not say, 'When you are about to go through a gate, ask who is there; when you are about to ascend a hall, you must make a sound; when you are about to go through a door, you must look down, lest you surprise someone who is unprepared'? Now you went to her place of respite and privacy, going through her door without a sound. That she was seen squatting is (the result of) your lack of ritual. It is not your wife's lack of ritual."

Thereupon Mencius blamed himself and did not dare expel his wife.

STRATAGEMS OF THE WARRING STATES (EXCERPTS)

The state of Zhao seized the sacrificial grounds of Zhou. The King of Zhou was upset by this and told Zheng Chao. Zheng Chao said, "Lord, do not be upset. Let me take (the grounds) back with (merely) thirty pieces of gold."

The Lord of Zhou granted him (the gold). Zheng Chao presented it to the Grand Diviner of Zhao and told him about the matter of the sacrificial grounds. When the King (of Zhao) became ill, he sent for a divination. The Grand Diviner upbraided him, saying, "The sacrificial grounds of Zhou constitute an evil influence." So Zhao returned (the grounds).

When Gan Mao was Prime Minister in Qin, the King of Qin favored Gongsun Yan. One time when they were standing together at leisure, (the king) addressed (Gongsun Yan), saying, "I am about to make you Prime Minister."

One of Gan Mao's functionaries heard this while he was passing by and told Gan Mao. Gan Mao then went in to have an audience with the king. He said, "Your Majesty, you have gained a worthy Prime Minister. I venture to pay my respects and congratulate you."

The king said, "I have entrusted the state to you; why do I need another worthy Prime Minister?"

He replied, "Your Majesty, you are about to make the *xishou* [Gongsun Yan] your Prime Minister."

The king said, "How did you hear that?"

He replied, "The *xishou* told me."

The king was enraged that the *xishou* should have leaked (this information), so he banished him.

King Xuan of Jing asked his flock of ministers, saying, "I have heard that the north fears Zhao Xixu [commander-in-chief of the army]. Verily, how shall we (proceed)?"

None of the ministers answered. Then Jiang Yi said, "A tiger was seeking out the Hundred Beasts and eating them when he caught a fox. The fox said, 'You dare not eat me. Di in Heaven has made me the leader of the Hundred Beasts. If you were to eat me, you would be opposing the command of Di. If you think I am being untrustworthy, I shall walk ahead of you, and you will follow behind me. Observe whether there are any of the Hundred Beasts that dare not flee when they see me!' The tiger doubted the fox, so he walked with him. When the beasts saw them, they fled. The tiger did not know that the beasts fled because they were afraid of him, but thought they were afraid of the fox.

"Now, your Majesty, your territory is five thousand tricents square and contains a million armed (soldiers). But they have all been assigned to Zhao Xixu alone. Thus, when the north fears Zhao Xixu, in reality they fear your Majesty's armed troops, as the Hundred Beasts fear the tiger.

The King of Wei sent a beautiful woman to the King of Chu; the King of Chu was pleased by her. His wife, Zheng Xiu, knew that the king was pleased by the new woman, and that he was very kind to her. Whatever clothing or baubles (the new woman) liked, (Zheng Xiu) gave her; whatever rooms and bed-furnishings she liked, (Zheng Xiu) gave her. She was kinder to her than the king was.

The king said, "A wife serves her husband with sex, but jealousy is her essence. Now you, Zheng Xiu, know that I am pleased by the new woman, and you are kinder to her than I am. This is how a filial son would serve his parents, how a loyal minister would serve his lord."

Relying on her knowledge that the king did not consider her jealous, Zheng Xiu addressed the new woman, saying, "The king loves your beauty! Though this is so, he dislikes your nose. When you see the king, you must cover your nose." So the new woman would cover her nose whenever she went to see the king.

The king addressed Zheng Xiu, saying, "Why does the new woman cover her nose when she sees me?

Zheng Xiu said, "I know why."

The king said, "You must say it even if it is horrible."

Zheng Xiu said, "It seems she hates to smell your odor."

The king said, "Shrew!" He ordered (the new woman's) nose cut off, and would not allow anyone to disobey the command.

There was a man who presented an herb of immortality to the King of Jing. The visitor was holding it in his hand as he entered, and a Mid-Rank Servitor asked, "Can it be eaten?"

(The visitor) said, "It can."

Thereupon (the servitor) snatched it and ate it. The king was enraged and sent men to kill the Mid-Rank Servitor. The Mid-Rank Servitor sent a messenger to persuade the king, saying, "Your servant asked the visitor, and the visitor said it could be eaten; thus your servant ate it. Because of this, your servant is without guilt; the guilt is with the visitor. Furthermore, the guest was presenting an herb of immortality. If your servant eats it and you, king, kill your servant, then it must be an 'herb of mortality.' King, you will be killing a guiltless servant as well as making it plain that people deceive you." Thus the king did not kill him.

The state of Zhao was about to attack Yan. Su Dai addressed King Hui (of Zhao) on behalf of Yan, saying, "As I was coming here today, I passed the Yi River. A mussel had just come out (of its shell) to bask when a heron began to peck at its flesh; the mussel thereupon snapped closed on (the bird's) beak. The heron said, 'If it does not rain today or tomorrow, there will be a dead mussel.' The mussel said to the heron, 'If I do not come out today or tomorrow, there will be a dead heron.' Neither was willing to let the other go, and a fisherman was able to catch both of them.

"Now Zhao is about to attack Yan. Yan and Zhao will withstand each other for a long time, thereby straining their large populations. I fear that mighty Qin will be the fisherman. I request that you cook this plan through."

King Hui said, "Very well." Thereupon he desisted.

READING AND DISCUSSION QUESTIONS

1. How do the figures in these passages achieve their goals? What does this suggest about the personal traits that were valued in this time period?

2. What do these passages reveal about the nature of government in China during the Warring States Period? How did government operate? Who were the chief officials and what were their duties?

COMPARATIVE QUESTIONS

1. Compare the advice given to rulers in the *Book of Documents* and the *Dao De Jing*. What does this suggest about the similarities and differences between Confucianism and Daoism?

2. How did government impact the lives of ordinary Chinese people during the Shang Dynasty (as conveyed in the *Book of Documents* excerpt) as compared to the Warring States Period? How did the treatment and role of royal advisors differ in each period?

3. What roles could women inhabit in Chinese society, as conveyed in the *Book of Songs* and the anecdotes from the Warring States Period?

CHAPTER 4

The Greek Experience

ca. 3500–146 B.C.E.

Greek civilization supplied Rome and much of Europe with a cultural foundation in art, literature, architecture, and philosophy. The fundamentals of Greek life and religious beliefs were laid out in poetry, the earliest form of Greek literature, during the Archaic Age (800–500 B.C.E.) by authors such as Homer, Hesiod, and Sappho, while philosophy took root under the Pre-Socratics. During the Classical Period (500–338 B.C.E.), authors including Herodotus, Thucydides, Sophocles, and Euripides created new genres such as history and drama, while philosophers like Socrates, Plato, and Aristotle established the course of Western philosophy. The following four documents present two of these cultural innovations: poetry and philosophy. The selections from Homer and Sappho provide a glimpse into everyday life and desires, while Plato attempts to define wisdom and Aristotle describes the differences between various forms of government.

DOCUMENT 4-1

HOMER

From Iliad: *Hector Prepares to Meet His Destiny*

ca. 750 B.C.E.

Homer (ca. 800–700 B.C.E.) is the traditional name of the blind, possibly illiterate, author of the two most important epics in Greek literature, the Iliad *and the* Odyssey. *The* Iliad *takes place in the final year of the Trojan War (ca. 1250 B.C.E.), a Greek assault against the Trojans waged to avenge Paris of Troy's kidnapping of Helen from her husband, the king of the Greek*

Homer, *The Iliad*, bk. 21, in Fred Morrow Fling, ed., *A Source Book of Greek History* (Boston: D. C. Heath and Company, 1907), 6–7.

city-state of Sparta. In his final exchange with his wife, the Trojan hero Hector prepares to face the greatest Greek warrior, Achilles, in battle. Hector will ultimately fall and then be publicly defiled by Achilles, who drags his body behind a chariot around the city of Troy.

Then great Hector of the glancing helm answered her: "Surely I take thought for all these things, my wife; but I have very sore shame of the Trojans and Trojan dames with trailing robes, if like a coward I shrink away from battle. Moreover mine own soul forbiddeth me, seeing I have learned ever to be valiant and fight in the forefront of the Trojans, winning my father's great glory and mine own.

"Yea of a surety I know this in heart and soul; the day shall come for holy Ilios [Troy] to be laid low and Priam [King of Troy, Hector and Paris's father] and the folk of Priam of the good ashen spear. Yet doth the anguish of the Trojans hereafter not so much trouble me, neither Hekabe's [Queen of Troy's] own, neither King Priam's, neither my brethren's, the many and brave that shall fall in the dust before their foemen, as doth thy anguish in the day when some mailclad Achaian [Greek] shall lead thee weeping and rob thee of the light of freedom. So shalt thou abide in Argos [a Greek city near Sparta] and play the loom at another woman's bidding, and bear water from fount Messeis or Hypereia, being grievously entreated, and sore constraint shall be laid upon thee. And then shall one say that beholdeth thee weep: 'This is the wife of Hector, that was foremost in battle of the horse-taming Trojans when men fought about Ilios.' Thus shall one say hereafter, and fresh grief shall be thine for lack of such an husband as thou hadst to ward off the day of thraldom. But me in death may the heaped-up earth be covering, ere I hear thy crying and thy carrying into captivity."

So spake glorious Hector, and stretched out his arm to his boy. But the child shrunk crying to the bosom of his fair-girdled nurse, dismayed at his dear father's aspect, and in dread at the bronze and horse-hair crest that he beheld nodding fiercely from the helmet's top. Then his dear father laughed aloud, and his lady mother; forthwith glorious Hector took the helmet from his head, and laid it, all gleaming, upon the earth; then kissed he his dear son and dandled him in his arms, and spake in prayer to Zeus and all the gods: "O Zeus and all ye gods, vouchsafe ye that this my son may likewise prove even as I, preeminent amid the Trojans, and as valiant in might, and be a great king of Ilios. Then may men say of him, 'Far greater is he than his father,' as he returneth home from battle; and may he bring with him blood-stained spoils from the foeman that he has slain, and may his mother's heart be glad."

So spake he, and laid his son in his dear wife's arms; and she took him to her fragrant bosom, smiling tearfully. And her husband had pity to see her, and caressed her with his hand, and spake and called upon her name: "Dear one, I pray thee be not of oversorrowful heart; no man against my fate shall hurl me to Hades; only destiny, I ween, no man hath escaped, be he coward or be he valiant, when once he hath been born. But go thou to thine house and see to mine own tasks, the loom and distaff,[1] and bid thy handmaidens ply their work; but for war shall men provide, and I in chief of all men that dwell in Ilios."

So spake glorious Hector, and took up his horse-hair crested helmet; and his dear wife departed to her home oft looking back, and letting fall big tears.

READING AND DISCUSSION QUESTIONS

1. Why is Hector compelled to fight against the Greeks? Why does he give in to destiny?

2. According to the passage, what are the highest goals for a Greek man?

3. What was the status of women in Trojan society? What was their role in the family and during war?

DOCUMENT 4-2

SAPPHO

A Lyric Poem Laments an Absent Lover

ca. 590 B.C.E.

Sappho (ca. 625–570 B.C.E.) remains the most famous female writer from antiquity; however, only a small selection of her work has survived on papyri or cited as grammatical examples by later writers. Much of Sappho's extant

---

Sappho no. 31 (*Greek Lyrics*, vol. 1, Loeb Classical Library) in Jeffrey M. Duban, trans., *Ancient and Modern Images of Sappho* (Lanham, Md.: University Press of America, 1983), 51.

[1] **distaff**: woman's work, related to spinning thread.

poetry describes love and desire between women, leading many modern read-ers to describe her as a lesbian (the term is derived from the island of her birth, Lesbos). Ancient sexuality, however, differed greatly from sexuality in modernity, and strict labels of homo- or heterosexuality are inadequate to explain sexual dynamics in antiquity. For example, Sappho's poems men-tion her daughter, Cleïs, indicating that she was probably married.

Equal to the gods does he appear
that man who sits close to you,
hears the sound of your sweet voice,
— intently near —
and your delightful laughter. That sight,
I swear, sets my heartbeat pounding;
the slightest glance at you puts my
speech to flight!
My tongue unhinges, a delicate
flame slips racing beneath my skin,
I see nothing, am blinded, my ears
ring, pulsate,
a cold sweat commands me, dread
grasps at my heart. More pallid
than grass, I appear to myself
nearly dead.

READING AND DISCUSSION QUESTIONS

1. How does Sappho describe the qualities of being in love?
2. What do Sappho's poems suggest about the education and status of women in Greek society?

DOCUMENT 4-3

PLATO

From Apologia

ca. 399 B.C.E.

Plato (427–347 B.C.E.), a classical Greek philosopher and founder of the Academy philosophical school, was a pupil of the philosopher Socrates (ca. 470–399 B.C.E.), and sought to preserve his mentor's contribution to Athenian life. As Socrates recorded nothing, we must rely on Plato's documentation of Socrates' teachings. In the following speech, Socrates presents his defense in Athenian court against the charges that he was impious and corrupted the youth. It is unclear to what extent the Apologia *represents his actual words or merely Plato's re-imagining of them. Although the exact date of the* Apologia *is unknown, Plato recorded this speech after Socrates' conviction and execution.*

Men of Athens, do not interrupt me with noise, even if I seem to you to be boasting; for the word that I speak is not mine, but the speaker to whom I shall refer it is a person of weight. For of my wisdom — if it is wisdom at all — and of its nature, I will offer you the god of Delphi[2] as a witness. You know Chaerephon, I fancy. He was my comrade from a youth and the comrade of your democratic party.[3] . . . Well, once he went to Delphi and made so bold as to ask the oracle this question; and, gentlemen, don't make a disturbance at what I say; for he asked if there were anyone wiser than I. Now the Pythia[4] replied that there was no one wiser. And about these things his brother here will bear you witness, since Chaerephon is dead.

But see why I say these things; for I am going to tell you from where the prejudice against me has arisen. For when I heard this, I thought to

---

Plato, *Apologia*, in F. J. Church, trans. *The Trial and Death of Socrates* (London: MacMillan, 1880).

[2] **Delphi**: The location of the most important oracle in the Greek world, which was dedicated to the god Apollo.
[3] **your democratic party**: Socrates did not support Athens's democratic faction.
[4] **Pythia**: The priestess at Delphi who spoke for the god Apollo.

myself: "What in the world does the god mean, and what riddle is he pro-pounding?[5] For I am conscious that I am not wise to any degree. What then does he mean by declaring that I am the wisest? He certainly cannot be lying, for that is not possible for him." And for a long time I was at a loss as to what he meant; then with great reluctance I proceeded to investigate him somewhat as follows.

I went to one of those who had a reputation for wisdom, thinking that there, if anywhere, I should prove the utterance wrong and should show the oracle "This man is wiser than I, but you said I was wisest." So exam-ining this man — for I need not call him by name, but it was one of the public men with regard to whom I had this kind of experience, men of Athens — and conversing with him, this man seemed to me to seem to be wise to many other people and especially to himself, but not to be so; and then I tried to show him that he thought he was wise, but was not. As a result, I became hateful to him and to many of those present; and so, as I went away, I thought to myself, I am wiser than this man; for neither of us really knows anything fine and good, but this man thinks he knows some-thing when he does not, whereas I, as I do not know anything, do not think I do either. I seem, then, in just this little thing to be wiser than this man at any rate, that what I do not know I do not think I know either." From him I went to another of those who were reputed to be wiser than he, and these same things seemed to me to be true; and there I became hateful both to him and to many others. . . .

Now from this investigation, men of Athens, many enmities have arisen against me, and such as are most harsh and grievous, so that many prejudices have resulted from them and I am called a wise man. For on each occasion those who are present think I am wise in the matters in which I confute someone else; but the fact is, gentlemen, it is likely that the god is really wise and by his oracle means this: "Human wisdom is of little or no value." And it appears that he does not really say this of Socrates, but merely uses my name, and makes me an example, as if he were to say: "This one of you, O human beings, is wisest, who, like Socrates, recog-nizes that he is in truth of no account in respect to wisdom."

Therefore I am still even now going about and searching and investi-gating at the god's behest anyone, whether citizen or foreigner, who I think

---

[5] **what riddle . . . propounding?**: The Pythia at Delphi was known for answering questions in the form of riddles.

is wise; and when he does not seem so to me, I give aid to the god and show that he is not wise. And by reason of this occupation I have no leisure to attend to any of the affairs of the state worth mentioning, or of my own, but am in vast poverty on account of my service to the god.[6]

And in addition to these things, the young men who have the most leisure, the sons of the richest men, accompany me of their own accord, find pleasure in hearing people being examined, and often imitate me themselves, and then they undertake to examine others; and then, I fancy, they find a great plenty of people who think they know something, but know little or nothing. As a result, therefore, those who are examined by them are angry with me, instead of being angry with themselves, and say that "Socrates is a most abominable person and is corrupting the youth."

And when anyone asks them "by doing or teaching what?" they have nothing to say, but they do not know, and that they may not seem to be at a loss, they say these things that are handy to say against all the philosophers, "the things in the air and the things beneath the Earth" and "not to believe in the gods" and "to make the weaker argument the stronger." For they would not, I fancy, care to say the truth, that it is being made very clear that they pretend to know, but know nothing. . . . If you should say to me . . . "Socrates, this time we will not do as Anytus[7] says, but we will let you go, on this condition, however, that you no longer spend our time in this investigation or in philosophy ["love of wisdom"], and if you are caught doing so again you shall die"; if you should let me go on this condition which I have mentioned, I should say to you, "Men of Athens, I respect and love you, but I shall obey the god [Apollo] rather than you, and while I live and am able to continue, I shall never give up philosophy or stop exhorting you and pointing out the truth to any one of you whom I may meet, saying in my accustomed way: "Most excellent man, are you who are a citizen of Athens, the greatest of cities and the most famous for wisdom and power, not ashamed to care for the acquisition of wealth and for reputation and honor, when you neither care nor take thought for wisdom and truth and the perfection of your soul?" And if any of you argues the point, and says he does care, I shall not let him go at once, nor shall I go away, but I shall question and examine and cross-examine him, and if I

---

[6] **my service to the god**: Socrates performed his civic duty for Athens as a soldier and as an officeholder.

[7] **Anytus**: The person who brought charges against Socrates.

find that he does not possess virtue, but says he does, I shall rebuke him for scorning the things that are of most importance and caring more for what is of less worth. This I shall do to whomever I meet, young and old, foreigner and citizen, but most to the citizens, inasmuch as you are more nearly related to me. For know that the god commands me to do this, and I believe that no greater good ever came to pass in the city than my service to the god. For I go about doing nothing else than urging you, young and old, not to care for your persons or your property more than for the perfection of your souls, or even so much; and I tell you that virtue does not come from money, but from virtue comes money and all other good things to man, both to the individual and to the state. If by saying these things I corrupt the youth, these things must be injurious, but if anyone asserts that I say other things than these, he says what is untrue. Therefore I say to you, men of Athens, either do as Anytus tells you, or not, and either acquit me, or not, knowing that I shall not change my conduct even if I am to die many times over. . . .

For know that if you kill me, I being such a man as I say I am, you will not injure me so much as yourselves. . . . And so, men of Athens, I am now making my defense not for my own sake, as one might imagine, but far more for yours, that you may not by condemning me err in your treatment of the gift the god gave you. For if you put me to death, you will not easily find another, who, to use a rather absurd figure, attaches himself to the city as a gadfly to a horse, which, though large and well bred, is sluggish on account of his size and needs to be aroused by stinging. I think the god fastened me upon the city in some such capacity, and I go about arousing, and urging and reproaching each one of you, constantly alighting upon you everywhere the whole day long. Such another is not likely to come to you, gentlemen; but if you take my advice, you will spare me. But you, perhaps, might be angry, like people awakened from a nap, and might slap me, as Anytus advises, and easily kill me; then you would pass the rest of your lives in slumber, unless the god, in his care for you, should send someone else to sting you. And that I am, as I say, a kind of gift from the god, you might understand from this; for I have neglected all my own affairs and have been enduring the neglect of my concerns all these years, but I am always busy in your interest, coming to each one of you individually like a father or an elder brother and urging you to care for virtue; now that is not like human conduct. If I derived any profit from this and received pay for these exhortations, there would be some sense in it; but now you yourselves see that my accusers, though they accuse me of everything else in such a shameless way, have not been able to work themselves up to such a pitch of shamelessness as to produce a witness to testify that I ever exacted or asked pay of anyone. For I think I have a sufficient witness that I speak the truth, namely, my poverty. . . .

I was never any one's teacher. If any one, whether young or old, wishes to hear me speaking and pursuing my mission, I have never objected, nor do I converse only when I am paid and not otherwise, but I offer myself alike to rich and poor; I ask questions, and whoever wishes may answer and hear what I say. And whether any of them turns out well or ill, I should not justly be held responsible, since I never promised or gave any instruction to any of them;[8] but if any man says that he ever learned or heard anything privately from me, which all the others did not, be assured that he is lying.

But why then do some people love to spend much of their time with me? You have heard the reason, men of Athens; for I told you the whole truth; it is because they like to listen when those are examined who think they are wise and are not so; for it is amusing.

READING AND DISCUSSION QUESTIONS

1. How does Socrates defend himself against the charges of impiety and corrupting the youth? Do you find his argument convincing?

2. Socrates was convicted and later sentenced to death. Why might the Athenians have found him guilty?

3. How does Socrates define and seek wisdom?

4. What tactics did Socrates use to question people? Why might he have attracted so many followers? Conversely, what elements of Socrates method might have created enemies?

---

[8] **I was never any one's teacher . . . them**: Socrates contrasts himself with the Sophists who charged money for their instruction.

DOCUMENT 4-4

ARISTOTLE

From Politics

ca. 340 B.C.E.

Plato's Academy attracted a number of students, including Aristotle (384–322 B.C.E.). Following Plato's death in 347 B.C.E., Aristotle left the Academy, tutored the young Alexander before he became "the Great," and eventually founded his own school, the Lyceum in Athens. Aristotle disagreed with Plato on a number of basic philosophical points, most importantly in methodology, for Aristotle believed that direct observation and experiments were the source of true knowledge. In Politics, *he compared information from numerous constitutions and sought to understand the difference between a "good" government, which enhanced everyone's life, and a "bad" government, which enriched the lives of a few.*

Having established these particulars, we come to consider next the different number of governments which there are, and what they are; and first, what are their excellencies: for when we have determined this, their defects will be evident enough.

It is evident that every form of government or administration, for the words are of the same import, must contain a supreme power over the whole state, and this supreme power must necessarily be in the hands of one person, or a few, or many; and when either of these apply their power for the common good, such states are well governed; but when the interest of the one, the few, or the many who enjoy this power is alone consulted, then ill; for you must either affirm that those who make up the community are not citizens, or else let these share in the advantages of government. We usually call a state which is governed by one person for the common good, a kingdom; one that is governed by more than one, but by a few only, an aristocracy; either because the government is in the hands of the most worthy citizens, or because it is the best form for the city and its inhabitants. When the citizens at large govern for the public good, it is called a state; which is also a common name for all other governments,

Aristotle, *Politics* 3:7, 10, trans. J. E. C. Welldon (London: Macmillan, 1883), 78–79, 84.

and these distinctions are consonant to reason; for it will not be difficult to find one person, or a very few, of very distinguished abilities, but almost impossible to meet with the majority of a people eminent for every virtue; but if there is one common to a whole nation it is valor; for this is created and supported by numbers: for which reason in such a state that profession of arms will always have the greatest share in the government.

Now the corruptions attending each of these governments are these; a kingdom may degenerate into a tyranny, an aristocracy into an oligarchy, and a state into a democracy. Now a tyranny is a monarchy where the good of one man only is the object of government, an oligarchy considers only the rich, and a democracy only the poor; but neither of them have a common good in view. . . .

It may also be a doubt where the supreme power ought to be lodged. Shall it be with the majority, or the wealthy, with a number of proper persons, or one better than the rest, or with a tyrant? But whichever of these we prefer some difficulty will arise. For what? Shall the poor have it because they are the majority? They may then divide among themselves what belongs to the rich: nor is this unjust; because truly it has been so judged by the supreme power. But what avails it to point out what is the height of injustice if this is not? Again, if the many seize into their own hands everything which belongs to the few, it is evident that the city will be at an end. But virtue will never destroy what is virtuous; nor can what is right be the ruin of the state: therefore such a law can never be right, nor can the acts of a tyrant ever be wrong, for of necessity they must all be just; for he, from his unlimited power, compels every one to obey his command, as the multitude oppress the rich. Is it right then that the rich, the few, should have the supreme power? And what if they be guilty of the same rapine [theft] and plunder the possessions of the majority, that will be as right as the other: but that all things of this sort are wrong and unjust is evident. Well then, these of the better sort shall have it: but must not then all the other citizens live unhonored, without sharing the offices of the city; for the office of a city are its honors, and if one set of men are always in power, it is evident that the rest must be without honor. Well then, let it be with one person of all others the fittest for it: but by this means the power will be still more contracted, and a greater number than before continue unhonored. But some one may say, that it is wrong to let man have the supreme power and not the law, as his soul is subject to so many passions. But if this law appoints an aristocracy, or a democracy, how will it help us in our present doubts? For those things will happen which we have already mentioned.

READING AND DISCUSSION QUESTIONS

1. According to Aristotle, what are the different types of governments and how are they defined?

2. Aristotle believes that one of the chief problems in organizing a government is determining who should rule. How does Aristotle solve this problem and what is his argument?

3. Aristotle argues that governments tend to become corrupt; for example, a kingdom becomes a tyranny, an aristocracy becomes an oligarchy, and a state becomes a democracy. What is the problem with these corrupt governments? How might good governments be corrupted?

COMPARATIVE QUESTIONS

1. How are the gods charaterized in these passages? Specifically, how are the gods in Plato's *Apologia* similar to or different from those in Homer's works?

2. How do the techniques that Socrates and Aristotle used to understand the world differ?

3. What aspects of everyday life are visible in these passages? What aspects are unexamined?

4. Greek civilization is often described as "rational." In what ways do each of these passages support or challenge that characterization?

CHAPTER 5

The World of Rome

753 B.C.E.–479 C.E.

According to tradition, the twins Romulus and Remus, abandoned as infants, founded the city of Rome in 753 B.C.E. on the site where they were discovered and nurtured by a she-wolf. Rome was at first controlled by kings, the last of whom was overthrown in 509 B.C.E., but the founding of the republic put power in the hands of elected officials and the Senate. Over the next five centuries, Rome defeated Carthage and the Hellenistic states, taking complete control of the Mediterranean world. While these victories brought immense wealth to Rome, its powerful leaders plunged the republic into civil war. In 31 B.C.E., the adoptive son of Julius Caesar, who was later known as Augustus, founded the Roman Empire. The Roman Empire expanded its territory even further, moving west and north into Gaul and Britain and eastward into Asia, while emperors consolidated power for themselves, slowly restricting the powers of the senatorial class.

DOCUMENT 5-1

The Twelve Tables

ca. 450 B.C.E.

By tradition, Roman laws were not written down and were only interpreted by the patricians (upper class men) and the priests. In 451 B.C.E., a panel of ten men was appointed to inscribe the laws on stone, possibly to placate plebeian (lower class) hostility to arbitrary justice. The panel initially produced ten tables and added two more in 450. The original Twelve Tables were destroyed when the city of Rome was sacked by the Gauls in the early fourth

Oliver J. Thatcher, ed., *The Library of Original Sources* (Milwaukee, Wis.: University Research Extension Co., 1901), Vol. III: *The Roman World*, 9–11. [Modernized by J. S. Arkenberg].

century B.C.E. *and were gradually superseded by later laws. For these reasons, only fragments of the Twelve Tables survive.*

TABLE I.

1. If anyone summons a man before the magistrate, he must go. If the man summoned does not go, let the one summoning him call the bystanders to witness and then take him by force.
2. If he shirks or runs away, let the summoner lay hands on him.
3. If illness or old age is the hindrance, let the summoner provide a team. He need not provide a covered carriage with a pallet unless he chooses.
4. Let the protector of a landholder be a landholder; for one of the proletariat, let anyone that cares, be protector. . . .
6–9. When the litigants settle their case by compromise, let the magistrate announce it. If they do not compromise, let them state each his own side of the case, in the *comitium*[1] of the forum before noon. Afterwards let them talk it out together, while both are present. After noon, in case either party has failed to appear, let the magistrate pronounce judgment in favor of the one who is present. If both are present the trial may last until sunset but no later.

TABLE II.

2. He whose witness has failed to appear may summon him by loud calls before his house every third day.

TABLE III.

1. One who has confessed a debt, or against whom judgment has been pronounced, shall have thirty days to pay it in. After that forcible seizure of his person is allowed. The creditor shall bring him before the magistrate. Unless he pays the amount of the judgment or some one in the presence of the magistrate interferes in his behalf as protector the creditor so shall take him home and fasten him in stocks or fetters. He shall fasten him with not less than fifteen pounds of weight or, if he choose, with more. If the prisoner choose, he may

---

[1] *comitium*: A location in the forum in front of the Senate building where speeches were delivered and judicial business was conducted.

furnish his own food. If he does not, the creditor must give him a pound of meal daily; if he choose he may give him more.

2. On the third market day let them divide his body among them. If they cut more or less than each one's share it shall be no crime.

3. Against a foreigner the right in property shall be valid forever.

TABLE IV.

1. A dreadfully deformed child shall be quickly killed.

2. If a father sell his son three times, the son shall be free from his father.

3. As a man has provided in his will in regard to his money and the care of his property, so let it be binding. If he has no heir and dies intestate, let the nearest agnate [male relative] have the inheritance. If there is no agnate, let the members of his gens [families belonging to one ancestral group] have the inheritance.

4. If one is mad but has no guardian, the power over him and his money shall belong to his agnates and the members of his gens.

5. A child born after ten months since the father's death will not be admitted into a legal inheritance.

TABLE V.

1. Females should remain in guardianship even when they have attained their majority.

TABLE VI.

1. When one makes a bond and a conveyance of property, as he has made formal declaration so let it be binding. . . .

3. A beam that is built into a house or a vineyard trellis one may not take from its place. . . .

5. *Usucapio* [obtaining ownership] of movable things requires one year's possession for its completion; but *usucapio* of an estate and buildings two years.

6. Any woman who does not wish to be subjected in this manner to the hand of her husband should be absent three nights in succession every year, and so interrupt the *usucapio* of each year.

TABLE VII.

1. Let them keep the road in order. If they have not paved it, a man may drive his team where he likes. . . .

9. Should a tree on a neighbor's farm be bend crooked by the wind and lean over your farm, you may take legal action for removal of that tree.

10. A man might gather up fruit that was falling down onto another man's farm.

TABLE VIII.

2. If one has maimed a limb and does not compromise with the injured person, let there be retaliation. If one has broken a bone of a freeman with his hand or with a cudgel, let him pay a penalty of three hundred coins. If he has broken the bone of a slave, let him have one hundred and fifty coins. If one is guilty of insult, the penalty shall be twenty-five coins.

3. If one is slain while committing theft by night, he is rightly slain.

4. If a patron shall have devised any deceit against his client, let him be accursed.

5. If one shall permit himself to be summoned as a witness, or has been a weigher, if he does not give his testimony, let him be noted as dishonest and incapable of acting again as witness. . . .

10. Any person who destroys by burning any building or heap of corn deposited alongside a house shall be bound, scourged [whipped], and put to death by burning at the stake provided that he has committed the said misdeed with malice aforethought; but if he shall have committed it by accident, that is, by negligence, it is ordained that he repair the damage or, if he be too poor to be competent for such punishment, he shall receive a lighter punishment. . . .

12. If the theft has been done by night, if the owner kills the thief, the thief shall be held to be lawfully killed.

13. It is unlawful for a thief to be killed by day. . . . unless he defends himself with a weapon; even though he has come with a weapon, unless he shall use the weapon and fight back, you shall not kill him. And even if he resists, first call out so that someone may hear and come up. . . .

23. A person who had been found guilty of giving false witness shall be hurled down from the Tarpeian Rock.[2] . . .

26. No person shall hold meetings by night in the city.

---

[2]**Tarpeian Rock**: A cliff located on the Capitoline Hill close to the temple of Jupiter. Those convicted of murder or treason during the republic were thrown off of it.

TABLE IX.

4. The penalty shall be capital [i.e., execution] for a judge or arbiter legally appointed who has been found guilty of receiving a bribe for giving a decision.
5. Treason: he who shall have roused up a public enemy or handed over a citizen to a public enemy must suffer capital punishment.
6. Putting to death of any man, whosoever he might be unconvicted is forbidden.

TABLE X.

1. None is to bury or burn a corpse in the city.
3. The women shall not tear their faces nor wail on account of the funeral.
5. If one obtains a crown himself, or if his chattel does so because of his honor and valor, if it is placed on his head, or the head of his parents, it shall be no crime.

TABLE XI.

1. Marriages should not take place between plebeians and patricians.

TABLE XII.

2. If a slave shall have committed theft or done damage with his master's knowledge, the action for damages is in the slave's name. . . .
5. Whatever the people had last ordained should be held as binding by law.

READING AND DISCUSSION QUESTIONS

1. From reading the Twelve Tables, what impression do you get of the Roman family? What power did men have over their children and wives?
2. What do these laws tell us about Roman society?
3. What was Roman justice like?

DOCUMENT 5-2

PLUTARCH

On Julius Caesar, A Man of Unlimited Ambition

ca. 44 C.E.

Plutarch's Parallel Lives *served as the greatest source of knowledge about the ancient world for people of the Renaissance and for Shakespeare, even though its original intent was not to preserve history, but rather to examine moral virtues and vices. Plutarch was committed to supporting the Roman Empire and later became a priest at the Greek oracle shrine at Delphi. The following document, written about 150 years after the death of Julius Caesar, describes Roman attitudes toward the power that Julius Caesar gained following a civil war victory against the general Pompey.*

But that which brought upon him the most apparent and mortal hatred was his desire of being king;[3] which gave the common people the first occasion to quarrel with him, and proved the most specious pretence to those who had been his secret enemies all along. Those who would have procured him that title gave it out that it was foretold in the Sibyls' books[4] that the Romans should conquer the Parthians[5] when they fought against them under the conduct of a king, but not before. And one day, as Caesar was coming down from Alba to Rome, some were so bold as to salute him by the name of king; but he, finding the people disrelish it, seemed to resent it himself, and said his name was Caesar, not king. Upon this there was a general silence, and he passed on looking not very well pleased or contented. Another time, when the senate had conferred on him some extravagant honors, he chanced to receive the message as he was sitting on the rostra [podium], where, though the consuls [highest elected officials]

Plutarch, *Parallel Lives*, "Julius Caesar," trans. John Dryden, rev. Arthur Hugh Clough (New York: Modern Library, n.d.), 888–890.

[3] **his desire of being king**: The Romans feared the tyranny of kings.
[4] **Sybils' books**: Books of prophecy that were consulted in Rome during times of crisis.
[5] **Parthians**: The only civilized power on Rome's frontiers, the Parthians controlled Mesopotamia and Persia. They were famous horsemen and developed the "Parthian shot," which allowed them to shoot arrows while riding away from attackers.

and praetors [elected ministers of justice] themselves waited on him, attended by the whole body of the senate, he did not rise, but behaved himself to them as if they had been private men, and told them his honors wanted rather to be retrenched then increased. This treatment offended not only the senate, but the commonalty too, as if they thought the affront upon the senate equally reflected upon the whole republic; so that all who could decently leave him went off, looking much discomposed. Caesar, perceiving the false step he had made, immediately retired home; and laying his throat bare, told his friends that he was ready to offer this to any one would give the stroke. But afterwards he made the malady from which he suffered [epilepsy] the excuse for his sitting, saying that those who are attacked by it lose their presence of mind if they talk much standing; that they presently grow giddy, fall into convulsions, and quite lose their reason. But this was not the reality, for he would willingly have stood up to the senate, had not Cornelius Balbus, one of his friends, or rather flatterers, hindered him. "Will you not remember," said he, "you are Caesar, and claim the honor which is due to your merit?"

He gave a fresh occasion of resentment by his affront to the tribunes.[6] The Lupercalia were then celebrated, a feast at the first institution belonging, as some writers say, to the shepherds, and having some connection with the Arcadian Lycae. Many young noblemen and magistrates run up and down the city with their upper garments off, striking all they meet with thongs of hide, by way of sport; and many women, even of the highest rank, place themselves in the way, and hold out their hands to the lash, as boys in a school do to the master, out of a belief that it procures an easy labor to those who are with child, and makes those conceive who are barren. Caesar, dressed in a triumphal robe, seated himself in a golden chair at the rostra to view this ceremony. Antony [i.e., Mark Antony, Caesar's closest ally], as consul, was one of those who ran this course, and when he came into the forum, and the people made way for him, he went up and reached to Caesar a diadem wreathed with laurel [like a king's crown]. Upon this there was a shout, but only a slight one, made by the few who were planted there for that purpose; but when Caesar refused it, there was universal applause. Upon the second offer, very few, and upon the second refusal, all again applauded. Caesar finding it would not take, rose up, and

---

[6] **tribunes**: Tribunes of the Plebs, which were originally created to defend the plebian class of citizens against the patricians who dominated the early Roman government and which could veto actions and laws they thought would harm the plebians. By the time of Caesar, the Tribunes of the Plebs were often working for their own benefit.

ordered the crown to be carried into the capitol. Caesar's statues were afterwards found with royal diadems on their heads. Flavius and Marullus, two tribunes of the people, went presently and pulled them off, and having apprehended those who first saluted Caesar as king committed them to prison. The people followed them with acclamations, and called them by the name of Brutus, because Brutus was the first who ended the succession of kings,[7] and transferred the power which before was lodged in one man into the hands of the senate and people. Caesar so far resented this, that he displaced Marullus and Flavius; and in urging his charges against them, at the same time ridiculed the people, by himself giving the men more than once the names of Bruti and Cumaei.[8]

This made the multitude turn their thoughts to Marcus Brutus, who, by his father's side, was thought to be descended from that first Brutus, and by his mother's side from the Servilii, another noble family, being besides nephew and son-in-law to Cato. But the honors and favors he had received from Caesar took off the edge from the desires he might himself have felt for overthrowing the new monarchy. For he had not only been pardoned himself after Pompey's defeat at Pharsalia, and had procured the same grace for many of his friends, but was one in whom Caesar had a particular confidence. He had at that time the most honorable praetorship for the year, and was named for the consulship four years after, being preferred before Cassius, his competitor. Upon the question as to the choice, Caesar, it is related, said that Cassius had the fairer pretensions, but that he could not pass by Brutus. Nor would he afterwards listen to some who spoke against Brutus, when the conspiracy against him was already afoot, but laying his hand on his body, said to the informers, "Brutus will wait for this skin of mine," intimating that he was worthy to bear rule on account of his virtue, but would not be base and ungrateful to gain it. Those who desired a change, and looked on him as the only, or at least the most proper, person to effect it, did not venture to speak with him; but in the night-time laid papers about his chair of state, where he used to sit and determine causes, with such sentences in them as, "You are asleep, Brutus," "You are no longer Brutus." Cassius, when he perceived his ambition a little raised upon this, was more instant than before to work him yet

---

[7] **was the first . . . kings**: In 509 B.C.E., Lucius Brutus removed the last king from Rome.

[8] **Bruti and Cumaei**: Both names suggest that Caesar was calling the people stupid. The name Brutus means "stupid" and people from Cumae were thought to lack intelligence.

further, having himself a private grudge against Caesar[9] for some reasons that we have mentioned in the Life of Brutus.[10] Nor was Caesar without suspicions of him, and said once to his friends, "What do you think Cassius is aiming at? I don't like him, he looks so pale." And when it was told him that Antony and Dolabella[11] were in a plot against him, he said he did not fear such fat, luxurious men, but rather the pale, lean fellows, meaning Cassius and Brutus.

READING AND DISCUSSION QUESTIONS

1. What was the Roman attitude toward Caesar becoming king? What difference do you detect between the views of the senators and of the common people?

2. How did the plot against Caesar develop? What justification did Brutus and Cassius use to support their assassination of Caesar?

DOCUMENT 5-3

LIVY

On the Founding of Rome and the Rape of the Sabine Women

27–25 B.C.E.

Titus Livius (59 B.C.E.–17 C.E.) lived through the end of the Roman civil wars and became a confidant and loyal critic of the emperor Augustus. Livy composed 142 books of Roman history going back to the founding of the city of Rome, but less than 30 survive intact. Based on oral tradition dating back

Livy, *Roman History*, trans. John Henry Freese, Alfred John Church, and William Jackson Brodribb (New York: D. Appleton and Company, 1898), 4–7, 10–12.

[9] **a private grudge against Caesar**: Cassius was angry that Caesar had promoted Brutus over him.

[10] **Life of Brutus**: Another one of Plutarch's *Parallel Lives*.

[11] **Dolabella**: A general who originally sided with Pompey, but later joined with Caesar who rewarded him with the consulship.

over seven hundred years, the following passage is Livy's retelling of two leg-
ends concerning the earliest history of the Roman people — the founding of
the city by Romulus and Remus and the rape of the Sabine women.

My opinion, however, is that the origin of so great a city and an empire
next in power to that of the gods was due to the fates. The Vesta Rea[12] was
ravished by force and having brought forth twins, declared Mars [Roman
god of war] to be the father of her illegitimate offspring, either because
she really imagined it to be the case, or because it was less discreditable
to have committed such an offense with a god. But neither gods nor men
protected either her or her offspring from the king's cruelty. The priestess was bound and cast into prison; the king ordered the children to be
thrown into the flowing river. By some chance which Providence seemed
to direct, the Tiber,[13] having overflown its banks, thereby forming stagnant
pools could not be approached at the regular course of its channel;
notwithstanding it gave the bearers of the children hope that they could be
drowned in its water however calm. Accordingly, as if they had executed
the king's orders, they exposed the boys in the nearest land-pool, where
now stands the ficus Ruminalis [a fig tree], which they say was called
Romularis [after Romulus]. At that time the country in those parts was a
desolate wilderness. The story goes, that when the shallow water, subsid-
ing, had left the floating trough, in which the children had been exposed,
on dry ground, a thirsty she-wolf from the mountains around directed her
course toward the cries of the infants, and held down her teats to them
with such gentleness, that the keeper of the king's herd found her licking
the boys with her tongue. They say that his name was Faustulus; and that
they were carried by him to his homestead and given to his wife Larentia
to be brought up. Some are of the opinion that Larentia was called Lupa[14]
among the shepherds from her being a common prostitute; and hence an
opening was afforded for the marvellous story. The children, thus born and
thus brought up, as soon as they reached the age of youth, did not lead a
life of inactivity at home or amid the flocks, but, in the chase, scoured the
forests. Having thus gained strength, both in body and spirit, they now

[12] **Vesta Rea**: Rea, a vestal virgin. Vestal virgins had to remain sexually pure during
their thirty-year service to the goddess of the hearth, Vesta. Those who did not were
buried alive.

[13] **Tiber**: A river in central Italy on which Rome was later founded.

[14] **Lupa**: The Latin name for either a she-wolf or a prostitute.

were not only able to withstand wild beasts, but attacked robbers laden with booty, and divided the spoils with the shepherds, in whose company, as the number of their young associates increased daily, they carried on business and pleasure.

Even in these early times it is said that the festival of the Lupercal,[15] as now celebrated, was solemnized on the Palatine Hill.[16] . . . When they were engaged in this festival, as its periodical solemnization was well known, a band of robbers, enraged at the loss of some booty, lay in wait for them, and took Remus prisoner, Romulus having vigorously defended himself: the captive Remus they delivered up to King Amulius,[17] and even went so far as to bring accusations against him. They made it the principal charge that having made incursions into Numitor's [King of Alba Longa] lands, and, having assembled a band of young men, they had driven off their booty after the manner of enemies. Accordingly, Remus was delivered up to Numitor for punishment. Now from the very first Faustulus [the shepherd who found Romulus and Remus] had entertained hopes that the boys who were being brought up by him, were of royal blood: for he both knew that the children had been exposed by the king's orders, and that the time, at which he had taken them up, coincided exactly with that period: but he had been unwilling to disclose the matter, as yet not ripe for discovery, till either a fitting opportunity or the necessity for it should arise. Necessity came first. Accordingly, urged by fear, he disclosed the whole affair to Romulus. By accident also, Numitor, while he had Remus in custody, having heard that the brothers were twins, by comparing their age and their natural disposition entirely free from servility, felt his mind struck by the recollection of his grandchildren, and by frequent inquiries came to the conclusion he had already formed, so that he was not far from openly acknowledging Remus. Accordingly a plot was concerted against the king on all sides. Romulus, not accompanied by a body of young men — for he was not equal to open violence — but having commanded the shepherds to come to the palace by different roads at a fixed time, made an attack upon the king, while Remus, having got together another party from Numitor's house, came to his assistance; and so they slew the king.

---

[15] **Lupercal**: Festival celebrated during February in which naked young men lightly whipped young women to enhance their fertility.

[16] **Palatine Hill**: One of the seven hills of Rome; it overlooks the Roman Forum. Augustus's house was located on Palatine Hill.

[17] **King Amulius**: Uncle of Rea, mother of Romulus and Remus, and younger brother of her father Numitor. He took the throne of Alba Longa from Numitor.

Numitor, at the beginning of the fray, giving out that enemies had invaded the city and attacked the palace, after he had drawn off the Alban youth to the citadel to secure it with an armed garrison, when he saw the young men, after they had compassed the king's death, advancing toward him to offer congratulations, immediately summoned a meeting of the people, and recounted his brother's unnatural behavior toward him, the extraction of his grandchildren, the manner of their birth, bringing up, and recognition, and went on to inform them of the king's death, and that he was responsible for it. The young princes advanced through the midst of the assembly with their band in orderly array, and, after they had saluted their grandfather as king, a succeeding shout of approbation, issuing from the whole multitude, ratified for him the name and authority of sovereign. The government of Alba being thus entrusted to Numitor, Romulus, and Remus were seized with the desire of building a city on the spot where they had been exposed and brought up. Indeed, the number of Alban and Latin inhabitants was too great for the city; the shepherds also were included among that population, and all these readily inspired hopes that Alba and Lavinium [city of the Latin people near Rome] would be insignificant in comparison with that city, which was intended to be built. But desire of rule, the bane of their grandfather, interrupted these designs, and thence arose a shameful quarrel from a sufficiently amicable beginning. For as they were twins, and consequently the respect for seniority could not settle the point, they agreed to leave it to the gods, under whose protection the place was, to choose by augury which of them should give a name to the new city, and govern it when built. Romulus chose the Palatine and Remus the Aventine [a hill southwest of the Palatine], as points of observation for taking the auguries [a form of divination].

It is said that an omen came to Remus first, six vultures; and when, after the omen had been declared, twice that number presented themselves to Romulus, each was hailed king by his own party, the former claiming sovereign power on the ground of priority of time, the latter on account of the number of birds. Thereupon, having met and exchanged angry words, from the strife of angry feelings they turned to bloodshed: there Remus fell from a blow received in the crowd. A more common account is that Remus, in derision of his brother, leaped over the newly-erected walls, and was thereupon slain by Romulus in a fit of passion, who, mocking him, added words to this effect: "So perish every one hereafter, who shall leap over my walls." Thus Romulus obtained possession of supreme power for himself alone. The city, when built, was called after the name of its founder. . . .

By this time the Roman state was so powerful, that it was a match for any of the neighboring states in war: but owing to the scarcity of women its greatness was not likely to outlast the existing generation, seeing that the Romans had no hope of issue at home, and they did not intermarry with their neighbors. So then, by the advice of the senators, Romulus sent around ambassadors to the neighboring states, to solicit an alliance and the right of intermarriage for his new subjects, saying, that cities, like everything else, rose from the humblest beginnings: next, that those which the gods and their own merits assisted, gained for themselves great power and high renown: that he knew full well that the gods had aided the first beginnings of Rome and that merit on their part would not be wanting: therefore, as men, let them not be reluctant to mix their blood and stock with men. The embassy nowhere obtained a favorable hearing: but, although the neighboring peoples treated it with such contempt, yet at the same time they dreaded the growth of such a mighty power in their midst to the danger of themselves and of their posterity. In most cases when they were dismissed they were asked the question, whether they had opened a sanctuary for women also: for that in that way only could they obtain suitable matches. The Roman youths were bitterly indignant at this, and the matter began unmistakably to point to open violence.

Romulus, in order to provide a fitting opportunity and place for this, dissembling his resentment, with this purpose in view, instituted games to be solemnized every year in honor of Neptunus Equester [the horse god Neptune], which he called Consualia ["God of good counsel"]. He then ordered the show to be proclaimed among the neighboring peoples; and the Romans prepared to solemnize it with all the pomp with which they were then acquainted or were able to exhibit, in order to make the spectacle famous, and an object of expectation. Great numbers assembled, being also desirous of seeing the new city, especially all the nearest peoples, the Caeninenses, Crustumini, and Antemnates: the entire Sabine population [a people near Rome] attended with their wives and children. They were hospitably invited to the different houses: and, when they saw the position of the city, its fortified walls, and how crowded with houses it was; they were astonished that the power of Rome had increased so rapidly. When the time of the show arrived, and their eyes and minds alike were intent upon it, then, according to preconcerted arrangement, a disturbance was made, and, at a given signal, the Roman youths rushed in different directions to carry off the unmarried women. A great number were carried off at hap-hazard, by those into whose hands they severally fell: some of the common people, to whom the task had been assigned, conveyed to their homes certain women of surpassing beauty, who were destined for the leading senators. . . . The festival being disturbed by the alarm thus caused, the sorrowing parents of the maidens retired, complaining of the violated compact of hospitality, and invoking the god, to whose solemn festival and games they had come, having been deceived by the pretence of religion and good faith. Nor did the maidens entertain better hopes for themselves, or feel less indignation. Romulus, however, went about in person and pointed out that what had happened was due to the pride of their fathers, in that they had refused the privilege of intermarriage to their neighbors; but that, notwithstanding, they would be lawfully wedded, and enjoy a share of all their possessions and civil rights, and — a thing dearer than all else to the human race — the society of their common children: only let them calm their angry feelings, and bestow their affections on those on whom fortune had bestowed their bodies. Esteem (said he) often arose subsequent to wrong: and they would find them better husbands for the reason that each of them would endeavor, to the utmost of his power, after having discharged, as far as his part was concerned, the duty of a husband, to quiet the longing for country and parents. To this the blandishments of the husbands were added, who excused what had been done on the plea of passion and love, a form of entreaty that works most successfully upon the feelings of women.

READING AND DISCUSSION QUESTIONS

1. According to this passage, how was the city of Rome founded? What elements make this story seem credible or unlikely? What, if any, parallel foundation myths does it resemble?

2. One of Livy's primary reasons for writing about the history of Rome was to provide moral examples. What kind of moral examples are included in these passages?

3. In what ways is this retelling of Roman history a justification for the Roman conquest of the Mediterranean and for the establishment of a king?

4. How are women portrayed in this passage?

DOCUMENT 5-4

TACITUS

On the Roman Empire

98 C.E.

The historian Tacitus (ca. 56–118 C.E.) was born in Gaul (modern France), moved to Rome, and held several important positions, including the office of consul. He wrote a number of books about the early history of the Roman Empire, but the following passage comes from his biography of his father-in-law, Agricola, who served as the governor of Britain. During Agricola's tenure, he fought against native British groups and in the following passage Tacitus recounts a speech he attributes to the British leader Galgacus. However, Galgacus did not deliver this actual speech; it is based on what Tacitus believed opponents of the Roman Empire thought.

Upwards of thirty thousand men appeared in arms, and their force was increasing every day. The youth of the country poured in from all quarters, and even the men in years, whose vigor was still unbroken, repaired to the army, proud of their past exploits, and the ensigns of honor which they had gained by their martial spirit. Among the chieftains, distinguished by their birth and valor, the most renowned was Galgacus. The multitude gathered around him, eager for action, and burning with uncommon ardor. He harangued them to the following effect:

"When I consider the motives that have roused us to this war; when I reflect on the necessity that now demands our firmest vigor, I expect every thing great and noble from that union of sentiment that pervades us all. From this day I date the freedom of Britain. We are the men, who never crouched in bondage. Beyond this spot there is no land, where liberty can find a refuge. Even the sea is shut against us, while the Roman fleet is hovering on the coast. To draw the sword in the cause of freedom is the true glory of the brave, and, in our condition, cowardice itself would throw away the scabbard. In the battles, which have been hitherto fought with alternate vicissitudes of fortune, our countrymen might well repose some

Tacitus, *The Works of Cornelius Tacitus*, 2d ed., trans. by Arthur Murphy (Washington, D.C.: Davis & Force, D. Rapine, P. Thomson, B. P. French, 1822), 42–45.

hopes in us; they might consider us as their last resource; they knew us to be the noblest sons of Britain, placed in the last recesses of the land, in the very sanctuary of liberty. We have not so much as seen the melancholy regions, where slavery has debased mankind. We have lived in freedom, and our eyes have been unpolluted by the sight of ignoble bondage.

The extremity of the earth is ours: defended by our situation, we have to this day preserved our honor and the rights of men. But we are no longer safe in our obscurity: our retreat is laid open; the enemy rushes on, and, as things unknown are ever magnified, he thinks a mighty conquest lies before him. But this is the end of the habitable world, and rocks and brawling waves fill all the space behind. The Romans are in the heart of our country; no submission can satisfy their pride; no concessions can appease their fury. While the land has any thing left, it is the theater of war; when it can yield no more they explore the seas for hidden treasure. Are the nations rich? Roman avarice is their enemy. Are they poor? Roman ambition lords it over them. The east and the west have been rifled, and the spoiler is still insatiate. The Romans, by a strange singularity of nature, are the only people who invade, with equal ardor, the wealth and the poverty of nations. To rob, to ravage, and to murder, in their imposing language, are the arts of civil policy. When they have made the world a solitude, they call it peace.

Our children and relatives are dear to us all. It is an affection planted in our breast by the hand of nature. And yet those tender pledges are ravished from us to serve in distant lands. Are our wives, our sisters, and our daughters safe from brutal lust and open violation? The insidious conqueror, under the mask of hospitality and friendship, brands them with dishonor. Our money is conveyed into their treasury, and our corn into their granaries. Our limbs and bodies are worn out in clearing woods, and draining marshes: and what have been our wages! Stripes [whipping scars] and insult. The lot of the meanest slave, born in servitude, is preferable to ours: he is sold but once, and his master maintains him; but Britain every day invites new tyrants, and every day pampers their pride. In a private family the slave "who is last bought in, provokes the mirth and ridicule of the whole domestic crew; and in this general servitude, to which Rome has reduced the world, the case is the same: we are treated, at first, as objects of derision, and then marked out for destruction." . . .

READING AND DISCUSSION QUESTIONS

1. According to this speech, what motivated the Romans to expand their empire?

2. How is life under the Roman Empire described?

3. Although this speech was written by Tacitus, what elements might reflect the feelings of conquered peoples? Other parts reflect concerns felt by Romans — especially the fear of tyranny. Why might Romans living during the Roman Empire feel this way?

4. Why do you think Tacitus wanted to give voice to an enemy of the Roman Empire?

COMPARATIVE QUESTIONS

1. How do the writings of Plutarch, Livy, and Tacitus reflect changing attitudes toward the rule of one man (king, dictator, and emperor) during different periods of Roman history?

2. How does Livy's depiction of family and gender relations differ from that of the Twelve Tables?

3. What role does violence play in Roman society, as depicted in these passages?

4. Based on the other documents, how do you think Romans in Tacitus's time and earlier would have responded to Galgacus's criticisms of the Roman Empire?

CHAPTER 6

East Asia and the Spread of Buddhism

256 B.C.E.–800 C.E.

T he Qin Dynasty (221–206 B.C.E.) conquered the "warring states" of China and created what Qin Shihuangdi (259–210 B.C.E.) hoped would be an empire that would last for 10,000 years. However, the brutal strategies of control espoused by Legalism, a philosophy that called for strict adherence to laws and a ruler with absolute power, ended the dynasty in just fourteen years. When the Han Dynasty (206 B.C.E.–220 C.E.) took control of China, they maintained a traditional focus on Confucianism and rejected the Qin's harsh punishments. Following the Han's collapse, nomadic groups from Central Asia took power in northern China, while southern China was ruled by a succession of unsuccessful dynasties. Buddhism became increasingly influential in this "Age of Division" (220–589 C.E.); Islam and Christianity also appeared in China but were less popular. When the Sui (581–618 C.E.) and Tang (618–907 C.E.) dynasties reestablished formal control over all of China, neighboring societies in Korea, Tibet, Vietnam, and Japan began to imitate Chinese rule and culture.

DOCUMENT 6-1

BAN ZHAO

From Lessons for Women

ca. 80 C.E.

Although women in traditional Confucian society were regarded as subservient to men, a few women achieved distinction in their literary pursuits

Nancy Lee Swann, trans., *Pan Chao: Foremost Woman Scholar of China* (New York: Century Co., 1932), 111–114.

and roles in government. Ban Zhao (ca. 45–120 C.E.) was the daughter of a famous writer and administrator and sister to Ban Gu, who served as the court historian for Emperor He (r. 89–105 C.E.). The privileged Ban Zhao was educated at an early age. When Ban Gu died, Ban Zhao finished his history of the Han Dynasty and served as an advisor to Emperor He and the Empress Deng. Ban Zhao's best-known work, Lessons for Women, *served as an advice manual for women in China until the twentieth century.*

I, the unworthy writer, am unsophisticated, unenlightened, and by nature unintelligent, but I am fortunate both to have received not a little favor from my scholarly father, and to have had a cultured mother and instructresses upon whom to rely for a literary education as well as for training in good manners. More than forty years have passed since at the age of fourteen I took up the dustpan and the broom in the Cao family.[1] During this time with trembling heart I feared constantly that I might disgrace my parents, and that I might multiply difficulties for both the women and the men of my husband's family. Day and night I was distressed in heart, but I labored without confessing weariness. Now and hereafter, however, I know how to escape from such fears.

Being careless, and by nature stupid, I taught and trained my children without system. Consequently I fear that my son Gu may bring disgrace upon the Imperial Dynasty by whose Holy Grace he has unprecedentedly received the extraordinary privilege of wearing the Gold and the Purple,[2] a privilege for the attainment of which by my son, I a humble subject never even hoped. Nevertheless, now that he is a man and able to plan his own life, I need not again have concern for him. But I do grieve that you, my daughters, just now at the age for marriage, have not at this time had gradual training and advice; that you still have not learned the proper customs for married women. I fear that by failure in good manners in other families you will humiliate both your ancestors and your clan. I am now seriously ill, life is uncertain. As I have thought of you all in so untrained a state, I have been uneasy many a time for you. At hours of leisure I have composed . . . these instructions under the title, "Lessons for Women." In order that you may have something wherewith to benefit your

---

[1] **took up the dustpan . . . family**: Ban Zhao had become a wife.
[2] **the Gold and the Purple**: The colors worn by the elite administrants of the Chinese realm.

persons, I wish every one of you, my daughters, each to write out a copy for yourself.

From this time on every one of you strive to practice these lessons.

HUMILITY

On the third day after the birth of a girl the ancients observed three customs: first to place the baby below the bed; second to give her a potsherd [shard of pottery] with which to play; and third to announce her birth to her ancestors by an offering. Now to lay the baby below the bed plainly indicated that she is lowly and weak, and should regard it as her primary duty to humble herself before others. To give her potsherds with which to play indubitably signified that she should practice labor and consider it her primary duty to be industrious. To announce her birth before her ancestors clearly meant that she ought to esteem as her primary duty the continuation of the observance of worship in the home.

These three ancient customs epitomize a woman's ordinary way of life and the teachings of the traditional ceremonial rites and regulations. Let a woman modestly yield to others; let her respect others; let her put others first, herself last. Should she do something good, let her not mention it; should she do something bad, let her not deny it. Let her bear disgrace; let her even endure when others speak or do evil to her. Always let her seem to tremble and to fear. When a woman follows such maxims as these, then she may be said to humble herself before others.

Let a woman retire late to bed, but rise early to duties; let her not dread tasks by day or by night. Let her not refuse to perform domestic duties whether easy or difficult. That which must be done, let her finish completely, tidily, and systematically. When a woman follows such rules as these, then she may be said to be industrious.

Let a woman be correct in manner and upright in character in order to serve her husband. Let her live in purity and quietness of spirit, and attend to her own affairs. Let her love not gossip and silly laughter. Let her cleanse and purify and arrange in order the wine and the food for the offerings to the ancestors. When a woman observes such principles as these, then she may be said to continue ancestral worship.

No woman who observes these three fundamentals of life has ever had a bad reputation or has fallen into disgrace. If a woman fails to observe them, how can her name be honored; how can she but bring disgrace upon herself?

Husband and Wife

The Way of husband and wife is intimately connected with *Yin* and *Yang*,[3] and relates the individual to gods and ancestors. Truly it is the great principle of Heaven and Earth, and the great basis of human relationships. Therefore the "Rites"[4] honor union of man and woman; and in the "Book of Poetry"[5] the "First Ode" manifests the principle of marriage. For these reasons the relationship cannot but be an important one.

If a husband is unworthy, then he possesses nothing by which to control his wife. If a wife is unworthy, then she possesses nothing with which to serve her husband. If a husband does not control his wife, then the rules of conduct manifesting his authority are abandoned and broken. If a wife does not serve her husband, then the proper relationship between men and women and the natural order of things are neglected and destroyed. As a matter of fact the purpose of these two [the controlling of women by men, and the serving of men by women] is the same.

Now examine the gentlemen of the present age. They only know that wives must be controlled, and that the husband's rules of conduct manifesting his authority must be established. They therefore teach their boys to read books and study histories. But they do not in the least understand that husbands and masters must also be served, and that the proper relationship and the rites should be maintained.

Yet only to teach men and not to teach women — is that not ignoring the essential relation between them? According to the "Rites," it is the rule to begin to teach children to read at the age of eight years, and by the age of fifteen years they ought then to be ready for cultural training. Only why should it not be that girls' education as well as boys' be according to this principle?

Respect and Caution

As *Yin* and *Yang* are not of the same nature, so man and woman have different characteristics. The distinctive quality of the *Yang* is rigidity; the

---

[3] *Yin* and *Yang*: An important concept in Chinese culture that originated in Daoism (see Document 3-3). Yin and yang are oppositional forces that are bound together and create each other.

[4] the "Rites": The *Book of Rites* is one of the five classics of Confucianism. It deals with li or "rules of conduct," and provides instructions for the correct observation of rituals.

[5] Book of Poetry: The *Book of Songs* is another of the five classics of Confucianism (see Document 3-2).

function of the *Yin* is yielding. Man is honored for strength; a woman is beautiful on account of her gentleness. Hence there arose the common saying: "A man though born like a wolf may, it is feared, become a weak monstrosity; a woman though born like a mouse may, it is feared, become a tiger."

Now for self-culture nothing equals respect for others. To counteract firmness nothing equals compliance. Consequently it can be said that the Way of respect and acquiescence is woman's most important principle of conduct. So respect may be defined as nothing other than holding on to that which is permanent; and acquiescence nothing other than being liberal and generous. Those who are steadfast in devotion know that they should stay in their proper places; those who are liberal and generous esteem others, and honor and serve them.

If husband and wife have the habit of staying together, never leaving one another, and following each other around within the limited space of their own rooms, then they will lust after and take liberties with one another. From such action improper language will arise between the two. This kind of discussion may lead to licentiousness. Out of licentiousness will be born a heart of disrespect to the husband. Such a result comes from not knowing that one should stay in one's proper place.

Furthermore, affairs may be either crooked or straight; words may be either right or wrong. Straightforwardness cannot but lead to quarreling; crookedness cannot but lead to accusation. If there are really accusations and quarrels, then undoubtedly there will be angry affairs. Such a result comes from not esteeming others, and not honoring and serving them.

If wives suppress not contempt for husbands, then it follows that such wives rebuke and scold their husbands. If husbands stop not short of anger, then they are certain to beat their wives. The correct relationship between husband and wife is based upon harmony and intimacy, and conjugal love is grounded in proper union. Should actual blows be dealt, how could matrimonial relationship be preserved? Should sharp words be spoken, how could conjugal love exist? If love and proper relationship both be destroyed, then husband and wife are divided.

WOMANLY QUALIFICATIONS

A woman ought to have four qualifications: (1) womanly virtue; (2) womanly words; (3) womanly bearing; and (4) womanly work. Now what is called womanly virtue need not be brilliant ability, exceptionally different from others. Womanly words need be neither clever in debate nor keen in conversation. Womanly appearance requires neither a pretty nor a perfect face and form. Womanly work need not be work done more skillfully than that of others.

To guard carefully her chastity; to control circumspectly her behavior; in every motion to exhibit modesty; and to model each act on the best usage, this is womanly virtue.

To choose her words with care; to avoid vulgar language; to speak at appropriate times; and not to weary others with much conversation, may be called the characteristics of womanly words.

To wash and scrub filth away; to keep clothes and ornaments fresh and clean; to wash the head and bathe the body regularly; and to keep the person free from disgraceful filth, may be called the characteristics of womanly bearing.

With whole-hearted devotion to sew and to weave; to love not gossip and silly laughter; in cleanliness and order to prepare the wine and food for serving guests, may be called the characteristics of womanly work.

These four qualifications characterize the greatest virtue of a woman. No woman can afford to be without them. In fact they are very easy to possess if a woman only treasure them in her heart. The ancients had a saying: "Is Love afar off? If I desire love, then love is at hand!" So can it be said of these qualifications. . . .

IMPLICIT OBEDIENCE

Whenever the mother-in-law says, "Do not do that," and if what she says is right, unquestionably the daughter-in-law obeys. Whenever the mother-in-law says, "Do that," even if what she says is wrong, still the daughter-in-law submits unfailingly to the command.

Let a woman not act contrary to the wishes and the opinions of parents-in-law about right and wrong; let her not dispute with them what is straight and what is crooked. Such docility may be called obedience which sacrifices personal opinion. Therefore the ancient book, "A Pattern for Women," says: "If a daughter-in-law who follows the wishes of her parents-in-law is like an echo and a shadow, how could she not be praised?"

READING AND DISCUSSION QUESTIONS

1. What is the status of women in Chinese society? How does the treatment of infant daughters convey this status?
2. What are the duties of a husband and a wife?

3. What are the four qualifications to be a good woman? What does this imply about education regarding women and daughters?

4. How does this document, although written by a woman, support a patriarchal social structure?

DOCUMENT 6-2

From Chronicles of Japan

ca. 720 C.E.

In 720 C.E., Prince Toneri (676–735 C.E.) completed editing a vast compilation of Japanese history, the Hihonji, *or* Chronicles. *The* Chronicles *were written in Chinese because Japan adopted writing from China for official documents; only later did the Japanese develop a system for writing their own language. The text traces the history of Japan back to the seventh century* B.C.E., *but the earliest reigns mentioned are most likely based on myths. Indeed, the majority of the text is based on uncertain historical foundations, as emperors did not begin to keep written records until the sixth century* C.E. *The following passage, issued by Prince Shotoku in 604* C.E., *guided Japanese government until the nineteenth century.*

The Prince Imperial [Prince Shotoku] in person prepared for the first time laws. There were seventeen clauses as follows: —

1. Harmony is to be valued, and an avoidance of wanton opposition to be honored. All men are influenced by class-feelings, and there are few who are intelligent. Hence there are some who disobey their lords and fathers, or who maintain feuds with the neighboring villages. But when those above are harmonious and those below are friendly, and there is concord in the discussion of business, right views of things spontaneously gain acceptance. Then what is there which cannot be accomplished!

"Chronicles of Japan," in W. G. Aston, trans., *Nihongi: Chronicles of Japan from the Earliest Times to* A.D. *697*, 2 vols. (London: Kegan, Paul, Trench, Truebner, 1896), 2:128–133.

2. Sincerely reverence the three treasures. The three treasures: the Buddha, the Law, and the Priesthood,[6] are the final refuge . . . and are the supreme objects of faith in all countries. What man in what age can fail to reverence this law? Few men are utterly bad. They may be taught to follow it. But if they do not go to the three treasures, how shall their crookedness be made straight?

3. When you receive the Imperial commands, fail not scrupulously to obey them. The lord is Heaven, the vassal is Earth. Heaven overspreads, and Earth upbears. When this is so, the four seasons follow their due course, and the powers of Nature obtain their efficacy. If the Earth attempted to overspread, Heaven would simply fall in ruin. Therefore is it that when the lord speaks, the vassal listens; when the superior acts, the inferior yields compliance. Consequently when you receive the Imperial commands, fail not to carry them out scrupulously. Let there be a want of care in this matter, and ruin is the natural consequence.

4. The Ministers and functionaries should make decorous behavior their leading principle, for the leading principle of the government of the people consists in decorous behavior. If the superiors do not behave with decorum, the inferiors are disorderly: if inferiors are wanting in proper behavior, there must necessarily be offenses. Therefore it is that when lord and vassal behave with propriety, the distinctions of rank are not confused: when the people behave with propriety, the Government of the Commonwealth proceeds of itself. . . .

6. Chastise that which is evil and encourage that which is good. This was the excellent rule of antiquity. Conceal not, therefore, the good qualities of others, and fail not to correct that which is wrong when you see it. Flatterers and deceivers are a sharp weapon for the overthrow of the State, and a pointed sword for the destruction of the people. Sycophants are also fond, when they meet, of speaking at length to their superiors on the errors of their inferiors; to their inferiors, they censure the faults of their superiors. Men of this kind are all wanting in fidelity to their lord, and in benevolence toward the people. From such an origin great civil disturbances arise.

7. Let every man have his own charge, and let not the spheres of duty be confused. When wise men are entrusted with office, the sound of

---

[6] **the Buddha, the Law, and the Priesthood**: The Buddha himself, the Law of Dharma, and the Sangha, which are monastic communities.

praise arises. If unprincipled men hold office, disasters and tumults are multiplied. In this world, few are born with knowledge: wisdom is the product of earnest meditation. In all things, whether great or small, find the right man, and they will surely be well managed: on all occasions, be they urgent or the reverse, meet but with a wise man, and they will of themselves be amenable. In this way will the State be lasting and the Temples of the Earth and of Grain[7] will be free from danger. Therefore did the wise sovereigns of antiquity seek the man to fill the office, and not the office for the sake of the man. . . .

10. Let us cease from wrath, and refrain from angry looks. Nor let us be resentful when others differ from us. For all men have hearts, and each heart has its own leanings. Their right is our wrong, and our right is their wrong. We are not unquestionably sages, nor are they unquestionably fools. Both of us are simply ordinary men. How can any one lay down a rule by which to distinguish right from wrong? For we are all, one with another, wise and foolish, like a ring which has no end. Therefore, although others give way to anger, let us on the contrary dread our own faults, and though we alone may be in the right, let us follow the multitude and act like them.

11. Give clear appreciation to merit and demerit, and deal out to each its sure reward or punishment. In these days, reward does not attend upon merit, nor punishment upon crime. You high functionaries who have charge of public affairs, let it be your task to make clear rewards and punishments. . . .

15. To turn away from that which is private, and to set our faces toward that which is public — this is the path of a Minister. Now if a man is influenced by private motives, he will assuredly feel resentments, and if he is influenced by resentful feelings, he will assuredly fail to act harmoniously with others. If he fails to act harmoniously with others, he will assuredly sacrifice the public interest to his private feelings. When resentment arises, it interferes with order, and is subversive of law. . . .

16. Let the people be employed [in forced labor] at seasonable times. This is an ancient and excellent rule. Let them be employed, therefore, in the winter months, when they are at leisure. But from Spring to Autumn, when they are engaged in agriculture or with the

---

[7]**Temples of the Earth and of Grain**: Shinto shrines to the gods of agriculture.

mulberry trees,[8] the people should not be so employed. For if they do not attend to agriculture, what will they have to eat? If they do not attend to the mulberry trees, what will they do for clothing?

17. Decisions on important matters should not be made by one person alone. They should be discussed with many. But small matters are of less consequence. It is unnecessary to consult a number of people. It is only in the case of the discussion of weighty affairs, when there is a suspicion that they may miscarry, that one should arrange matters in concert with others, so as to arrive at the right conclusion.

READING AND DISCUSSION QUESTIONS

1. What does this document reveal about the political and social structure of Japan? What Chinese influence can you detect on these structures?

2. How effective do you think these laws would be for administering Japan?

3. These seventeen laws influenced Japanese government until in the nineteenth century. Why might they have had such lasting appeal?

DOCUMENT 6-3

BISHOP ADAM
From The Christian Monument
ca. 781 C.E.

Following the legalization of Christianity, bishops and emperors in the Roman Empire began to dictate orthodox, *or "correct," belief. The followers of Nestorianism, a branch of Christianity that was deemed heretical and*

Bishop Adam, "The Christian Monument," in P. Y. Saeki, *The Nestorian Documents and Relics in China* (Tokyo: Maruzen, 1951), 56–61.

[8] **engaged . . . with the mulberry trees**: Silkworms eat the leaves of mulberry trees and their cocoons are spun into silk.

banned in 381 C.E., were driven out of the Roman Empire and found refuge in Iran. From Iran, Nestorian Christians traveled throughout Asia and one named Aluoben gained an audience with the Chinese emperor Taizong (r. 526–649). The following stone inscription illustrates Aluoben's achievements and the impact of Chinese politics on the spread of Christianity. Bishop Adam, who composed this inscription, appears to have been born in China to Persian immigrants who were employed in the Chinese administration.

"The *Way*"[9] would not have spread so widely had it not been for the Sage,[10] and the Sage would not have been so great were it not for "The *Way*." Ever since the Sage and "The *Way*" were united together as the two halves of an indentured deed [two identical copies] would agree, then the world became refined and enlightened.

When the accomplished Emperor Taizong began his magnificent career in glory and splendor over the (recently) established dynasty[11] and ruled his people with intelligence, he proved himself to be a brilliant Sage.

And behold there was a highly virtuous man named Aluoben in the Kingdom of Daqin.[12] Auguring (of the Sage, i.e., Emperor) from the azure sky, he decided to carry the true Sutras [the Bible] (of the True Way) with him, and observing the course of the winds, he made his way (to China) through difficulties and perils. Thus in the ninth year of the period named Zhenguan (635 C.E.) he arrived at Chang'an [capital of Tang China]. The Emperor dispatched his Minister, Duke Fang Xuanling, with a guard of honor, to the western suburb to meet the visitor and conduct him to the Palace. The Sutras (Scriptures) were translated in the Imperial Library. (His Majesty) investigated "The *Way*" in his own forbidden apartments, and being deeply convinced of its correctness and truth, he gave special orders for its propagation.

---

[9] "The *Way*": Nestorian Christianity. Adam is playing on the fact that Daoism was known as "the Way."

[10] the Sage: The Emperor Taizong (599–649 C.E.), second ruler of the Tang Dynasty and considered to be one of the greatest rulers in Chinese history. Adam continues his metaphor because Laozi, founder of Daoism (see Document 3-3) was often referred to as the Sage.

[11] (recently) established dynasty: Emperor Taizong played an important role in overthrowing the Sui Dynasty and placing his father on the thrown.

[12] Kingdom of Daqin: Syria or possibly modern Iraq or Iran.

In the twelfth year of the Zhenguan Period (638 C.E.) in the seventh month of Autumn, the following Imperial Rescript was issued: —

"'The Way' had not, at all times and in all places, the selfsame name; the Sage had not, at all times and in all places, the selfsame human body. (Heaven) caused a suitable religion to be instituted for every region and clime so that each one of the races of mankind might be saved. Bishop Aluoben of the kingdom of Daqin, bringing with him the Sutras and Images,[13] has come from afar and presented them at our Capital. Having carefully examined the scope of his teaching, we find it to be mysteriously spiritual and of silent operation. Having observed its principal and most essential points, we reached the conclusion that they cover all that is most important in life. Their language is free from perplexing expressions; their principles are so simple that they 'remain as the fish would remain even after the net (of the language) were forgotten.' This Teaching is helpful to all creatures and beneficial to all men. So let it have free course throughout the Empire."

Accordingly, the proper authorities built a Daqin monastery in the Yining Ward in the Capital and twenty-one priests were ordained and attached to it. The virtue of the honored House of Zhou had died away;[14] (the rider on) the black chariot had ascended to the West.[15] But (virtue revived) and "The *Way*" was brilliantly manifested again at the moment when the Great Tang began its rule, whilst the breezes of the Luminous (Religion) came eastward to fan it.[16] Immediately afterwards, the proper officials were again ordered to take a faithful portrait of the Emperor, and to have it copied on the walls of the monastery. The celestial beauty appeared in its variegated colors, and the dazzling splendor illuminated the Luminous "portals" (i.e., congregation). The sacred features (lit., footprints) (thus preserved) conferred great blessing (on the monastery), and illuminated the Church for evermore. . . .

The great Emperor Gaozong (650–683 C.E.) succeeded most respectfully to his ancestors; and giving the True Religion the proper elegance and finish, he caused monasteries of the Luminous Religion to be founded

---

[13] **Sutras and Images**: Icons that were thought to provide a direct connection to saints.

[14] **the virtue . . . had died away**: The Zhou Dynasty claimed that they restored virtue after defeating the Shang Dynasty.

[15] **(the rider on) . . . the West**: A legend in which Laozi, sage of Daoism, left China to travel in the West.

[16] **But . . . came eastward to fan it**: Adam connects the coming of Christianity from the West with Laozi.

in every prefecture. Accordingly, he honored Aluoben by conferring on him the office of the Great Patron and Spiritual Lord of the Empire. The Law (of the Luminous Religion) spread throughout the ten provinces, and the Empire enjoyed great peace and concord. Monasteries were built in many cities, whilst every family enjoyed the great blessings (of Salvation).

During the period of Shengli[17] (698–699 C.E.),the Buddhists, taking advantage of these circumstances, and using all their strength raised their voices (against the Luminous Religion) in the Eastern Zhou,[18] and at the end of the Xiandian Period (712 C.E.) some inferior scholars [probably Confucians] ridiculed and derided it, slandering and speaking against it in the Western Hao.[19] But there came the Head-priest (or Archdeacon) Luohan, Bishop Jilie, and others, as well as Noblemen from the "Golden" region [the West] and the eminent priests who had forsaken all worldly interests. All these men co-operated in restoring the great fundamental principles and united together to re-bind the broken ties.

The Emperor Xuanzong,[20] who was surnamed "the Perfection of the Way," ordered the Royal prince, the King of Ningguo and four other Royal princes to visit the blessed edifices (i.e., monastery) personally and to set up altars therein. Thus the "consecrated rafters," which had been temporarily bent, were once more straightened and strengthened, whilst the sacred foundation-stones which for a time had lost the right position were restored and perfected. In the early part of the period Tianbao (742 C.E.) he gave orders to his general Gao Lishi to carry the faithful portraits of the Five Emperors [mythical rulers] and to have them placed securely in the monastery, and also to take the Imperial gift of one hundred pieces of silk with him. Making the most courteous and reverent obeisance to the Imperial portraits, we feel as though "we were in a position to hang on to the Imperial bow and sword, in case the beard of the Dragon[21] should be out of reach." Although the solar horns shine forth with such dazzling brilliance, yet the gracious Imperial faces are so gentle that they may be gazed upon at a distance less than a foot.

---

[17] period of Shengli: Empress Wu Zeitan (r. 690–705) ruled China during this period.

[18] Eastern Zhou: Empress Wu Zeitan changed the name of her dynasty to Zhou and moved the capital to Luoyang.

[19] slandering . . . in the Western Hao: There were riots in the capital against the Christians and the monastery in the capital was attacked.

[20] Emperor Xuanzong: Ruled 712 to 756 C.E., during the height of the Tang Dynasty.

[21] Dragon: The symbol of the emperor.

In the third year of the same period (744 C.E.) there was a priest named Jihe in the Kingdom of Daqin. Observing the stars, he decided to engage in the work of conversion; and looking toward the sun (i.e., eastward), he came to pay court to the most honorable Emperor. The Imperial orders were given to the Head-priest (Archdeacon) Luohan, priest Pulun and others, seven in all, to perform services to cultivate merit and virtue with this Bishop Jihe in the Xingqing Palace. Thereupon the monastery-names, composed and written by the Emperor himself, began to appear on the monastery gates; and the front-tablets to bear the Dragon-writing (i.e., the Imperial hand-writing). The monastery was resorted to by (visitors) whose costumes resembled the shining feathers of the king-fisher bird whilst all (the buildings) shone forth with the splendor of the sun. The Imperial tablets hung high in the air and their radiance flamed as though vying with the sun. The gifts of the Imperial favor are immense like the highest peak of the highest mountains in the South, and the food of its rich benevolence is as deep as the depths of the Eastern sea.

There is nothing that "The Way" cannot effect (through the Sage); and whatever it effects, it is right of us to define it as such (in eulogy). There is nothing that the Sage cannot accomplish (through "The Way"); and whatever He accomplishes, it is right we should proclaim it in writing (as the Sage's work).[22]

READING AND DISCUSSION QUESTIONS

1. Why does Adam begin and end his inscription using Daoist terms to discuss Christianity?

2. What did Christianity in China owe to imperial support? What happened when imperial support was taken away? What does this suggest about the popularity of Christianity in China during the Tang Dynasty?

---

[22] (**as the Sage's work**): Adam finishes the inscription by returning to his initial parody of Daoism.

> DOCUMENT 6-4

HAN YU

Memorial on Buddhism

ca. 819 C.E.

Buddhism entered China during the Han Dynasty, spreading from Central Asia along the Silk Road. Although conversion to Buddhism was slow at first, later dynasties such as the Wei (386–534 C.E.) adopted and promoted Buddhism. The continued political division of China and concurrent chaos prompted many to seek spiritual refuge in the Buddha. When the Tang Dynasty took control of China Buddhism was firmly established, but criticism of it remained. The celebrated writer Han Yu (768–824 C.E.) was prompted to write this essay when Emperor Tang Xuanzong (r. 805–820 C.E.) brought veneration of the finger of Buddha, one of the most famous relics of the Buddha, to China.

MEMORIAL ON BUDDHISM

Your servant submits that Buddhism is but one of the practices of barbarians [non-Chinese speakers] which has filtered into China since the Later Han. In ancient times there was no such thing. . . . In those times the empire was at peace, and the people, contented and happy, lived out their full complement of years. . . . The Buddhist doctrine had still not reached China, so this could not have been the result of serving the Buddha.

The Buddhist doctrine first appeared in the time of the Emperor Ming (57–75 C.E.) of the Han Dynasty, and the Emperor Ming was a scant eighteen years on the throne. Afterwards followed a succession of disorders and revolutions, when dynasties did not long endure. From the time of the dynasties Song, Qi, Liang, Chen, and Wei,[23] as they grew more zealous in the service of the Buddha, the reigns of kings became shorter. There was only the Emperor Wu (502–549) of the Liang who was on the throne for

---

Han Yu, "Memorial on Buddhism" from *Ennin's Travels in T'ang China*, by Edwin O. Reischauer, (New York: John Wiley & Sons, Inc., 1955), 221–224.

[23] **Song, Qi, Liang, Chen, and Wei**: These dynasties ruled from the fourth through sixth centuries C.E., after the collapse of the Han Dynasty.

forty-eight years. First and last, he thrice abandoned the world and dedicated himself to the service of the Buddha. He refused to use animals in the sacrifices in his own ancestral temple. His single meal a day was limited to fruits and vegetables. In the end he was driven out and died of hunger. His dynasty likewise came to an untimely end. In serving the Buddha he was seeking good fortune, but the disaster that overtook him was only the greater. Viewed in the light of this, it is obvious that the Buddha is not worth serving.

When Gaozu [Li Yuan, the first Tang emperor] first succeeded to the throne of the Sui [whom the Tangs had overthrown], he planned to do away with Buddhism, but his ministers and advisors were short-sighted men incapable of any real understanding of the Way of the Former Kings, or of what is fitting for past and present; they were unable to apply the Emperor's ideas so as to remedy this evil, and the matter subsequently came to naught — many the times your servant has regretted it. I venture to consider that Your Imperial Majesty, shrewd and wise in peace and war, with divine wisdom and heroic courage, is without an equal through the centuries. When first you came to the throne, you would not permit laymen to become monks or nuns or Daoist priests, nor would you allow the founding of temples or cloisters. It constantly struck me that the intention of Gaozu was to be fulfilled by Your Majesty. Now even though it has not been possible to put it into effect immediately, it is surely not right to remove all restrictions and turn around and actively encourage them.

Now I hear that by Your Majesty's command a troupe of monks went to Fengxiang to get the Buddha-bone [the finger of Buddha], and that you viewed it from a tower as it was carried into the Imperial Palace; also that you have ordered that it be received and honored in all the temples in turn. Although your servant [i.e., the author Han Yu] is stupid, he cannot help knowing that Your Majesty is not misled by this Buddha, and that you do not perform these devotions to pray for good luck. But just because the harvest has been good and the people are happy, you are complying with the general desire by putting on for the citizens of the capital this extraordinary spectacle which is nothing more than a sort of theatrical amusement. How could a sublime intelligence like yours consent to believe in this sort of thing?

But the people are stupid and ignorant; they are easily deceived and with difficulty enlightened. If they see Your Majesty behaving in this fashion, they are going to think you serve the Buddha in all sincerity. All will say, "The Emperor is wisest of all, and yet he is a sincere believer. What are we common people that we still should grudge our lives?" Burning heads and searing fingers by the tens and hundreds, throwing away their clothes and scattering their money, from morning to night emulating one another and fearing only to be last, old and young rush about, abandoning their work and place; and if restrictions are not immediately imposed, they will increasingly make the rounds of temples and some will inevitably cut off their arms and slice their flesh in the way of offerings. Thus to violate decency and draw the ridicule of the whole world is no light matter.

Now the Buddha was of barbarian origin. His language differed from Chinese speech; his clothes were of a different cut; his mouth did not pronounce the prescribed words of the Former Kings, his body was not clad in the garments prescribed by the Former Kings. He did not recognize the relationship between prince and subject, nor the sentiments of father and son. Let us suppose him to be living today, and that he come to court at the capital as an emissary of his country. Your Majesty would receive him courteously. But only one interview in the audience chamber, one banquet in his honor, one gift of clothing, and he would be escorted under guard to the border that he might not mislead the masses.

How much the less, now that he has long been dead, is it fitting that his decayed and rotten bone, his ill-omened and filthy remains, should be allowed to enter in the forbidden precincts of the Palace? Confucius said, "Respect ghosts and spirits, but keep away from them."[24] The feudal lords of ancient times, when they went to pay a visit of condolence in their states, made it their practice to have exorcists go before with rush-brooms and peachwood branches[25] to dispel unlucky influences. Only after such precautions did they make their visit of condolence. Now without reason you have taken up an unclean thing and examined it in person when no exorcist had gone before, when neither rush-broom nor peachwood branch had been employed. But your ministers did not speak of the wrong nor did the censors call attention to the impropriety; I am in truth ashamed of them. I pray that Your Majesty will turn this bone over to the officials that it may be cast into water or fire, cutting off for all time the root and so dispelling the suspicions of the empire and preventing the befuddlement of later generations. Thereby men may know in what manner a great sage acts who a million times surpasses ordinary men. Could this be anything but ground for prosperity? Could it be anything but a cause for rejoicing?

---

[24] **"Respect ghosts . . . from them"**: Quoted from the *Analects*, the recorded teachings of Confucius.

[25] **rush-brooms and peachwood branches**: The ancient Chinese believed that these objects could ward off bad spirits.

If the Buddha has supernatural power and can wreak harm and evil, may any blame or retribution fittingly fall on my person. Heaven be my witness: I will not regret it. Unbearably disturbed and with the utmost sincerity I respectfully present my petition that these things may be known.

Your servant is truly alarmed, truly afraid.

READING AND DISCUSSION QUESTIONS

1. Why does Han Yu attack the veneration of the finger of the Buddha? What kinds of arguments does he make?

2. Why would the emperor continue to support the spread of Buddhism in China, even in the face of opposition from Confucian scholars?

3. Why might Buddhism have been so appealing to the Chinese people?

COMPARATIVE QUESTIONS

1. What role did the Chinese government play in promoting religion throughout China?

2. Based on each of these documents, how would you describe the social and political structures of China and Japan?

3. How does the status and daily life of women in China as described by Ban Zhao compare to that of women in India according to *The Laws of Manu* (Document 2-4)?

4. How do the ideas of effective and prosperous rule described in the *Chronicles of Japan* compare to those in ancient Assyria (Document 1-7) and republican Rome (Document 5-1)?

CHAPTER 7

Europe and Western Asia

ca. 350–850

I n the fourth century, the Roman emperor Constantine legalized Christianity, and by the fifth century it was the official religion of the empire.
This change transformed the previously illegal and persecuted religion
into the most important cultural force throughout the Mediterranean
world. While Christian devotion flourished during the fifth century, the
Roman Empire at large began to disintegrate. Rome was sacked twice and
by the end of the century the western portion of the empire was in the
hands of Germanic-speaking Christian peoples such as the Goths, Lombards, and Franks. These usurping kingdoms encouraged the spread of
Christianity into new territories, such as Saxony in modern Germany.
Despite Rome's loss of the western Mediterranean, the eastern part of the
empire, called the Byzantine Empire by modern scholars, endured until
the Ottoman Turks captured Constantinople in 1453.

DOCUMENT 7-1

TERTULLIAN

From Apologia

ca. 197

*The earliest Christians originated in the Near East and the entire New Tes-
tament of the Christian Bible was composed in the koine (common) Greek
spoken throughout eastern provinces of the Roman Empire. However, by the
late second century, Christianity had attracted a number of converts in the
western half of the empire as well. One of these converts, Tertullian (ca. 160–
240), was the first Christian of note who wrote in Latin. His most famous work,
the Apologia, presents a defense of Christianity against Roman persecution*

and is excerpted below. Tertullian would exert enormous influence on later Christians in the West, including Saint Augustine (Document 7-2).

Magistrates of the Roman Empire! You who are seated for the administration of justice in almost the highest position of the state[1] and under the gaze of everyone! If you are not allowed to conduct an open examination, face to face, into the truth regarding the Christians, if in this case alone you fear or are ashamed to exercise your authority to conduct a public investigation with the care that justice demands, if, finally, the extreme hatred shown this group (as happened recently in the domestic courts) has been raised to such a level that it inhibits their defense, then let the truth reach your ears by the secret pathway of silent literature. . . .

If it is certain that we are the most criminal of people, why do you treat us differently from others of our kind, namely all other criminals? The same crime should receive the same treatment. When others are charged with the same crimes imputed to us, they are permitted to use their own mouths and the hired advocacy of others to plead their innocence. They have full freedom to answer the charge and to cross-examine. In fact, it is against the law to condemn anyone without a defense and a hearing. Only Christians are forbidden to say anything in defense of the truth that would clear their case and assist the judge in avoiding an injustice. All that they care about (and this by itself is enough to arouse public hatred) is a confession to bearing the name "Christian," not an investigation of the charge. Now, let us assume you are trying any other criminal. If he confesses to the crime of murder, or sacrilege, or sexual debauchery, or treason — to cite the crimes of which we stand accused — you are not content to pass sentence immediately. Rather, you weigh the relevant circumstances: the nature of the deed; how often, where, how, and when it was committed; the co-conspirators and the partners-in-crime. Nothing of this sort is done in our case. Yet, whenever that false charge is brought against us, we should equally be made to confess: How many murdered babies has one eaten? How many illicit sexual acts has one performed under cover of darkness? Which cooks and which dogs were there? Oh, how great would be the glory of that governor who should bring to light a Christian who has already devoured 100 babies!

---

[1] **You who are seated . . . state**: In theory, a Roman citizen could appeal a judgment made by a provincial governor to the emperor.

To the contrary, we find that it is forbidden to hunt us down. When Pliny the Younger was a provincial governor [in modern Turkey] and had condemned some Christians to death and had intimidated others to abandon the steadfastness of their faith, he was still concerned by their sheer numbers and worried about what to do in the future. So he consulted Trajan, the reigning emperor [ca. 98–117]. Pliny explained that, other than their obstinate refusal to offer sacrifice,[2] he had learned nothing else about their religious ceremonies, except that they met before daybreak to sing hymns to Christ and God and to bind themselves by oath to a way of life that forbids murder, adultery, fraud, treachery, and all other crimes. Trajan then wrote back that people of this sort should not be hunted down, but, when brought to court, they should be punished.

What a decision! How inevitably self-contradictory! He declares that they should not be hunted down, as though they are innocent. Then he prescribes that they be punished, as though they are guilty. He spares them, yet he directs his anger upon them. He pretends to shut his eyes, yet he calls attention to them. Judges, why do you tie yourself up in knots? If you condemn them why not hunt them down? If you do not hunt them down, why not also find them innocent?

Throughout all the provinces, soldiers are assigned by lot to hunt down bandits. When it comes to traitors and public enemies each person is a soldier. Inquiry extends even to one's associates and confederates. The Christian alone may not be hunted down, but he may be brought to court, as if hunting down led to anything other than being haled [hauled] into court. So, you condemn someone who is haled into court, although no one wished to seek him out. He has not merited punishment, I suppose, because he is guilty, but because, forbidden to be looked for, he was found! . . .

A person shouts out, "I am a Christian." He says what he is. You want to hear what he is not. You preside to extort the truth, yet in our case alone you take infinite pains to hear a lie. "I am," he says, "what you ask if I am. Why torture me to twist the fact around? I confess, and you torture me. What would you do if I denied?" Clearly when others deny you do not readily believe them. In our case, when we deny, you immediately believe us. . . .

Inasmuch as you treat us differently from all other criminals, which you do by concentrating on disassociating us from that name (for we are

---

[2] **refusal to offer sacrifice**: All inhabitants of the Roman Empire were supposed to make sacrifices for the well-being of the emperor and the empire, usually of incense. Some groups, such as the Jews, were exempted.

cut off from the name "Christian" only if we do what non-Christians do),
you must know that there is no crime whatsoever in our case. It is only a
name. . . .

So much for my preface, as it were, which is intended to beat into submission the injustice of the public hatred felt for us. Now I take the stand
to plead our innocence. . . .

We are said to be the worst of criminals because of our sacramental
baby-killing and the baby-eating that accompanies it and the sexual license
that follows the banquet, where dogs are our pimps in darkness when they
overturn candles and procure a certain modesty for our impious lusts.[3] We
are always spoken of in this way, yet you take no pains to investigate the
charges that you have made against us for so long. If you believe them,
investigate them. Otherwise, stop believing what you do not investigate.
The fact that you look the other way suggests that the evil that you yourselves dare not investigate does not exist. . . .

You say, "You do not worship the [traditional Greek and Roman] gods,
and you do not offer sacrifices for the emperors." It follows logically that
we do not offer sacrifices for others because we do not do so even for
ourselves. All of this is a consequence of our not worshipping the gods.
So we are accused of sacrilege and treason. This is the chief case against
us. In fact, it is the whole case. . . . Your gods we cease to worship from
the moment we recognize they are not gods. So that is what you ought
to require us to prove — that those gods do not exist and for that reason should not be worshipped because they deserve worship only if they
are gods.

READING AND DISCUSSION QUESTIONS

1. According to Tertullian, what proof was necessary to convict someone
    of being a Christian? Of what crimes were Christians accused?

2. What problems does Tertullian describe concerning the persecution
    of Christians? How were Christian court cases unique?

3. Why did the Christians refuse to make sacrifices to the emperors?
    How did the Roman authorities interpret this defiance?

---

[3] **where . . . impious lusts**: A rumor stated that dogs were used to extinguish the
candles. Strings were attached to the dog's tails and to the candles so that when the
dogs were thrown food the dogs would leap and cause the candles to fall over.

DOCUMENT 7-2

SAINT AUGUSTINE

From City of God: A Denunciation of Paganism

ca. 413–426

No author had more influence throughout the Western Middle Ages than Saint Augustine (354–430), bishop of Hippo. Though he was a late convert to Christianity, Augustine became a devout Catholic in 386. His most important work, City of God, *was written in response to the Goth's sack of Rome in 410. Unlike Augustine, pagans blamed the spread of the Christian faith and the rejection of the old Roman gods for sapping the strength of the Roman Empire.*

Cicero,[4] a weighty man, and a philosopher in his way, when about to be made edile,[5] wished the citizens to understand that, among the other duties of his magistracy, he must propitiate Flora [honor the goddess of flowers and spring] by the celebration of games. And these games are reckoned devout in proportion to their lewdness. In another place, and when he was now consul,[6] and the state in great peril, he says that games had been celebrated for ten days together, and that nothing had been omitted which could pacify the gods: as if it had not been more satisfactory to irritate the gods by temperance, than to pacify them by debauchery; and to provoke their hate by honest living, than soothe it by such unseemly grossness. . . .

They [the pagan gods], then, are but abandoned and ungrateful wretches, in deep and fast bondage to that malign spirit, who complain and murmur that men are rescued by the name of Christ from the hellish thraldom of these unclean spirits, and from a participation in their punishment, and are brought out of the night of pestilential ungodliness into the light of most healthful piety. Only such men could murmur that the masses flock to the churches and their chaste acts of worship, where a

---

Augustine, *City of God*, 27–29, in Philip Schaff, ed., *Library of Nicene and Post-Nicene Fathers*, 1st ser. (New York, 1890), 3:41–43.

[4] **Cicero**: Roman philosopher in the first century B.C.E. who is often considered one of the best writers in Latin.

[5] **edile**: A lower elected office in the Roman Republic.

[6] **consul**: The highest elected officer in the Roman Republic.

seemly separation of the sexes is observed; where they learn how they may so spend this earthly life, as to merit a blessed eternity hereafter; where Holy Scripture and instruction in righteousness are proclaimed from a raised platform in presence of all, that both they who do the word may hear to their salvation, and they who do it not may hear to judgment. And though some enter who scoff at such precepts, all their petulance [childish irritation] is either quenched by a sudden change, or is restrained through fear or shame. For no filthy and wicked action is there set forth to be gazed at or to be imitated; but either the precepts of the true God are recommended, His miracles narrated, His gifts praised, or His benefits implored.

This, rather, is the religion worthy of your desires, O admirable Roman race, — the progeny of your Scaevolas and Scipios, of Regulus, and of Fabricius.[7] This rather covet, this distinguish from that foul vanity and crafty malice of the devils. If there is in your nature any eminent virtue, only by true piety is it purged and perfected, while by impiety it is wrecked and punished. Choose now what you will pursue, that your praise may be not in yourself, but in the true God, in whom is no error. For of popular glory you have had your share; but by the secret providence of God, the true religion was not offered to your choice. Awake, it is now day; as you have already awaked in the persons of some in whose perfect virtue and sufferings for the true faith we glory: for they, contending on all sides with hostile powers, and conquering them all by bravely dying, have purchased for us this country of ours with their blood; to which country we invite you, and exhort you to add yourselves to the number of the citizens of this city, which also has a sanctuary of its own in the true remission of sins. Do not listen to those degenerate sons of thine who slander Christ and Christians, and impute to them these disastrous times, though they desire times in which they may enjoy rather impunity for their wickedness than a peaceful life. Such has never been Rome's ambition even in regard to her earthly country. Lay hold now on the celestial country, which is easily won, and in which you will reign truly and for ever. For there shalt thou find no vestal fire,[8] no Capitoline stone,[9] but the one true God.

---

[7] **Scaevolas . . . Fabricius**: The Scaevolas and Scipios were important families during the Roman Republic. Regulus was a consul during the Punic Wars between Rome and Carthage, and Fabricius was a general of the early republic who also served as a censor.

[8] **vestal fire**: Virgin priestesses tended a fire dedicated to Vesta, goddess of the hearth and home.

[9] **Capitoline stone**: The temple dedicated to the Roman triad of deities — Jupiter, Juno, and Minerva — was located on the Capitoline Hill, which also overlooked the Roman Forum.

No date, no goal will here ordain:
But grant an endless, boundless reign.

No longer, then, follow after false and deceitful gods; abjure them rather, and despise them, bursting forth into true liberty. Gods they are not, but malignant spirits, to whom your eternal happiness will be a sore punishment.

READING AND DISCUSSION QUESTIONS

1. How does Augustine describe the Roman pagan gods? What are his major problems with them?

2. What evidence does Augustine use to support the worship of the Christian God?

3. What do Augustine's descriptions of the pagan gods and the Christian God suggest about changing ideas of morality in the weakened Roman Empire?

DOCUMENT 7-3

SAINT BENEDICT OF NURSIA
The Rule of Saint Benedict: Work and Pray
529

Christian monasticism developed in the Egyptian desert at the turn of the fourth century C.E. *as a solitary activity of self-denial. In the early fourth century; however, groups of monks began to come together to live in self-sufficient communities. These groups required regulation, leading to the creation of monastic "rules." Saint Benedict (480–547), who turned his country estate at Monte Cassino, Italy, into a monastery, developed the most important rule for Western European monks. It guided medieval monasticism and helped shape the early Catholic Church.*

E. F. Henderson, ed., *Select Historical Documents of the Middle Ages* (London: G. Bell, 1892), 597–598.

Concerning the daily manual labor. Idleness is the enemy of the soul. And therefore, at fixed times, the brothers ought to be occupied in manual labor; and again, at fixed times, in sacred reading. Therefore we believe that, according to this disposition, both seasons ought to be arranged; so that, from Easter until the Calends of October,[10] going out early, from the first until the fourth hour they shall do what labor may be necessary. Moreover, from the fourth hour until about the sixth, they shall be free for reading. After the meal of the sixth hour, moreover, rising from table, they shall rest in their beds with all silence; or, perchance, he that wishes to read may so read to himself that he do not disturb another. And the nona[11] shall be gone through with more moderately about the middle of the eighth hour; and again they shall work at what is to be done until Vespers.[12] But, if the exigency or poverty of the place demands that they be occupied by themselves in picking fruits, they shall not be dismayed: for then they are truly monks if they live by the labors of their hands; as did also our fathers and the apostles. Let all things be done with moderation, however, on account of the faint-hearted. . . . [There follows a slightly different schedule for the winter months from October to Easter.] But in the days of Lent,[13] from dawn until the third full hour, they shall be free for their readings; and, until the tenth full hour, they shall do the labor that is enjoined on them. In which days of Lent they shall all receive separate books from the library; which they shall read entirely through in order. These books are to be given out on the first day of Lent. Above all there shall certainly be appointed one or two elders, who shall go round the monastery at the hours in which the brothers are engaged in reading, and see to it that no troublesome brother chance to be found who is open to idleness and trifling, and is not intent on his reading; being not only of no use to himself, but also stirring up others. If such a one — may it not happen — be found, he shall be admonished once and a second time. If he do not amend, he shall be subject under the Rule to such punishment that the others may have fear. . . . On feeble or delicate brothers such a labor or art is to be imposed, that they shall neither be idle, nor shall they be so oppressed by the violence of labor as to be driven to take flight. Their weakness is to be taken into consideration by the abbot.

---

[10] **Calends of October**: The first day of the month of October.

[11] **nona**: The second meal of the day.

[12] **Vespers**: Evening prayers.

[13] **Lent**: The forty days leading up to Easter, normally spent in self-denial, fasting, and prayer.

READING AND DISCUSSION QUESTIONS

1. How would you describe the daily life of a monk?

2. Why might there be so much emphasis on reading in the monastery?

DOCUMENT 7-4

CHARLEMAGNE

From Capitulary on Saxony *and* A *Letter to Pope Leo III*

785, 796

During the collapse of the western half of the Roman Empire in the fifth century the Franks took control of northern Gaul, now called France. By the middle of the eighth century the Franks had become the most powerful of the Germanic kingdoms. In 751, Pippin the Short (714–768) was accepted by the pope as king of the Franks. His successor Charlemagne (747–814), Charles the Great, was crowned Roman Emperor on Christmas Day in 800. In exchange for their new authority, both Pippin and Charlemagne prom-ised to protect the pope from the Muslims, internal Italian conflicts, and the Byzantine Empire. Under Charlemagne, the kingdom of the Franks reached its apex and expanded into Italy, Germany, and Spain.

CAPITULARY ON SAXONY

First, concerning the greater chapters [capital offenses] it has been enacted:

1. It is pleasing to all that the churches of Christ, which are now being built in Saxony [located in modern northwest Germany] and con-secrated to God, should not have less, but greater and more illustri-ous honor than the shrines of the idols have had.

Oliver J. Thatcher and Edgar H. McNeal, trans., *A Source Book for Medieval History* (New York: Charles Scribner's Sons, 1905), 107; D. C. Munro, trans., *University of Pennsylvania Translations and Reprints* (Philadelphia: University of Pennsylvania, 1900), 6(5):16–27.

2. If any one shall have fled to a church for refuge, let no one presume to expel him from the church by violence, but he shall be left in peace until he shall be brought to the judicial assemblage; and on account of the honor due to God and the saints, and the reverence due to the church itself, let his life and all his members be granted to him. Moreover, let him plead his cause as best he can and he shall be judged; and so let him be led to the presence of the lord king, and the latter shall send him where it shall seem fitting to his clemency.

3. If any one shall have entered a church by violence and shall have carried off anything in it by force or theft, or shall have burned the church itself, let him be punished by death.

4. If any one, out of contempt for Christianity, shall have despised the holy Lenten fast and shall have eaten flesh, let him be punished by death. But, nevertheless, let it be taken into consideration by a priest lest perhaps any one from necessity has been led to eat flesh.

5. If any one shall have killed a bishop or priest or deacon let him likewise be punished capitally.

6. If any one, deceived by the devil, shall have believed, after the manner of the pagans, that any man or woman is a witch and eats men, and on this account shall have burned the person, or shall have given the person's flesh to others to eat, or shall have eaten it himself, let him be punished by a capital sentence.

7. If any one, in accordance with pagan rites, shall have caused the body of a dead man to be burned, and shall have reduced his bones to ashes, let him be punished capitally.

8. If any one of the race of the Saxons hereafter, concealed among them, shall have wished to hide himself unbaptized, and shall have scorned to come to baptism, and shall have wished to remain a pagan, let him be punished by death.

9. If any one shall have sacrificed a man to the devil, and, after the manner of the pagans, shall have presented him as a victim to the demons, let him be punished by death.

10. If any one shall have formed a conspiracy with the pagans against the Christians, or shall have wished to join with them in opposition to the Christians, let him he punished by death; and whosoever shall have consented fraudulently to this same against the king and the Christian people, let him be punished by death.

11. If any one shall have shown himself unfaithful to the lord king, let him be punished with a capital sentence. . . .

13. If any one shall have killed his lord or lady, let him be punished in a like manner.

14. If, indeed, for these mortal crimes secretly committed any one shall have fled of his own accord to a priest, and after confession shall have wished to do penance, let him be freed by the testimony of the priest from death. . . .

18. On the Lord's day no meetings or public judicial assemblages shall be held, unless perchance in a case of great necessity, or when war compels it, but all shall go to church to hear the word of God, and shall be free for prayers or good works. Likewise, also, on the special festivals they shall devote themselves to God and to the services of the Church, and shall refrain from secular assemblies.

19. Likewise, it has been pleasing to insert in these decrees that all infants shall be baptized within a year; we have decreed this, that if any one shall have refused to bring his infant to baptism within the course of a year, without the advice or permission of the priest, if he is a noble he shall pay 120 *solidi* to the treasury; if a freeman, 60; if a *litus*,[14] 30. . . .

21. If any one shall have made a vow at springs or trees or groves, or shall have made an offering after the manner of the heathen and shall have partaken of a repast in honor of the demons, if he shall be a noble, 60 *solidi*; if a freeman, 30; if a *litus*, 15. If, indeed, they have not the means of paying at once, they shall be given into the service of the Church until the *solidi* are paid.

22. We command that the bodies of Saxon Christians shall be carried to the church cemeteries, and not to the mounds of the pagans.

23. We have ordered that diviners and soothsayers shall be handed over to the churches and priests.

24. Concerning robbers and malefactors who shall have fled from one county to another, if any one shall receive them into his protection and shall keep them with him for seven nights, except for the purpose of bringing them to justice, let him pay our ban. Likewise, if a count[15] shall have concealed them, and shall be unwilling to bring them forward so that Justice may be done, and is not able to excuse himself for this, let him lose his office. . . .

---

[14] *litus*: A social status between free person and slave.

[15] count: One of Charles's political governors, assigned to the counties.

34. We have forbidden that Saxons shall hold public assemblies in general, unless perchance our *missus*[16] shall have caused them to come together in accordance with our command; but each count shall hold judicial assemblies and administer justice in his jurisdiction. And this shall be cared for by the priests, lest it be done otherwise.

A LETTER TO POPE LEO III

Charles, by the grace of God king of the Franks and Lombards, and patrician of the Romans, to his holiness, Pope Leo, greeting. . . . Just as I entered into an agreement with the most holy father, your predecessor, so also I desire to make with you an inviolable treaty of mutual fidelity and love; that, on the one hand, you shall pray for me and give me the apostolic benediction, and that, on the other, with the aid of God I will ever defend the most holy seat of the holy Roman Church. For it is our part to defend the holy Church of Christ from the attacks of pagans and infidels from without, and within to enforce the acceptance of the Catholic faith. It is your part, most holy father, to aid us in the good fight by raising your hands to God as Moses did [Exo. 17:11] so that by your intercession the Christian people under the leadership of God may always and everywhere have the victory over the enemies of His holy name, and the name of our Lord Jesus Christ may be glorified throughout the world. Abide by the canonical law in all things and obey the precepts of the Holy Fathers always, that your life may be an example of sanctity to all, and your holy admonitions be observed by the whole world, and that your light may so shine before men that they may see your good works and glorify your father who is in Heaven [Matt. 5:16]. May omnipotent God preserve your holiness unharmed through many years for the exalting of His holy Church.

READING AND DISCUSSION QUESTIONS

1. When Charlemagne conquered Saxony, the territory was not completely Christianized. What did Charlemagne do to convert the population?

2. In his letter to Pope Leo III, what did Charlemagne believe were the Pope's duties? What in turn were his responsibilities?

3. Considering his letter to the pope, why did Charlemagne go to such lengths to bring Christianity to Saxony?

---

[16] **missus**: Special envoys or commissioners who oversaw the counts and ecclesiastical authorities.

LIUDPRAND OF CREMONA
A Report on the Embassy to Constantinople
968–969

In 751, the Byzantine Empire lost the last of its possessions in Italy to a Germanic kingdom ruled by the Lombards. This kingdom was in turn conquered by the Franks under Charlemagne, and in the tenth century conquered again by the king of Germany, Otto I (912–973). In 962, Otto was crowned emperor of the Roman Empire, placing him in direct conflict with the Byzantine Empire. To lessen tension, he sent Liudprand, bishop of Cremona, to the Byzantine court of Nicephoros II Phocas (963–969). Liudprand spoke Greek and had been an ambassador to the Byzantines for previous kings of Italy. An admirer of the Byzantine Empire, he was shocked by the treatment he received.

Weakened therefore by my own tribulations and those of my companions,[17] I called in our warden, or rather my persecutor, and by prayers and bribes induced him to take the following letter to the emperor's brother:

Bishop Liudprand to Leo, chancellor and marshal of the palace [and brother of the Byzantine emperor],

"If his serene highness the emperor intends to grant the request for which I came,[18] then the sufferings I am now enduring shall not exhaust my patience; my master [the Holy Roman emperor Otto], however, must be informed by letter and messenger that my stay is not useless. On the other hand, if a refusal is contemplated, there is a Venetian merchantman in the harbor here just about to start. Let him permit me as a sick man to

---

Liudprand of Cremona, "A Report of the Embassy to Constantinople" in F. A. Wright, trans., *The Works of Liudprand of Cremona* (New York: E. P. Dutton & Co., 1930), 243–245.

[17]**Weakened . . . my companions:** Liudprand had recently dined with the Byzantine emperor, Nicephorus, who insulted him and his companions. They were banished to their rooms.

[18]**the request for which I came:** Liudprand was sent by the Holy Roman emperor Otto to arrange a marriage between Otto's son and the daughter of Nicephorus.

go on board, so that, if the time of my dissolution is at hand, my native land may at least receive my corpse."

Leo read my letter and gave me an audience four days later. In accordance with their rule, their wisest men, strong in Attic[19] eloquence sat with him to discuss your request, namely Basil the chief chamberlain, the chief secretary, the chief master of the wardrobe, and two other dignitaries. They began their discourse as follows: "Tell us, brother, the reason that induced you to take the trouble to come here." When I told them that it was on account of the marriage which was to be the ground for a lasting peace, they said: "It is unheard of that a daughter born in the purple of an emperor born in the purple[20] should contract a foreign marriage. Still, great as is your demand, you shall have what you want, if you give what is proper: Ravenna,[21] namely, and Rome with all the adjoining territories from thence to our possessions. If you desire friendship without the marriage, let your master permit Rome to be free, and hand over to their former lord [the Byzantine Emperor] the princes of Capua and Benevento, who were formerly slaves of our holy empire and are now rebels."

To this I answered: "Even you cannot but know that my master rules over Slavonian princes[22] who are more powerful than Peter, king of the Bulgarians, who has married the daughter of the emperor Christopher." "Ah," said they, "but Christopher was not born in the purple."[23]

"As for Rome," I went on, "for whose freedom you are so noisily eager; who is her master? To whom does she pay tribute? Was she not formerly enslaved to harlots? And while you were sleeping, nay powerless, did not my master the august emperor free her from that foul servitude?[24]

---

[19] **Attic**: Form of Greek spoken in classical Athens for more than a thousand years prior to Liudprand's visit. Attic Greek was considered the most elegant of the many dialects spoken in ancient Greece.

[20] **born in the purple**: Born to a reigning emperor in a special room decorated only with purple marble. Purple was the color reserved for emperors.

[21] **Ravenna**: The capital of the last Western Roman emperors in the fifth century. Ravenna was located near Venice and served as the Byzantine capital of Italy until it was captured by the Lombards in 751.

[22] **my master rules over Slavonian princes**: Otto did exert influence in Eastern Europe, where the Holy Roman Empire and the Byzantine Empire vied for power.

[23] **Christopher . . . purple**: Christopher was the brother-in-law of Emperor Constantine VII Porphyrogenitos, so Christopher was not "born in the purple" but only connected by marriage. Christopher and his father, Romanus, served as co-rulers, but Christopher died before he could reign on his own.

[24] **that foul servitude**: The city of Rome was controlled by Pope John XII who had tried to revolt against Otto's control with help from the Byzantine Empire.

Constantine, the august emperor who founded this city and called it after his name, as ruler of the world made many offerings to the holy Roman apostolic Church, not only in Italy but in almost all the western kingdoms, as well as those in the east and south, in Greece, Judaea, Persia, Mesopotamia, Babylonia, Egypt, Libya, as his own special regulations testify that are preserved in our country. In Italy, in Saxony, in Bavaria, and in all my master's realms, everything that belongs to the Church of the blessed apostles has been handed over to the vicar of those holy apostles [the pope]. And if my master has kept back a single city, farm, vassal or slave, then I have denied God. Why does not your emperor do the same? Why does he not restore to the apostolic Church what lies in his kingdoms and thereby himself increase the richness and freedom that it already owes to my master's exertions and generosity?"

"He will do so," said the chief chamberlain Basil, "when Rome and the Roman Church shall be so ordered as he wishes." Then said I: "A certain man having suffered much injury from another, approached God with these words: 'Lord, avenge me upon my adversary.' To whom the Lord said: 'I will do so on the day when I shall render to each man according to his works.' 'How late that day will be!' the man replied."

At that everyone except the emperor's brother burst into laughter. Then they broke off the discussion and ordered me to be taken back to my detestable dwelling place and to be carefully guarded until the day of the apostles, a feast that all religious persons duly observe.[25] At the ceremony the emperor commanded me, though I was very ill at the time, together with the Bulgarian envoys who had arrived the day before, to meet him at the Church of the Holy Apostles. After some verbose chants had been sung and mass celebrated, we were invited to table, where I found placed above me on my side of the long narrow board the Bulgarian envoy. He was a fellow with his hair cut in the Hungarian fashion, girt about with a brazen chain and, as I fancy, just admitted into the Christian faith. The preference given to him over me was plainly meant as an insult to you, my august masters. On your account I was despised, rejected, and scorned. I thank the Lord Jesus Christ, whom you serve with all your heart, that I have been considered worthy to suffer insults for your sake. However, my masters, I considered that the insult was done to you, not to me, and I therefore left the table. I was just going indignantly away when Leo, the emperor's brother and marshal of the court, and Simeon, the chief secre-

---

[25] **day of the apostles . . . duly observe**: A feast day in both the Catholic and Eastern Orthodox calendars.

tary, came after me, howling: "When Peter, king of the Bulgarians, married Christopher's daughter, a mutual agreement was sworn to on both sides to the effect that envoys of the Bulgarians should with us be preferred, honored, and esteemed above the envoys of all other nations. What you say is true: the Bulgarian envoy over there has his hair cut short, he has not washed himself, and his girdle consists of a brass chain. But nevertheless he is a patrician [of elite status], and we are definitely of the opinion that it would be wrong to give a bishop, especially a Frankish [Western] bishop, preference over him. We have noticed your show of indignation, and we are not going to allow you to return to your lodgings, as you suppose; we shall force you to take food with the emperor's servants in an inn."

My mental anguish was so unparalleled that I could not answer them back but did what they ordered, judging that table no fit place for me, seeing that a Bulgarian envoy was preferred, I will not say to myself personally, that is, to Bishop Liudprand, but to your representative. But my indignation was appeased by a handsome present! The sacred emperor sent me one of his most delicate dishes, a fat goat, of which he himself had partaken, richly stuffed with garlic, onion, and leeks and swimming in fish sauce. I wish, sires, that you could have had it on your table. The sight of it, I am sure, would have banished any incredulity you have felt concerning the sacred emperor's luxurious ways.

When eight days had passed and the Bulgarians had left the city, Nicephorus, thinking that I esteemed his table highly, compelled me, in spite of my ill health, to dine with him again in the same place. The patriarch[26] with several other bishops was present, and before them he propounded to me many questions concerning the Holy Scriptures, which, under the inspiration of the Holy Spirit, I elegantly answered. Finally, wishing to make merry of you, he asked which synods[27] we recognized. Those of Nicaea, Chalcedon, Ephesus, Carthage, Antioch, Ancyra, and Constantinople, I replied. "Ha, ha," he said, "you have forgotten to mention Saxony.[28] If you ask me, the reason why our books do not mention it either is that the Christian faith there is too young." . . .

I answered: "On that member of the body where the malady has its seat a cautery[29] must be used. All the heresies [against orthodox beliefs] have emanated from you and among you have flourished; by our Western

---

[26] **patriarch**: Head of the Byzantine church who was based at Constantinople.

[27] **synods**: Church councils where orthodox belief was institutionalized.

[28] **you have forgotten . . . Saxony**: There was never a major church council at Saxony.

[29] **cautery**: A hot iron used to cauterize a wound, burning the flesh to prevent infection.

peoples they have been either strangled or killed. Synods have often been held at Rome or Pavia, but I do not count them here. It was a Roman cleric, he whom you call Dialogus, who afterwards became the universal Pope Gregory (590–604), who freed the heretic Eutychius (552–565 and 577–582), patriarch of Constantinople, from his error. Eutychius said, and not only said but in his teachings, sermons, and writings proclaimed, that at the Resurrection [the rising of the dead on Judgment Day] we should put on not the real flesh that we have here but a certain fantastic substance of his own imagination. The book that set forth this heresy was burned in the interests of orthodoxy by Gregory. Moreover, Ennodius, bishop of Pavia, was sent here, that is, to Constantinople, by the patriarch of Rome [the pope] to deal with a certain other heresy, which he repressed, and he restored the orthodox catholic doctrine. As for the Saxon people, ever since they received holy baptism and the knowledge of God, they have not been stained by any heresy which rendered a synod necessary for its correction; of heresies we have had none. You declare that our Saxon faith is young, and I agree. Faith in Christ is always young and not old among people whose faith is seconded by works. Here faith is old, not young; works do not accompany it, and by reason of its age it is held in light esteem like a worn-out garment. I know for certain of one synod held in Saxony where it was enacted and decreed that it was more seemly to fight with the sword than with the pen, and better to face death than to fly before a foe. Your own army is finding that out now." And in my own mind I said: "May it soon find out by experience how warlike our men are."

READING AND DISCUSSION QUESTIONS

1. How was Liudprand treated by the Byzantine emperor and officials? What does this indicate about the status of Westerners in the Byzantine Empire?

2. How does Liudprand portray the Byzantine court and society? Is his description positive or negative?

3. What role does Christianity, specifically different ideas of "orthodox" Christianity, play in the passage?

COMPARATIVE QUESTIONS

1. What do the documents in this chapter reveal about the political, cultural, and religious changes that had taken place since the time of ancient Rome (Chapter 5)?

2. What values did Christians profess according to Saints Augustine and Benedict? How might these values have affected their society? In what ways were those Christian values implemented by Charlemagne?

3. Can you detect any ways in which Augustine was influenced by Tertullian? How do their attitudes toward paganism differ? How does this compare to Charlemagne's treatment of pagans in Saxony?

4. How does Charlemagne's *Capitulary on Saxony* compare to Hammurabi's law code (Document 1-3) or the Twelve Tables (Document 5-1)? How can you account for the similarities and the differences?

5. How might Liudprand of Cremona reflect on Charlemagne's charge in the wake of his diplomatic visit to the Byzantine capital?

CHAPTER 8

The Islamic World

ca. 600–1400

I n the sixth century, the city of Mecca rose to prominence in the Arabian peninsula due to the popularity of its religious shrine, the Ka'ba, and its trade with the Byzantine and Persian Empires. The Prophet Muhammad (ca. 570–632) began his adult life working Mecca's caravans, but on turning forty he began to have revelations that formed the basis for the Qur'an. In 622, Muhammad was forced out of Mecca and led his followers to Medina, where he settled disputes between Jewish merchant groups and eventually became the leader of the city. Muhammad later captured the city of Mecca and united the nomadic tribes of the Arabian peninsula. Under Muhammad's successors, the caliphs, Islamic armies conquered the Middle East, North Africa, Spain, and portions of northern India. In so doing, the Muslims encountered Jews and Christians — honored as fellow "people of the book" — as well as polytheists, who they persecuted. During the Umayyad (661–750) and the Abbasid (750–1258) Dynasties, the Islamic caliphate dominated the world in economic activity, scientific development, and culture.

DOCUMENT 8-1

MUHAMMAD

Qur'an: Muslim Devotion to God

ca. 650

The Prophet Muhammad urged "submission" (Islam) to God (Allah) and he demanded that the nomadic Arab tribes of the Arabian peninsula convert

James Harvey Robinson, ed., *Readings in European History* (Boston: Ginn, 1904), 1:116–120.

from polytheism. His revelations (Qur'an) delivered by the angel Gabriel accepted the authority of Jewish prophets and the teachings of Jesus, who was considered a prophet. However, Islamic faith holds that the Jewish and Christian scriptures are corrupt versions of God's teachings, which appear in their purest form in the Qur'an. While Muhammad lived, the Qur'an was passed orally or in short written sections, but during the reign of the caliph Uthman (644–656), these fragments were collected into a unified document.

IN THE NAME OF GOD, THE COMPASSIONATE, THE MERCIFUL

Praise be to God, the Lord of the Worlds!
> The Compassionate, the Merciful!
> King of the day of judgment!
> Thee we worship, and Thee we ask for help.
> Guide us in the straight way,
> The way of those to whom Thou art gracious;
> Not of those upon whom is Thy wrath, nor of the erring.

In the name of the merciful and compassionate God. That is the book! there is no doubt therein; a guide to the pious, who believe in the unseen, and are steadfast in prayer, and of what we have given them expend in alms; who believe in what is revealed to thee, and what was revealed before thee, and of the hereafter they are sure. These are in guidance from their Lord, and these are the prosperous.

Verily, those who misbelieve, it is the same to them if ye warn them or if ye warn them not, they will not believe. God has set a seal upon their hearts and on their hearing; and on their eyes is dimness, and for them is grievous woe. There are, indeed, those among men who say, "We believe in God and in the last day"; but they do not believe. They would deceive God and those who do believe; but they deceive only themselves and they do not perceive. In their hearts is a sickness, and God has made them still more sick, and for them is grievous woe because they lied. . . .

And if ye are in doubt of what we have revealed unto our servant, then bring a chapter like it, and call your witnesses other than God if ye tell truth. But if ye do it not, and ye shall surely do it not, then fear the fire, whose fuel is men and stones, prepared for misbelievers. But bear the glad tidings to those who believe and work righteousness, that for them are gardens beneath which rivers flow. Whenever they are provided with fruit therefrom they say, "This is what we were provided with before, and they shall be provided with the like; and there are pure wives for them therein, and they shall dwell therein for aye [forever]." . . .

In the Name of God, the Compassionate, the Merciful

Have we not made the earth as a bed? And the mountains as tent-pegs? and created you in pairs, and made you sleep for rest, and made the night for a mantle, and made the day for breadwinning, and built above you seven firmaments, and put therein a burning lamp, and sent down water pouring from the squeezed clouds to bring forth grain and herb withal, and gardens thick with trees?

Lo! the Day of Decision is appointed — the day when there shall be a blowing of the trumpet, and ye shall come in troops, and the heavens shall be opened, and be full of gates, and the mountains shall be removed, and turn into [mist]. Verily hell lieth in wait, the goal for rebels, to abide therein for ages; they shall not taste therein coolness nor drink, save scalding water and running sores, — a meet reward! Verily they did not expect the reckoning, and they denied our signs with lies; but everything have we recorded in a book: —

Then the people of the right hand — what people of good omen! And the people of the left hand — what people of ill omen! And the outstrippers, still outstripping: — these are the nearest [to God], in gardens of delight; a crowd of the men of yore, and a few of the latter days; upon inwrought couches, reclining thereon face to face. Youths ever young shall go unto them round about with goblets and ewers [pitchers] and a cup of flowing wine, — their heads shall not ache with it, neither shall they be confused; and fruits of their choice, and flesh of birds of their desire; and damsels with bright eyes like hidden pearls, — a reward for what they have wrought. They shall hear no folly therein, nor any sin, but only the greeting, "Peace! peace!"

And the people of the right hand — what people of good omen! Amid thornless lote-trees,[1] and bananas laden with fruit, and shade outspread, and water flowing, and fruit abundant, never failing, nor forbidden, . . . But the people of the left hand — what people of ill omen! — amid burning wind and scalding water, and a shade of black smoke, not cool or grateful! Verily before that they were prosperous; but they persisted in the most grievous sin, and used to say, "When we have died, and become dust and bones, shall we indeed be raised again, and our fathers, the men of yore." Say: Verily those of yore and of the latter days shall surely be gathered to the trysting-place of a day which is known. Then ye, O ye who err and call

---

[1] lote-trees: Mythical trees representing the boundary between humans and Allah and beyond which no mortal can pass; they mark the uppermost limit of human knowledge.

it a lie, shall surely eat of the tree of Zakkum, and fill your bellies with it, and drink upon it scalding water, — drink like the thirsty camel: — this shall be their entertainment on the Day of Judgment!

READING AND DISCUSSION QUESTIONS

1. How is God (Allah) described in this passage?

2. What is the fate for believers and unbelievers? In what ways does this contradict or support the idea of a compassionate, merciful God?

3. How might the idea of "submission" to God provide a critique of Christianity and Judaism?

DOCUMENT 8-2

MUHAMMAD

The Constitution of Medina: Muslims and Jews at the Dawn of Islam

ca. 625

In 622, Muhammad was invited by the Jewish tribes of Yathrib (Medina) to settle disputes that caused continual fighting among them. Because Muhammad's teaching faced growing persecution in Mecca, his entire community followed him to Medina. This "flight" (hijra) marks the beginning of the Islamic calendar. Muhammad became the most important leader in Medina as many of the Jewish tribes converted to Islam. Around 625, Muhammad and the remaining Jewish tribes signed the following treaty, which was originally recorded by the eighth-century Arabic historian Ibn Ishaq and preserved in the text of the ninth-century writer Ibn Hisham.

The Messenger of God [Muhammad] wrote a document, concerning the emigrants from Mecca and the helpers of Medina, in which he reconciled

---

J. A. Williams, *Themes in Islamic Civilization* (Berkeley and Los Angeles: University of California Press, 1971), 11–15.

the Jews and covenanted with them, letting them act freely in the religion
and possessions which they had, and stated reciprocal obligations.

IN THE NAME OF GOD, THE MERCIFUL, THE COMPASSIONATE!

This document is from Muhammad the Prophet, governing relations
among the Believers and the Muslims of Quraysh [Mecca] and Yathrib
(Medina) and those who followed them and joined with them and
struggled with them.

1. They are one Community (*umma*) to the exclusion of all other
   men. . . .
11. The Believers shall not desert any poor person among them, but
    shall pay his redemption or blood-money, as is proper.
12. No Believer shall seek to turn the auxiliary of another Believer
    against him.
13. God-fearing Believers will be against who-ever among them is rebel-
    lious or whoever seeks to sow injustice or sin or enmity among the
    Believers; every man's hand shall be against him, though he were
    the son of one of them.
14. No Believer shall kill a Believer for the sake of an unbeliever, or aid
    an unbeliever against a Believer.
15. The protection of God is one: even the least of them may extend it
    to a stranger. The Believers are friends to each other, to the exclu-
    sion of all other men.
16. The Jews who follow us shall have aid and equality, except those
    who do wrong or aid the enemies of the Muslims.
17. The peace of the Believers is one: no Believer shall make peace sep-
    arately where there is fighting for God's sake. Conditions (of peace)
    must be just and equitable to all.
18. In every raid, the riders shall ride close together.
19. And the Believers shall avenge one another's blood, if shed for God's
    sake, for the God-fearing have the best and strongest guidance.
20. No idolator [polytheist] (of Medina) shall take Qurayshi property or
    persons under his protection, nor shall he turn anyone against a
    Believer.
21. Whoever kills a Believer shall also be killed, unless the next of kin
    of the slain man is otherwise satisfied, and the Believers shall be
    against him altogether; no one is permitted to act otherwise.
22. No Believer who accepts this document and believes in God and
    Judgment is permitted to aid a criminal or give him shelter. The

curse of God and His wrath on the Day of Judgment shall fall upon whoever aids or shelters him, and no repentance or compensation shall be accepted from him if he does.

23. Whenever you differ about a case, it shall be referred to God and to Muhammad.

24. The Jews shall bear expenses with the Muslims as long as they fight along with them.

25. The Jews of the Banu 'Awf [one Jewish tribe] are one community with the Believers; the Jews have their religion and the Muslims have theirs. This is so for them and their clients, except for one who does wrong or treachery; he hurts only himself and his family. . . .

46. Everyone shall have his portion from the side to which he belongs; the Jews of al-Aws [another Jewish tribe], their clients and themselves, are in the same position as the people of this document. Honorable dealing is without treachery.

47. Whoever acquires any (guilt) does not acquire it for any but himself. God is the most just and loyal fulfiller of what is in this document. This writing will not protect a wrongdoer or a traitor. Whoever goes out is safe, and he who stays at home is safe in the town, unless he has done wrong or treachery. God is the protecting neighbor (*jar*) of whoever does good and fears Him, and Muhammad is the Messenger of God. Verily God is wrathful when His covenant is broken. Peace be upon you.

READING AND DISCUSSION QUESTIONS

1. What is the role of religion in administering justice for Muhammad and the tribes of Medina?

2. How is the relationship between Jews and Muslims defined here? What could negatively affect that relationship?

3. Muhammad, unlike Jesus, was a secular ruler in addition to being a religious teacher. How do you think this may have affected his teachings?

DOCUMENT 8-3

BENJAMIN BEN JONAH OF TUDELA
From Book of Travels
ca. 1159–1172

By the twelfth century, cultures throughout the Mediterranean were coming into contact with one another, largely as a consequence of the Crusades that began in 1095. Following in the paths of merchant vessels from Italian city-states and Crusader armies, travelers and pilgrims began to cross from Europe to the Middle East. One such traveler, Benjamin ben Jonah of Tudela, left his home in Christian-controlled Spain and visited Jewish communities throughout Europe and the Middle East. Benjamin's record of his journeys, the Book of Travels, *describes the social and religious customs at his various stops.*

Baghdad [is] . . . the royal residence of the Caliph[2] Emir al-Muminin al-Abbasi (1160–1170) of the family of Muhammad [Abbasid Dynasty]. He is at the head of the Muslim religion, and all the kings of Islam obey him; he occupies a similar position to that held by the pope over the Christians. He has a palace in Baghdad three miles in extent, wherein is a great park with all varieties of trees, fruit-bearing and otherwise, and all manner of animals. . . . There the great king, al-Abbasi the Caliph holds his court, and he is kind unto Israel [the Jewish people], and many belonging to the people of Israel are his attendants; he knows all languages, and is well versed in the Law of Israel. He reads and writes the holy language [Hebrew]. . . . He is truthful and trusty, speaking peace to all men. . . .

In Baghdad there are about forty thousand Jews,[3] and they dwell in security, prosperity, and honor under the great Caliph, and among them are great sages, the heads of Academies engaged in the study of the Law [Jewish law: the Torah and the Talmud]. In this city there are ten Acade-

---

Benjamin Ben Jonah, *The Itinerary of Benjamin of Tudela*, trans. Marcus N. Adler (London: H. Frowde, 1907), 35–42.

[2]**Caliph**: A successor of Muhammad; the title denotes the secular and religious leader of the Islamic community, or *umma*.

[3]**forty thousand Jews**: Some of these Jews were the descendants of families deported by Nebuchadnezzar during the Babylonian captivity (586–537 B.C.E.).

mies. . . . And at the head of them all is Daniel the son of Hisdai, who is styled "Our Lord the Head of the Captivity of all Israel." He possesses a book of pedigrees going back as far as David, King of Israel (ca. 1000–965 B.C.E.). The Jews call him "Our Lord, Head of the Captivity," and the Muslims call him "Saidna ben Daoud," ["Lord, son of David"] and he has been invested with authority over all the congregations of Israel at the hands of the Emir al-Muminin, the Lord of Islam. For thus Muhammad [not the Prophet, but a later Abbasid ruler of Baghdad] commanded concerning him and his descendants; and he granted him a seal of office over all the congregations that dwell under his rule, and ordered that every one, whether Muslim or Jew, or belonging to any other nation in his dominion, should rise up before him and salute him, and that any one who should refuse to rise up should receive one hundred stripes [public lashes].

And every fifth day when he goes to pay a visit to the great Caliph, horsemen, gentiles as well as Jews, escort him, and heralds proclaim in advance, "Make way before our Lord, the son of David, as is due unto him," the Arabic words being "Amilu tarik la Saidna ben Daud." He is mounted on a horse, and is attired in robes of silk and embroidery with a large turban on his head. . . . Then he appears before the Caliph and kisses his hand, and the Caliph rises and places him on a throne which Muhammad had ordered to be made for him, and all the Muslim princes who attend the court of the Caliph rise up before him. And the Head of the Captivity is seated on his throne opposite to the Caliph, in compliance with the command of Muhammad. . . . The authority of the Head of the Captivity extends over all the communities of Shinar,[4] Persia, Khurasan, and Sheba which is El-Yemen, and Diyar Kalach and the land of Aram Naharaim, and over the dwellers in the mountains of Ararat and the land of the Alans. . . . His authority extends also over the land of Siberia, and the communities in the land of the Togarmim unto the mountains of Asveh and the land of Gurgan, the inhabitants of which are called Gurganim who dwell by the river Gihon, and these are the Girgashites [Nubians and Ethiopians] who follow the Christian religion. Further it extends to the gates of Samarkand, the land of Tibet, and the land of India. In respect of all these countries the Head of the Captivity gives the communities power to appoint Rabbis and Ministers who come unto him to be consecrated and to receive his authority. They bring him offerings and gifts

---

[4] **the communities of Shinar**: The Head of the Captivity's reach extended through great stretches of Mesopotamia, Northeastern Iran, around the Black Sea, all the way to a city in central Asia along the Silk Road, then to Tibet and India.

from the ends of the earth. He owns hospices, gardens, and plantations in Babylon, and much land inherited from his fathers, and no one can take his possessions from him by force. He has a fixed weekly revenue arising from the hospices of the Jews, the markets and the merchants, apart from that which is brought to him from far-off lands. The man is very rich, and wise in the Scriptures as well as in the Talmud,[5] and many Israelites dine at his table every day.

At his installation, the Head of the Captivity gives much money to the Caliph, to the Princes, and to the Ministers. On the day that the Caliph performs the ceremony of investing him with authority, he rides in the second of the royal carriages, and is escorted from the palace of the Caliph to his own house with timbrels and fifes. The Exilarch [leader of the exile, Daniel the son of Hisdai] appoints the Chiefs of the Academies by placing his hand upon their heads, thus installing them in their office. The Jews of the city are learned men and very rich.

In Baghdad there are twenty-eight Jewish Synagogues, situated either in the city itself or in al-Karkh on the other side of the Tigris; for the river divides the metropolis into two parts. The great synagogue of the Head of the Captivity has columns of marble of various colors overlaid with silver and gold, and on these columns are sentences of the Psalms in golden letters. And in front of the ark are about ten steps of marble; on the topmost step are the seats of the Head of the Captivity and of the Princes of the House of David. The city of Baghdad is twenty miles in circumference, situated in a land of palms, gardens and plantations, the like of which is not to be found in the whole land of Shinar.

READING AND DISCUSSION QUESTIONS

1. What is the relationship between the Jewish and Muslim communities of Baghdad as described by Benjamin ben Jonah?

2. How would you describe the Jewish community and the social status of Daniel the son of Hisdai?

3. In this account, Benjamin ben Jonah appears to have exaggerated the power of the caliph, who had delegated authority to sultans through-

---

[5] **Talmud**: Writings that date after the Torah, but have a high authority. One collection was written in Babylon during the captivity, and the other was compiled later in Palestine.

out the caliphate. Why might Benjamin have portrayed the caliphate as more powerful than it really was?

4. What seems to be Benjamin's opinion of Baghdad? What does it suggest about the purpose of his travels?

ZAKARIYA AL-QAZWINI
From Monuments of the Lands: An Islamic View of the West
1275–1276

Zakariya al-Qazwini (1203–1283) was born in Persia and served as a professor of Islamic law who also cultivated interests in astronomy and geography. A prolific writer, he is best known for two works: Wonders of the Created Things *and* Monuments of the Lands (Athar al-bilad). *Monuments is a geographical text compiled from other sources, which suggests that al-Qazwini did not actually visit many of the peoples and places that he describes. In this passage, he describes "Frank-land," as the Muslims called Western Europe, in the aftermath of the Crusades.*

Frank-land, a mighty land and a broad kingdom in the realms of the Christians. Its cold is very great, and its air is thick because of the extreme cold. It is full of good things and fruits and crops, rich in rivers, plentiful of produce, possessing tillage and cattle, trees and honey. There is a wide variety of game there and also silver mines. They forge very sharp swords there, and the swords of Frank-land are keener than the swords of India.

Its people are Christians, and they have a king possessing courage, great numbers, and power to rule. He has two or three cities on the shore of the sea on this side,[6] in the midst of the lands of Islam, and he protects

---

Al-Qazwini, *Athar al-bilad*, in Bernard Lewis, ed. and trans., *Islam: From the Prophet Muhammed to the Capture of Constantinople* (New York: Walker, 1987), 2:123.

[6] **He has two or three . . . on this side**: Lands in the Middle East captured during the Crusades.

them from his side. Whenever the Muslims send forces to them to capture them, he sends forces from his side to defend them. His soldiers are of mighty courage and in the hour of combat do not even think of flight, rather preferring death. But you shall see none more filthy than they. They are a people of perfidy and mean character. They do not cleanse or bathe themselves more than once or twice a year, and then in cold water, and they do not wash their garments from the time they put them on until they fall to pieces. They shave their beards, and after shaving they sprout only a revolting stubble. One of them was asked as to the shaving of the beard, and he said, "Hair is a superfluity. You remove it from your private parts, so why should we leave it on our faces?"

READING AND DISCUSSION QUESTIONS

1. How does al-Qazwini describe the Frankish lands?
2. How does al-Qazwini describe the Frankish people?
3. What do his descriptions tell us about Muslim values?

COMPARATIVE QUESTIONS

1. How does the nature of the Muslims' relationship to God compare to that of the Jews (Document 1-6) and Christians (Document 7-2)?
2. How does Islam view non-Muslims, as described by Muhammad, Benjamin ben Jonah, and Zakariya al-Qazwini?
3. From these documents, what evidence can you find to explain the success of Islam? What factors might have influenced people to convert to Islam?

CHAPTER 9

African Societies and Kingdoms

ca. 400–1450

The history of Africa is as richly diverse as the continent itself. The period from the fifth to the fifteenth centuries saw the rise in influence of Islam in the north, the emergence of several major kingdoms in the west, and the transformative migrations of the Bantu-speaking people through the interior of the continent. Although written records for the period are often from the perspective of outsiders, such as Muslim merchants, they nonetheless point to the vitality and strength of African culture and society. The selections for this chapter reveal the critical role that trade routes played in the development of Africa, bringing African societies into contact with one another and connecting Africa to the larger world. The readings also document the introduction of Islam and Christianity to the continent, both of which significantly influenced the direction of the early kingdoms of Africa.

DOCUMENT 9-1

EZANA, KING OF AKSUM

Stele of Ezana

ca. 325

Trade was essential to the development of the kingdom of Aksum in northwestern Ethiopia, which served as a critical hub for trade routes between India and the Mediterranean, as well as between Africa and the Arabian peninsula. Aksum was also significant for its adoption of Christianity, which

---

H. Schäfer, *A History of Ancient Aethiopian Kingship* (London, 1905), 81–100.

*the kingdom maintained even after the introduction of Islam into Africa.
King Ezana of Aksum (r. 330–356) converted to Christianity during his reign
and conquered his Nubian neighbors. Ezana ordered the inscription of a
stele, excerpted below, to document these major events of his reign.*

Through the might of the Lord of All I took the field against the Noba
[Nubians] when the people of Noba revolted, when they boasted and "He
will not cross over the Takkaze [River]," said the Noba, when they did violence to the peoples Mangurto and Hasa and Barya, and the Black Noba
waged war on the Red Noba and a second and a third time broke their oath
and without consideration slew their neighbors and plundered our envoys
and messengers whom I had sent to interrogate them, robbing them of
their possessions and seizing their lances. When I sent again and they did
not hear me, and reviled me, and made off, I took the field against them.
And I armed myself with the power of the Lord of the Land and fought on
the Takkaze at the ford of Kemalke. And thereupon they fled and stood not
still, and I pursued the fugitives twenty-three days slaying them and cap-
turing others and taking plunder from them, where I came; while prisoners and plunder were brought back by my own people who marched out;
while I burnt their towns, those of masonry and those of straw, and seized
their corn and their bronze and the dried meat and the images in their
temples and destroyed the stocks of corn and cotton; and the enemy
plunged into the river Seda, and many perished in the water, the number
I know not, and as their vessels foundered a multitude of people, men and
women were drowned. . . .

READING AND DISCUSSION QUESTIONS

1. What role did Christianity play in Ezana's conquests?

2. Describe Ezana as a conqueror. How did he view the people and territories that he conquered? Why did Ezana attack his neighbors?

DOCUMENT 9-2

ABU UBAYDALLAH AL-BAKRI
From The Book of Routes and Realms
ca. 1067–1068

For centuries, the expansive Sahara desert isolated northern and western Africa from one another. In the fifth century C.E., *the introduction of the Arabian camel allowed for the establishment of regular trade routes across the Sahara. This trans-Sahara trade accelerated in the seventh and eight centuries as Arab Muslim forces conquered North Africa and turned to the western Sudan region for gold and slaves. In exchange for their precious goods, West Africans received items such as horses and salt, as well as exposure to the tenets of the Islamic faith. Excepted below are accounts by a Spanish Muslim of the West African kingdoms of Ghana and Mali.*

Ghana is a title given to their kings; the name of the region is Awkar, and their king today, namely in the year 460, is Tunka Manin. He ascended the throne in 455 [1063 C.E.]. The name of his predecessor was Basi and he became their ruler at the age of 85. He led a praiseworthy life on account of his love of justice and friendship for the Muslims. At the end of his life he became blind, but he concealed this from his subjects and pretended that he could see. When something was put before him he said: "This is good" or "This is bad." His ministers deceived the people by indicating to the king in cryptic words what he should say, so that the commoners could not understand. Basi was a maternal uncle of Tunka Manin. This is their custom and their habit, that the kingship is inherited only by the son of the king's sister. He has no doubt that his successor is a son of his sister, while he is not certain that his son is in fact his own, and he is not convinced of the genuineness of his relationship to him. This Tunka Manin is powerful, rules an enormous kingdom, and possesses great authority.

The city of Ghana consists of two towns situated on a plain. One of these towns, which is inhabited by Muslims, is large and possesses twelve mosques, in one of which they assemble for the Friday prayer. There are

N. Levtzion and J. F. P. Hopkins, eds., *Corpus of Early Arabic Sources for West African History*, trans. J. R. Hopkins (Cambridge, UK: Cambridge University Press, 1981), 78–83, 85–87.

salaried imams [mosque leaders] and muezzins [chanters who call Muslims to prayer], as well as jurists and scholars. In the environs are wells with sweet water, from which they drink and with which they grow vegetables. The king's town is six miles distant from this one and bears the name of Al-Ghaba ["the forest"]. Between these two towns there are continuous habitations. The houses of the inhabitants are of stone and acacia wood. The king has a palace and a number of domed dwellings all surrounded with an enclosure like a city wall. In the king's town, and not far from his court of justice, is a mosque where the Muslims who arrive at his court pray. Around the king's town are domed buildings and groves and thickets where the sorcerers of these people, men in charge of the religious cult, live. In them too are their idols and the tombs of their kings. These woods are guarded and none may enter them and know what is there. In them also are the king's prisons. If somebody is imprisoned there no news of him is ever heard. The king's interpreters, the official in charge of his treasury and the majority of his ministers are Muslims. Among the people who follow the king's religion[1] only he and his heir apparent (who is the son of his sister) may wear sewn clothes. All other people wear robes of cotton, silk, or brocade, according to their means. All of them shave their beards, and women shave their heads. The king adorns himself like a woman, wearing necklaces round his neck and bracelets on his forearms, and he puts on a high cap decorated with gold and wrapped in a turban of fine cotton. He sits in audience or to hear grievances against officials in a domed pavilion around which stand ten horses covered with gold-embroidered materials. Behind the king stand ten pages holding shields and swords decorated with gold, and on his right are the sons of the vassal kings of his country wearing splendid garments and their hair plaited with gold. The governor of the city sits on the ground before the king and around him are ministers seated likewise. . . . When people who profess the same religion as the king approach him they fall on their knees and sprinkle dust on their heads, for this is their way of greeting him. As for the Muslims, they greet him only by clapping their hands.

Their religion is paganism and the worship of idols. When their king dies they construct over the place where his tomb will be an enormous dome of wood. Then they bring him on a bed covered with a few carpets and cushions and place him beside the dome. At his side they place his ornaments, his weapons, and the vessels from which he used to eat and

---

[1] the king's religion: The king was not a Muslim. He followed the traditional religion of the Soninke.

drink, filled with various kinds of food and beverages. They place there too the men who used to serve his meals. They close the door of the dome and cover it with mats and furnishings. Then the people assemble, who heap earth upon it until it becomes like a big hillock and dig a ditch around it until the mound can be reached at only one place.

They make sacrifices to their dead and make offerings of intoxicating drinks.

On every donkey-load of salt when it is brought into the country their king levies one golden dinar, and two dinars when it is sent out. From a load of copper the king's due is five mithqals,[2] and from a load of other goods ten mithqals. The best gold found in his land comes from the town of Ghiyaru, which is eighteen days' traveling distant from the king's town over a country inhabited by tribes of the Sudan whose dwellings are continuous.

The nuggets found in all the mines of his country are reserved for the king, only this gold dust being left for the people. But for this the people would accumulate gold until it lost its value. The nuggets may weigh from an ounce to a pound. It is related that the king owns a nugget as large as a big stone. . . .

The king of Ghana, when he calls up his army, can put 200,000 men[3] into the field, more than 40,000 of them archers. . . .

On the opposite bank of the Nil [the Niger River] is another great kingdom, stretching a distance of more than eight days' marching, the king of which has the title of *Daw*. The inhabitants of this region use arrows when fighting. Beyond this country lies another called Malal [later Mali], the king of which is known as *al-musulmani* ["the Muslim"]. He is thus called because his country became afflicted with drought one year following another; the inhabitants prayed for rain, sacrificing cattle till they had exterminated almost all of them, but the drought and the misery only increased. The king had as his guest a Muslim who used to read the Quran and was acquainted with the Sunna [Islamic traditions]. To this man the king complained of the calamities that assailed him and his people. The man said: "O King, if you believed in God (who is exalted) and testified that He is One, and testified as to the prophetic mission of Muhammad (God bless him and give him peace) and if you accepted all the religious laws of Islam, I would pray for your deliverance from your

---

[2] **dinar . . . mithqals:** A dinar was a standard gold coin in the Islamic kingdom. It weighed one *mithqal*, or 4.72 grams.

[3] **200,000 men:** Surely an exaggeration. Ghana had no standing army.

plight and that God's mercy would envelop all the people of your country and that your enemies and adversaries might envy you on that account." Thus he continued to press the king until the latter accepted Islam and became a sincere Muslim. The man made him recite from the Quran some easy passages and taught him religious obligations and practices which no one may be excused from knowing. Then the Muslim made him wait till the eve of the following Friday [the Islamic day of rest], when he ordered him to purify himself by a complete ablution, and clothed him in a cotton garment which he had. The two of them came out towards a mound of earth, and there the Muslim stood praying while the king, standing at his right side, imitated him. Thus they prayed for a part of the night, the Muslim reciting invocations and the king saying "Amen." The dawn had just started to break when God caused abundant rain to descend upon them. So the king ordered the idols to be broken and expelled the sorcerers from his country. He and his descendants after him as well as his nobles were sincerely attached to Islam, while the common people of his kingdom remained polytheists. Since then their rulers have been given the title of *al-musulmani.*

READING AND DISCUSSION QUESTIONS

1. What evidence does al-Bakri provide to suggest that the king of Ghana wielded significant power and authority in his territory?

2. Describe the presence of Islam in Ghana. Who practiced Islam? How was the spread of Islam encouraged? What potential obstacles were there to the growth of Islam in Ghana?

3. Why did the king of Mali convert to Islam? What did he need to do in order to convert?

DOCUMENT 9-3

IBN BATTUTA

From Travels in Asia and Africa

ca. 1325–1354

Ibn Battuta (1304–1368) was a Muslim explorer from Tangier, Morocco. At the age of twenty-one, he left home to make the traditional Muslim pilgrimage to Mecca, a journey that sparked his lifelong interest in travel. Ibn Battuta became an explorer and spent more than three decades visiting much of the Islamic world, as well as India, East Asia, and parts of Europe, which he recorded extensively. Excerpted below are his impressions of the east coast of Africa, his description of the treacherous trip across the Sahara desert, and his thoughts on the Kingdom of Mali.

IBN BATTUTA SAILS ALONG THE EAST COAST OF AFRICA

I took ship at Aden, and after four days at sea reached Zayla [Zeila, on the Somalian coast], the town of the Berberah, who are a negro people. Their land is a desert extending for two months' journey from Zayla to Maqdashaw [Mogadishu]. Zayla is a large city with a great bazaar, but it is the dirtiest, most abominable, and most stinking town in the world. The reason for the stench is the quantity of its fish and the blood of the camels that they slaughter in the streets. When we got there, we chose to spend the night at sea, in spite of its extreme roughness, rather than in the town, because of its filth.

THE TOWN OF MOGADISHU IN SOMALIA

On leaving Zayla we sailed for fifteen days and came to Maqdasha [Mogadishu], which is an enormous town. Its inhabitants are merchants and have many camels, of which they slaughter hundreds every day [for food]. When a vessel reaches the port, it is met by sumbuqs, which are small boats, in each of which are a number of young men, each carrying a covered dish containing food. He presents this to one of the merchants on the ship saying "This is my guest," and all the others do the same. Each

---

Ibn Battuta, *Travels in Asia and Africa 1325–1354*, trans. and ed. H. A. R. Gibb (London: Broadway House, 1929), 110–112, 317–323.

merchant on disembarking goes only to the house of the young man who is his host, except those who have made frequent journeys to the town and know its people well; these live where they please. The host then sells his goods for him and buys for him, and if anyone buys anything from him at too low a price, or sells to him in the absence of his host, the sale is regarded by them as invalid. This practice is of great advantage to them.

We stayed there [in Mogadishu] three days, food being brought to us three times a day, and on the fourth, a Friday, the qadi [judge] and one of the wazirs [chief ministers] brought me a set of garments. We then went to the mosque and prayed behind the [sultan's] screen. When the Shaykh [elder] came out I greeted him and he bade me welcome. He put on his sandals, ordering the qadi and myself to do the same, and set out for his palace on foot. All the other people walked barefooted. Over his head were carried four canopies of colored silk, each surmounted by a golden bird. After the palace ceremonies were over, all those present saluted and retired. . . .

Ibn Battuta Prepares to Cross the Sahara

At Sijilmasa [at the edge of the desert] I bought camels and a four months' supply of forage for them. Thereupon I set out on the 1st Muharram of the year 53 [February 13, 1352] with a caravan including, amongst others, a number of the merchants of Sijilmasa.

The Saltworks at the Oasis of Taghaza

After twenty-five days [from Sijilmasa] we reached Taghaza, an unattractive village, with the curious feature that its houses and mosques are built of blocks of salt, roofed with camel skins. There are no trees there, nothing but sand. In the sand is a salt mine; they dig for the salt, and find it in thick slabs, lying one on top of the other, as though they had been tool-squared and laid under the surface of the earth. A camel will carry two of these slabs.

No one lives at Taghaza except the slaves of the Massufa tribe, who dig for the salt; they subsist on dates imported from Dar'a and Sijilmasa, camels' flesh, and millet imported from the Negrolands. The negroes come up from their country and take away the salt from there. At Iwalatan a load of salt brings eight to ten mithqals; in the town of Malli [Mali] it sells for twenty to thirty, and sometimes as much as forty. The negroes use salt as a medium of exchange, just as gold and silver is used [elsewhere]; they cut it up into pieces and buy and sell with it. The business done at Taghaza, for all its meanness, amounts to an enormous figure in terms of hundredweights of gold-dust.

We passed ten days of discomfort there, because the water is brackish and the place is plagued with flies. Water supplies are laid in at Taghaza for the crossing of the desert which lies beyond it, which is a ten-nights' journey with no water on the way except on rare occasions. We indeed had the good fortune to find water in plenty, in pools left by the rain. One day we found a pool of sweet water between two rocky prominences. We quenched our thirst at it and then washed our clothes. Truffles are plentiful in this desert and it swarms with lice, so that people wear string necklaces containing mercury, which kills them.

DEATH IN THE DESERT

At that time we used to go ahead of the caravan, and when we found a place suitable for pasturage we would graze our beasts. We went on doing this until one of our party was lost in the desert; after that I neither went ahead nor lagged behind. We passed a caravan on the way and they told us that some of their party had become separated from them. We found one of them dead under a shrub, of the sort that grows in the sand, with his clothes on and a whip in his hand. The water was only about a mile away from him.

THE OASIS OF TISARAHLA, WHERE THE CARAVAN HIRES A DESERT GUIDE

We came next to Tisarahla, a place of subterranean water-beds, where the caravans halt. They stay there three days to rest, mend their waterskins, fill them with water, and sew on them covers of sackcloth as a precaution against the wind.

From this point the "takshif" is despatched. The "takshif" is a name given to any man of the Massufa tribe who is hired by the persons in the caravan to go ahead to Iwalatan, carrying letters from them to their friends there, so that they may take lodgings for them. These persons then come out a distance of four nights' journey to meet the caravan, and bring water with them. Anyone who has no friend in Iwalatan writes to some merchant well known for his worthy character who then undertakes the same services for him.

It often happens that the "takshif" perishes in this desert, with the result that the people of Iwalatan know nothing about the caravan, and all or most of those who are with it perish. That desert is haunted by demons; if the "takshif" be alone, they make sport of him and disorder his mind, so that he loses his way and perishes. For there is no visible road or track in these parts, nothing but sand blown hither and thither by the wind. You see hills of sand in one place, and afterwards you will see them moved to quite another place. The guide there [sic] is one who has made the journey frequently in both directions, and who is gifted with a quick intelligence. I remarked, as a strange thing, that the guide whom we had was blind in one eye, and diseased in the other, yet he had the best knowledge of the road of any man. We hired the "takshif" on this journey for a hundred gold mithqals; he was a man of the Massufa. On the night of the seventh day [from Tasarahla] we saw with joy the fires of the party who had come out to meet us.

THE CARAVAN REACHES THE OASIS OF WALATA

Thus we reached the town of Iwalatan [Walata, in modern-day Mauritania] after a journey from Sijilmasa of two months to a day. Iwalatan is the northernmost province of the negroes, and the sultan's representative there was one Farba Husayn, "farba" meaning deputy. When we arrived there, the merchants deposited their goods in an open square, where the blacks undertook to guard them, and went to the farba. He was sitting on a carpet under an archway, with his guards before him carrying lances and bows in their hands, and the headmen of the Massufa behind him. The merchants remained standing in front of him while he spoke to them through an interpreter, although they were close to him, to show his contempt for them. It was then that I repented of having come to their country, because of their lack of manners and their contempt for the whites.

I went to visit Ibn Badda, a worthy man of Sala [Sallee, in modern-day Morocco], to whom I had written requesting him to hire a house for me, and who had done so. Later on the mushrif [inspector] of Iwalatan, whose name was Mansha Ju, invited all those who had come with the caravan to partake of his hospitality. At first I refused to attend, but my companions urged me very strongly, so I went with the rest. The repast was served — some pounded millet mixed with a little honey and milk, put in a half calabash shaped like a large bowl. The guests drank and retired. I said to them, "Was it for this that the black invited us?" They answered, "Yes; and it is in their opinion the highest form of hospitality." This convinced me that there was no good to be hoped for from these people, and I made up my mind to travel [back to Morocco at once] with the pilgrim caravan from Iwalatan. Afterwards, however, I thought it best to go to see the capital of their king [of the kingdom of Mali].

LIFE AT WALATA

My stay at Iwalatan lasted about fifty days; and I was shown honor and entertained by its inhabitants. It is an excessively hot place, and boasts a few small date-palms, in the shade of which they sow watermelons. Its water comes from underground waterbeds at that point, and there is plenty of mutton to be had. The garments of its inhabitants, most of whom belong to the Massufa tribe, are of fine Egyptian fabrics.

Their women are of surpassing beauty, and are shown more respect than the men. The state of affairs amongst these people is indeed extraordinary. Their men show no signs of jealousy whatever; no one claims descent from his father, but on the contrary from his mother's brother. A person's heirs are his sister's sons, not his own sons. This is a thing which I have seen nowhere in the world except among the Indians of Malabar. But those are heathens; these people are Muslims, punctilious in observing the hours of prayer, studying books of law, and memorizing the Koran. Yet their women show no bashfulness before men and do not veil themselves, though they are assiduous in attending the prayers. Any man who wishes to marry one of them may do so, but they do not travel with their husbands, and even if one desired to do so her family would not allow her to go.

The women there have "friends" and "companions" amongst the men outside their own families, and the men in the same way have "companions" amongst the women of other families. A man may go into his house and find his wife entertaining her "companion" but he takes no objection to it. One day at Iwalatan I went into the qadi's house, after asking his permission to enter, and found with him a young woman of remarkable beauty. When I saw her I was shocked and turned to go out, but she laughed at me, instead of being overcome by shame, and the qadi said to me "Why are you going out? She is my companion." I was amazed at their conduct, for he was a theologian and a pilgrim [to Mecca] to boot. I was told that he had asked the sultan's permission to make the pilgrimage that year with his "companion" — whether this one or not I cannot say — but the sultan would not grant it.

READING AND DISCUSSION QUESTIONS

1. What impact did trade routes have on the East African coast? What measures did trade cities take to ensure that they benefited from commerce in the area?

2. What were some of the dangers of crossing the Sahara? How did travelers and merchants protect themselves from these dangers?

3. As Ibn Battuta's chronicle makes clear, despite the introduction of Islam, local traditions persisted in the kingdom of Mali. What were some of these traditions? What does Ibn Battuta think of them?

COMPARATIVE QUESTIONS

1. What role did the introduction of Christianity and Islam play in the development of the kingdoms of Aksum, Ghana, and Mali? How did these religions influence the actions of the kings? How did they influence the economies of the territories?

2. Describe al-Bakri and Ibn Battuta's impressions of the sub-Saharan kingdoms of Ghana and Mali. What do they admire about these kingdoms? What local traditions do they criticize?

3. Identify the trade routes mentioned in the documents by al-Bakri and Ibn Battuta. What were the economic and cultural repercussions for Africa of such trade routes?

CHAPTER 10

Civilizations of the Americas

2500 B.C.E.–1500 C.E.

W ritten records of premodern societies in both Africa and the Americas typically come from the perspective of outsiders. While Muslim explorers and merchants created a record of African civilizations, European conquerors and missionaries wrote accounts of the American experience. These same Europeans also destroyed much of the writings of native American civilizations to discourage traditional practices and beliefs that opposed the spread of Christianity. This chapter explores the cultures of the Western Hemisphere, specifically the Mississippian societies of North America, the Mayans and Mexica of Mesoamerica, and the Inca in South America. In each case, the recently arrived Europeans provide the best surviving record of these civilizations, offering invaluable insights into religious beliefs, political and economic systems, and the everyday experiences of the early peoples of the Americas.

DOCUMENT 10-1

PEDRO DE CIEZA DE LEÓN
From Chronicles: *On the Inca*

ca. 1535

From the fifteenth to the early sixteenth century, the large Inca empire in western South America spanned an area that included modern-day Peru. Compared to other civilizations in the Americas, the Inca had a sophisticated bureaucracy. Their empire had four provinces that were each headed with a governor who reported back to the king, or Sapa Inca (God Emperor).

Pedro de Cieza de León, *Chronicles*, from *The Incas of Pedro de Cieza de León*, ed. Victor Wolfgang von Hagen, trans. Harriet de Onis (Norman: University of Oklahoma Press, 1959), 165–167, 169–174, 177–178.

In the following account, Pedro de Cieza de León (1520–1554), a Spanish conquistador who came to admire the Inca culture, describes the administration of the empire. In the case of the Inca, historians are particularly dependent on the Spanish record because no civilization from South America developed a form of writing.

It is told for a fact of the rulers of this kingdom that in the days of their rule they had their representatives in the capitals of all the provinces, . . . for in all these places there were larger and finer lodgings than in most of the other cities of this great kingdom, and many storehouses. They served as the head of the provinces or regions, and from every so many leagues around the tributes were brought to one of these capitals, and from so many others, to another. This was so well organized that there was not a village that did not know where it was to send its tribute. In all these capitals the Incas had temples of the sun, mints, and many silversmiths who did nothing but work rich pieces of gold or fair vessels of silver; large garrisons were stationed there, and, as I have said, a steward or representative who was in command of them all, to whom an accounting of everything that was brought in was made, and who, in turn, had to give one of all that was issued. And these governors could in no way interfere with the jurisdiction of another who held a similar post, but within his own, if there were any disorder or disturbance, he had authority to punish it[s perpetrators], especially if it were in the nature of a conspiracy or a rebellion, or failure to obey the Inca [i.e., Sapa Inca], for full power resided in these governors. And if the Incas had not had the foresight to appoint them and to establish the *mitimaes*,[1] the natives would have often revolted and shaken off the royal rule; but with the many troops and the abundance of provisions, they could not effect this unless they had all plotted such treason or rebellion together. This happened rarely, for these governors who were named were of complete trust, all of them *Orejones* [elite, and typically blood relations of the king], and most of them had their holdings, or *chacaras*, in the neighborhood of *Cuzco* [the capital city], and their homes and kinfolk. If one of them did not show sufficient capacity for his duties, he was removed and another put in his place.

When one of them came to Cuzco on private business or to see the Inca, he left a lieutenant in his place, not one who aspired to the post, but

---

[1] **establish the *mitimaes***: A reference to the practice of relocating the populations of recently conquered territories. By moving the population of the empire around, the Inca hoped to break down local customs and practices and create a unified culture for the entire empire.

one he knew would faithfully carry out what he was ordered to do and what was best for the service of the Inca. And if one of these governors or delegates died while in office, the natives at once sent word to the Inca how and of what he had died, and even transported the body by the post road if this seemed to them advisable. The tribute paid by each of these districts where the capital was situated and that turned over by the natives, whether gold, silver, clothing, arms, and all else they gave, was entered in the accounts of . . . [those] who kept the *quipus* [knotted strings used for accounting] and did everything ordered by the governor in the matter of finding the soldiers or supplying whomever the Inca ordered, or making delivery to Cuzco; but when they came from the city of Cuzco to go over the accounts, or they were ordered to go to Cuzco to give an accounting, the accountants themselves gave it by the quipus, or went to give it where there could be no fraud, but everything had to come out right. Few years went by in which an accounting of all these things was not made. . . .

Realizing how difficult it would be to travel the great distances of their land where every league and at every turn a different language was spoken, and how bothersome it would be to have to employ interpreters to understand them, these rulers, as the best measure, ordered and decreed, with severe punishment for failure to obey, that all the natives of their empire should know and understand the language of Cuzco, both they and their women. This was so strictly enforced that an infant had not yet left its mother's breast before they began to teach it the language it had to know. And although at the beginning this was difficult and many stubbornly refused to learn any language but their own, the Incas were so forceful that they accomplished what they had proposed, and all had to do their bidding. This was carried out so faithfully that in the space of a few years a single tongue was known and used in an extension of more than 1,200 leagues, yet, even though this language was employed, they all spoke their own [languages], which were so numerous that if I were to list them it would not be credited. . . .

[The Indians] had a method of knowing how the tributes of food supplies should be levied on the provinces when the Lord-Inca came through with his army, or was visiting the kingdom; or, when nothing of this sort was taking place, what came into the storehouses and what was issued to the subjects, so nobody could be unduly burdened. . . . This involved the quipus, which are long strands of knotted strings, and those who were the accountants and understood the meaning of these knots could reckon by them expenditures or other things that had taken place many years before. By these knots they counted from one to ten and from ten to a hundred, and from a hundred to a thousand. On one of these strands there is the account of one thing, and on the other of another, in such a way that what to us is a strange, meaningless account is clear to them. In the capital of each province there were accountants whom they called *quipu-camayocs*, and by these knots they kept the account of the tribute to be paid by the natives of that district in silver, gold, clothing, flocks, down to wood and other more insignificant things, and by these same quipus at the end of a year, or ten, or twenty years, they gave a report to the one whose duty it was to check the account so exact that not even a pair of sandals was missing. . . .

The *Orejones* of Cuzco who supplied me with information are in agreement that in olden times, in the days of the Lord-Incas, all the villages and provinces of Peru were notified that a report should be given to the rulers and their representatives each year of the men and women who had died, and all who had been born, for this was necessary for the levying of the tributes as well as to know how many were available for war and those who could assume the defense of the villages. This was an easy matter, for each province at the end of the year had a list by the knots of the quipus of all the people who had died there during the year, as well as of those who had been born. At the beginning of the new year they came to Cuzco, bringing their quipus, which told how many births there had been during the year, and how many deaths. This was reported with all truth and accuracy, without any fraud or deceit. In this way the Inca and the governors knew which of the Indians were poor, the women who had been widowed, whether they were able to pay their taxes, and how many men they could count on in the event of war, and many other things they considered highly important.

As this kingdom was so vast, as I have repeatedly mentioned, in each of the many provinces there were many storehouses filled with supplies and other needful things; thus, in times of war, wherever the armies went they drew upon the contents of these storehouses, without ever touching the supplies of their confederates or laying a finger on what they had in their settlements. And when there was no war, all this stock of supplies and food was divided up among the poor and the widows. These poor were the aged, or the lame, crippled, or paralyzed, or those afflicted with some other diseases; if they were in good health, they received nothing. Then the storehouses were filled up once more with the tributes paid the Inca. If there came a lean year, the storehouses were opened and the provinces were lent what they needed in the way of supplies; then, in a year of abundance, they paid back all they had received. Even though the tributes paid to the Inca were used only for the aforesaid purposes, they were employed to advantage, for in this way their kingdom was opulent and well supplied.

No one who was lazy or tried to live by the work of others was tolerated; everyone had to work. Thus on certain days each lord went to his lands and took the plow in hand and cultivated the earth, and did other things. Even the Incas themselves did this to set an example, for everybody was to know that there should be nobody so rich that, on this account, he might disdain or affront the poor. And under their system there was none such in all the kingdom, for, if he had his health, he worked and lacked for nothing; and if he was ill, he received what he needed from the storehouses. And no rich man could deck himself out in more finery than the poor, or wear different clothing, except the rulers and headmen, who, to maintain their dignity, were allowed great freedom and privilege, as well as the *Orejones*, who held a place apart among all the peoples.

READING AND DISCUSSION QUESTIONS

1. Describe the Inca bureaucracy. How did it enable the king to rule this large territory?

2. What role did the *quipu* [khipu] play in the administration of the Inca Empire?

3. Cieza mentions a law requiring that every person in the empire learn the Inca language. What does this law tell you about the priorities of the Inca government?

4. What services did the Inca government provide for the people of the empire? How were they able to offer such services?

DOCUMENT 10-2

DIEGO DURÁN

From Book of the Gods and Rites

ca. 1576–1579

The Mexica, or Aztecs, occupied a large section of modern-day central Mexico. Like their Mayan and Toltec predecessors in the area, the Aztecs practiced human sacrifice. This tradition drew on Mesoamerican creation myths,

---

Diego Durán, *Book of the Gods and Rites and the Ancient Calendar*, trans. Fernando Horcasitas and Doris Heyden (Norman: Oklahoma University Press, 1971), 137–139, 273–280, 284–286.

which often involved gods making the first sacrifice by offering their own blood in order to create humanity. Victims of human sacrifice were usually captured enemy soldiers sold in slave markets. In this excerpt, the Dominican priest Diego Durán (1537–1588) describes the role of the marketplace in Aztec society, as well as the practice of human sacrifice.

The markets in this land were all enclosed by walls and stood either in front of the temples of the gods or to one side. Market day in each town was considered a main feast in that town or city. And thus in that small shrine where the idol of the market stood were offered ears of corn, chili, tomatoes, fruit, and other vegetables, seeds, and breads — in sum, everything sold in the *tianguiz* [marketplace]. Some say that (these offerings) were left there until they spoiled; others deny this, saying that all was gathered up by the priests and ministers of the temples.

But, to return to what I said about the market day being a feast day, the following is the truth. One day I was informed in a personal way, and now I shall tell what took place between me and a lord of a certain village. When I begged him to finish a part of the church that was under construction, he answered: "Father, do you now know that tomorrow is a great feast in this town? How can you expect them to work? Leave it for another day." Then, very carefully, I looked at the calendar to see which saint's day it was, and I found none. Laughing at me, (the lord) said: "Do you not know that tomorrow is the feast of the *tianguiz* of this town? (Do you not know) that not a man or a woman will fail to pay it its due honor?" From these words I realized (how important) a feast and solemnity the market is for them. . . . .

Furthermore, a law was established by the state prohibiting the selling of goods outside the market place. Not only were there laws and penalties connected with this, but there was a fear of the supernatural, of misfortune, and of the ire and wrath of the god of the market. No one ventured, therefore, to trade outside (the market limits), and the custom has survived until these days. Many a time have I seen a native carry two or three hens or a load of fruit for sale in the market. On the road he meets a Spaniard who wants to buy them from him. The Spaniard offers the price which he would have received in the market. The native refuses and is unwilling to sell, even though he would save himself a league or two of walking. He begs the Spaniard to go to the market place to buy them there. . . . Even today, though they are Christians, the awe and fear of their ancient law is still strong. It must also be said that the planting of this awe and nonsense in these people brought a certain income from all that which was sold in the markets (in the form of taxes), which was divided between the lord and the community.

In this land the sovereigns had set up a regulation regarding the markets: they were to take the form of fairs or markets specializing in the selling of certain things. Some markets, therefore, became famous and popular for these reasons: it was commanded that slaves were to be sold at the fair in Azcapotzalco and that all the people of the land who had slaves for sale must go there and to no other place to sell. The same can be said of Itzocan. Slaves could be sold in these two places only. It was at these two fairs that slaves were sold so that those who needed them would go there and no other place to buy. In other places, such as Cholula, it was ordered that the merchandise must consist of jewels, precious stones, and fine featherwork. At others, such as Tetzcoco, cloth and fine gourds were sold, together with exquisitely worked ceramics, splendidly done in the native way. . . .

I would like to say some things regarding the slaves sold in the two markets I have mentioned, Azcapotzalco and Itzocan. Some things worthy of remembering can be said about these slaves. In the first place, it should be known that in honor of the gods (as has been noted) men and women were slain on all the feast days. Some of these were slaves bought in the market place for the special purpose of representing gods. When they had performed the representation, when those slaves had been purified and washed — some for an entire year, others for forty days, others for nine, others for seven — after having been honored and served in the name of the god they impersonated, at the end they were sacrificed by those who owned them.

Captives of another type were those taken as prisoners in war. These served exclusively as sacrifices for the man who had impersonated the god whose feast was being celebrated. Thus these were called the "delicious food of the gods." I do not have to deal with all of these, but only with the slaves who were sold in the market place for having broken the law or for the reasons I shall describe later. These were bought by rich merchants and by important chieftains, some to glorify their own names and others to fulfill their customary vows.

The masters took the slaves to the *tianguiz*: some took men, others women, others boys or girls, so that there would be variety from which to choose. So that they would be identified as slaves, they wore on their necks wooden or metal collars with small rings through which passed rods about one yard long. In its place I shall explain the reason for putting these collars on them. At the site where these slaves were sold (which stood at one side of the *tianguiz*, according to market regulations) the owners kept (the slaves) dancing and singing so that merchants would be attracted by the charm of their voices and their (dance) steps and buy them quickly. If one possessed this facility, therefore, he found a master immediately. This was not the case for those who lacked grace and were inept in these things. Thus they were presented many times at market places without anyone paying attention to them, though (occasionally) some bought them to make use of them (as domestic servants), since they were unfit to represent the gods. Singers and dancers were in demand because when they were garbed in the raiment of the gods they went about singing and dancing in the streets and the houses during the time of their impersonation. They entered (the houses) and the temples and (climbed to) the flat roofs of the royal houses and those of their masters. They were given all the pleasures and joys of the world — foods, drink, feasts — as if they had been the gods themselves. So it was that the merchants wished that, aside from being good dancers and singers, they were healthy, without blemish or deformity. . . . (These slaves) were therefore made to strip, and were examined from head to foot, member by member. They were forced to extend their hands and lift their feet (as is done today with) Negro (slaves), to determine whether they were crippled. If one was found healthy, he was bought; otherwise, no. For it was desired that the slaves to be purified to represent the gods (this ceremony belonging to their rites, religion and precepts) were healthy and without blemish, just as we read in the Holy Writ about the sacrifices of the Old Testament which were to be without blemish. These slaves were not strangers or foreigners or prisoners of war, as some have declared, but were natives of the same town. . . .

READING AND DISCUSSION QUESTIONS

1. What rules did the Aztec government establish to regulate the market-places?
2. What role did the markets play in Aztec society? Why would work stop on the day of the market?
3. How were slaves selected for human sacrifice? What qualities did they need to exhibit?
4. How were slaves treated before being sacrificed?

ANTONIO DE HERRERA Y TORDESILLAS
On the Mayan Ball Game Tlachtli
ca. 1598

The Mayan ballgame tlachtli *had social, political, and religious significance. Tlachtli courts were some of the most important structures in Mayan cities. Their size demonstrated the power and authority of the city, while decorative carvings highlighted key aspects of Mayan religion and myth. Tlachtli players tried to pass a rubber ball through tall rings without touching the ball with their hands. While winners became heroes, losers were typically sacrificed to the Mayan gods. The following description of this Mesoamerican sport was written by an official court historian to King Phillip II of Spain.*

The game was called "Tlachtli," which is the same as "Trinquete" in Spanish. The ball was made of the gum from a tree which grows in the hot country. This tree, when tapped, exudes some large white drops, which soon congeal and when mixed and kneaded become as black as pitch: of this material the balls are made, and, although heavy and hard to the hand, they bound and rebound as lightly as footballs, and are indeed better, as there is no need to inflate them. They do not play for "chases" but to make a winning stroke — that is, to strike the ball against or to hit it over the wall which the opposite party defend. The ball may be struck with any part of the body, either such part as is most convenient or such as each player is most skillful in using. Sometimes it is arranged that it should count against any player who touches the ball otherwise than with his hip, for this considered by them to show the greatest skill, and on this account they would wear a piece of stiff raw hide over the hips, so that the ball might better rebound. The ball might be struck as long as it bounded, and it made many bounds one after the other, as though it were alive.

They played in parties, so many on each side, and for such a stake as a parcel of cotton cloths, more or less, according to the wealth of the players. They also played for articles of gold and for feathers, and at times staked their own persons. The place where they played was a court on the level of

Alfred Percival Maudslay, *A Glimpse at Guatemala* (London: John Murray, 1899), 205–206.

the ground, long, narrow, and high, but wider above than below, and higher at the sides than at the ends. So that it should be better to play in, the court was well cemented, and the walls and floors made quite smooth. In the side walls were fixed two stones like millstones, with a hold pierced through the middle, through which there was just room for the ball to pass, and the player who hit the ball through the hole won the game; and as this was a rare victory, which few gained, by the ancient custom and law of the game, the victor had a right to the mantles of all the spectators. . . .

To those who saw the feat performed for the first time it seemed like a miracle, and they said that a player who had such good luck would become a thief or an adulterer, or would die soon. And the memory of such a victory lasted many days, until it was followed by another, which put it out of mind.

READING AND DISCUSSION QUESTIONS

1. How did Mayan society recognize and reward the winners of the ball-game? What does this recognition suggest about the role of the ball-game in Mayan society?

2. Describe the ballgame court. What does the court suggest about the building capabilities of the Mayans?

DOCUMENT 10-4

FATHER LE PETITE

On the Customs of the Natchez

1730

The Natchez occupied an area in the southern portion of the Mississippi River from around 700 until 1730, when they were attacked and dispersed by French forces. The Natchez, like the Hopewell in Ohio, were mound build-ers. For these groups, earthen mounds served as religious temples as well as

Reuben Goldthwaites, ed. *The Jesuit Relations and Allied Documents* (Cleveland: Murrow Brothers, 1900), 68:121–135.

burial chambers for elites. The following account comes from an eighteenth-century Jesuit missionary who lived among the Natchez until they were defeated by the French military. In the document, Father le Petite describes the religion and society of these native Americans.

My Reverend Father, This Nation of Savages inhabits one of the most beautiful and fertile countries in the World, and is the only one on this continent which appears to have any regular worship. Their Religion in certain points is very similar to that of the ancient Romans. They have a Temple filled with Idols, which are different figures of men and of animals, and for which they have the most profound veneration. Their Temple in shape resembles an earthen oven, a hundred feet in circumference. They enter it by a little door about four feet high, and not more than three in breadth. Above on the outside are three figures of eagles made of wood, and painted red, yellow, and white. Before the door is a kind of shed with folding-doors, where the Guardian of the Temple is lodged; all around it runs a circle of palisades, on which are seen exposed the skulls of all the heads which their Warriors had brought back from the battles in which they had been engaged with the enemies of their Nation. . . .

The Sun is the principal object of veneration to these people; as they cannot conceive of anything which can be above this heavenly body, nothing else appears to them more worthy of their homage. It is for the same reason that the great Chief of this Nation, who knows nothing on the earth more dignified than himself, takes the title of brother of the Sun, and the credulity of the people maintains him in the despotic authority which he claims.

The old men prescribe the Laws for the rest of the people, and one of their principles is . . . the immortality of the soul, and when they leave this world they go, they say, to live in another, there to be recompensed or punished.

In former times the Nation of the Natchez was very large. It counted sixty Villages and eight hundred Suns or Princes; now it is reduced to six little Villages and eleven Suns. (Its) Government is hereditary; it is not, however, the son of the reigning Chief who succeeds his father, but the son of his sister, or the first Princess of the blood.[2] This policy is founded

---

[2] **it is not, however, the son . . . blood**: Father le Petite fails to recognize that the Natchez practice matrilineal succession (through the line of the mother rather than father).

on the knowledge they have of the licentiousness of their women. They are not sure, they say, that the children of the chief's wife may be of the blood Royal, whereas the son of the sister of the great Chief must be, at least on the side of the mother.

READING AND DISCUSSION QUESTIONS

1. Describe the religious practices of the Natchez. Why might Father le Petite have believed that the Natchez would be easy converts to Christianity?

2. In what ways did Father le Petite's European background influence his understanding of the customs of the Natchez?

COMPARATIVE QUESTIONS

1. Compare and contrast the religious beliefs of the Natchez, as captured in Father le Petite's letter, with those of the Mexica in Diego Durán's description. How is their worship of their gods similar or different?

2. Taking into consideration the depictions of the Mexica marketplace and the Mayan ballgame, what benefits did entertainment provide to the civilizations of the Americas?

3. What role did law play in Mexica and Inca society? According to Durán and Cieza de León, how successful were the rulers of these civilizations in enforcing laws?

4. Compare the sources in this chapter to those on Africa (Chapter 9). Since most of the material from both chapters is written from the perspective of outsiders, in your opinion, can it be trusted? Why or why not? How might you verify the information in such sources?

CHAPTER 11

Central and Southern Asia

to 1400

During the medieval period, the climate of Central and Southern Asia was one of contact and transformation. A number of sea routes brought Indian merchants to Southeast Asia, where local populations adopted Buddhism and Hinduism and adapted Indian cultural influences in such varied fields as politics, music, and language. In Central Asia, nomadic groups of Turks and Mongols began to abandon their traditional transitory lifestyles as they came into contact with settled civilizations. The Mongols evolved into cultural brokers who facilitated the exchange of people and ideas throughout their far-reaching empire. The sources in this chapter examine the changes under way in Central and Southern Asia from approximately the fourth to the fifteenth century, with a special emphasis on the contact between civilizations.

DOCUMENT 11-1

FA-HSIEN

From A Record of Buddhistic Kingdoms

ca. 399–414

Buddhism entered China during the early days of the Han Dynasty (202
B.C.E.–220 C.E.), when Indian merchants and missionaries traveled along
the Silk Road to China, bringing the Buddhist religion with them. Fa-hsien
(ca. 337–422) is possibly the most famous of the Chinese Buddhists who
traveled the long distance in order to study with Indian religious scholars.
Like Marco Polo, Fa-hsien recorded his journey. A Record of Buddhistic

James Legge, trans., *A Record of Buddhistic Kingdoms: Being an Account by the Chinese Monk Fa-hsien of His Travels in India and Ceylon* (A.D. 399–414) *in Search of the Buddhist Books of Discipline* (New York: Paragon Book Reprint Corp., 1965).

Kingdoms describes Fa-hsien's trip to and from India and includes the description of Ceylon (modern-day Sri Lanka) excerpted below.

The country originally had no human inhabitants, but was occupied only by spirits and nagas [dragons], with which merchants of various countries carried on a trade. When the trafficking was taking place, the spirits did not show themselves. They simply set forth their precious commodities, with labels of the price attached to them; while the merchants made their purchases according to the price; and took the things away.

Through the coming and going of the merchants (in this way), when they went away, the people of (their) various countries heard how pleasant the land was, and flocked to it in numbers till it became a great nation. The (climate) is temperate and attractive, without any difference of summer and winter. The vegetation is always luxuriant. Cultivation proceeds whenever men think fit: there are no fixed seasons for it.

When Buddha came to this country,[1] wishing to transform the wicked nagas, by his supernatural power he planted one foot at the north of the royal city, and the other on the top of a mountain, the two being fifteen yojanas apart.[2] Over the footprint at the north of the city the king built a large tope, 400 cubits high,[3] grandly adorned with gold and silver, and finished with a combination of all the precious substances. By the side of the top he further built a monastery, called the Abhayagiri, where there are (now) five thousand monks. There is in it a hall of Buddha, adorned with carved and inlaid works of gold and silver, and rich in the seven precious substances, in which there is an image (of Buddha) in green jade, more than twenty cubits in height, glittering all over with those substances, and having an appearance of solemn dignity which words cannot express. In the palm of the right hand there is a priceless pearl. Several years had now elapsed since Fa-hien [Fa-hsien] left the land of Han; the men with whom he had been in intercourse had all been of regions strange to him; his eyes had not rested on an old and familiar hill or river, plant or tree; his fellow-travellers, moreover, had been separated from him, some by death, and others flowing off in different directions; no face or shadow was now with him but his own, and a constant sadness was in his heart. Suddenly (one

---

[1] **When Buddha came . . . country**: The Buddha probably never visited Sri Lanka.

[2] **the top of a mountain . . . apart**: A reference to Adam's Peak in central Sri Lanka, which bears a rock formation known as the "sacred footprint." A yojana is approximately 8–10 miles.

[3] **400 cubits high**: A cubit is approximately 18 inches, so the domed monument would have topped approximately 600 feet.

day), when by the side of this image of jade, he saw a [Chinese] merchant presenting as his offering a fan of white silk; and the tears of sorrow involuntarily filled his eyes and fell down.

A former king of the country had sent to Central India and got a slip of the patra tree,[4] which he planted by the side of the hall of Buddha, where a tree grew up to the height of about 200 cubits. As it bent on one side towards the south-east, the king, fearing it would fall, propped it with a post eight or nine spans round. The tree began to grow at the very heart of the prop, where it met (the trunk); (a shoot) pierced through the post, and went down to the ground, where it entered and formed roots, that rose (to the surface) and were about four spans round. Although the post was split in the middle, the outer portions kept hold (of the shoot), and people did not remove them. Beneath the tree there has been built a vihara [monastery], in which there is an image (of Buddha) seated, which the monks and commonalty reverence and look up to without ever becoming wearied. In the city there has been reared also the vihara of Buddha's tooth,[5] on which, as well as on the other, the seven precious substances have been employed.

The king practices the Brahmanical purifications, and the sincerity of the faith and reverence of the population inside the city are also great. Since the establishment of government in the kingdom there has been no famine or scarcity, no revolution or disorder. In the treasuries of the monkish communities there are many precious stones, and the priceless manis. One of the kings (once) entered one of those treasuries, and when he looked all round and saw the priceless pearls, his covetous greed was excited, and he wished to take them to himself by force. In three days, however, he came to himself, and immediately went and bowed his head to the ground in the midst of the monks, to show his repentance of the evil thought. As a sequel to this, he informed the monks (of what had been in his mind), and desired them to make a regulation that from that day forth the king should not be allowed to enter the treasury and see (what it contained), and that no bhikshu [male Buddhist monk] should enter it till after he had been in orders for a period of full forty years.

In the city there are many Vaisya[6] elders and Sabaean [likely Arab] merchants, whose houses are stately and beautiful. The lanes and passages are kept in good order. At the heads of the four principal streets there have been built preaching halls, where, on the eighth, fourteenth, and fifteenth

---

[4] **patra tree**: A pippala or the Bo tree, often associated with the Buddha.

[5] **Buddha's tooth**: A sacred relic of the Buddha.

[6] **Vaisya**: The third of the four traditional Hindu castes, usually merchants or farmers.

days of the month, they spread carpets, and set forth a pulpit, while the monks and commonalty from all quarters come together to hear the Law. The people say that in the kingdom there may be altogether sixty thousand monks, who get their food from their common stores. The king, besides, prepares elsewhere in the city a common supply of food for five or six thousand more. When any want, they take their great bowls, and go (to the place of distribution), and take as much as the vessels will hold, all returning with them full.

The tooth of Buddha is always brought forth in the middle of the third month. Ten days beforehand the king grandly caparisons a large elephant, on which he mounts a man who can speak distinctly, and is dressed in royal robes, to beat a large drum, and make the following proclamation: — "The Bodhisattva [Buddha], during three Asankhyeya-kalpas [great stretches of time], manifested his activity, and did not spare his own life. He gave up kingdom, city, wife, and son; he plucked out his eyes and gave them to another; he cut off a piece of his own flesh to ransom the life of a dove; he cut off his head and gave it as an alms; he gave his body to feed a starving tigress; he grudged not his marrow and his brains. In many such ways as these did he undergo pain for the sake of all living. And so it was, that, having become Buddha, he continued in the world for forty-five years, preaching his Law, teaching and transforming, so that those who had no rest found rest, and the unconverted were converted. When his connexion with the living was completed, he attained to pari-nirvana (and died). Since that event, for 1497 years, the light of the world has gone out, and all living beings have had long-continued sadness. Behold! ten days after this, Buddha's tooth will be brought forth, and taken to the Abhayagiri-vihara.[7] Let all and each, whether monks or laics [secular people], who wish to amass merit for themselves, make the roads smooth and in good condition, grandly adorn the lanes and by-ways, and provide abundant store of flowers and incense to be used as offerings to it."

When this proclamation is over, the king exhibits, so as to line both sides of the road, the five hundred different bodily forms in which the Bodhisattva has in the course of his history appeared: — here as Sudana, there as Sama; now as the king of elephants; and then as a stag or a horse.[8] All these figures are brightly colored and grandly executed, looking as if they were alive. After this the tooth of Buddha is brought forth, and is carried

---

[7] **Abhayagiri-vihara**: The main temple complex in the city of Anuradhapura.
[8] **the five hundred . . . stag or a horse**: References to the Buddha's numerous reincarnations.

along in the middle of the road. Everywhere on the way offerings are presented to it, and thus it arrives at the hall of Buddha in the Abhayagiri-vihara. There monks and laics are collected in crowds. They burn incense, light lamps, and perform all the prescribed services, day and night without ceasing, till ninety days have been completed, when (the tooth) is returned to the vihara within the city. On fast-days the door of that vihara is opened, and the forms of ceremonial reverence are observed according to the rules.

Forty le to the east of the Abhayagiri-vihara there is a hill, with a vihara on it, called the Chaitya, where there may be 2,000 monks. Among them there is a Sramana of great virtue, named Dharma-gupta,[9] honored and looked up to by all the kingdom. He has lived for more than forty years in an apartment of stone, constantly showing such gentleness of heart, that he has brought snakes and rats to stop together in the same room, without doing one another any harm.

READING AND DISCUSSION QUESTIONS

1. How does Fa-hsien describe the king of Ceylon? Which of the king's qualities does he admire?

2. According to Fa-hsien, how did Buddhism arrive in Ceylon? What impact did its introduction have on the territory?

3. Describe the festival involving the tooth of Buddha. What role does the king play in the festival?

DOCUMENT 11-2

To Commemorate Building a Well

1276

During the medieval period, India was in a persistent state of fragmentation and was divided into a number of kingdoms of various size and import. This

---

Pushpa Prasad, ed., *Sanskrit Inscriptions of Delhi Sultanate, 1191–1526* (New Delhi: Oxford University Press India, 1990), 12–15.

[9] **Dharma-gupta**: A famous Sramana, or wondering monk, in Ceylon around 400.

division ensured that regional rather than national concerns played an important role in Indian society. The following Sanskrit inscription describes the building of a well near modern-day Delhi. It captures the delicate balance between India's kings and the communities over which they reigned. The opening describes the king's capital city before turning to the local "householder" who authorized the digging of the well.

The metropolis of the lord of many hundreds of cities, the charming great city called Delhi, flourishes like a crescent-headed arrow on the side of his enemies. Like the earth, it is the storehouse of innumerable jewels; like the sky, a source of delight; like the nether regions, the abode of many Daityas[10]; like Maya herself, the most bewitching.

In that city of Delhi, renowned under the name Yoganipura, there was a householder who was the wealthy abode of innumerable good qualities, devoid of blemishes, wise, noble-minded, given to meritorious acts, named Uddhara.

Where the clear Candrabhaga joined the beautiful Vitasta, the Vipasa and Satadru; opposite is situated the Indus (Sindhu)[11], the good friend with its tributaries, without high waves. Honey is useless, sugar cane juice is useless, so is the nectar in Heaven. If one drinks the nectar of the Indus, even his nectar of knowledge becomes insipid. In this northernly region, in which the earth is washed by the divine nectar of Sindhu, which removes all kinds of distress, there is Uccapuri, which laughs at the city of gods that is situated on the banks of the heavenly Ganga.

In that city lived his father Haripala, whose father was Yasoraja. His father was Dallahara, whose father was Kipu. This is his genealogy on the father's side. Uddhara's mother was Candi, the daughter of Prthu, whose father was Hasiscandra; his father was Utshahana, the son of Sahadeva, who was the son of Tola. Tola's father was Vyagharahara, who was the son of Singha and grandson of Guara. In the work entitled *Vamsavali*, the two genealogies have been given in detail; here in this record, the names have been taken to the extent desired to recall them to memory.

He had three wives, embodiments, as it were, of will, wisdom, and energy. The eldest wife, Jajala, was accompanied by Rajasri and Katandevi. Her son was named Hariraja, pure in body, speech, and mind,

---

[10] **Daityas**: In Hindu mythology these demon giants opposed the gods.
[11] **Candrabhaga . . . Indus (Sindhu)**: All are rivers in the Punjab region where India and Pakistan meet.

renowned, the abode of the sixty-four arts, apparently like Vishnu, the sole protector of the universe. His two younger brothers, named Sthiraraja and Jaitra, shine forth along with a sister, Virada. The second wife also had at first a daughter, the liberal-minded Dhanavati. After her, Ratandevi had two sons, Gunaraja and Bhupati. There was also a son, Haradeva, known as Natha, and also another girl. She had also another son, Uttamaraja, and a daughter named Sadali. Thus, we have here the root, stem, branches, fruits, and flowers of this Wishing Tree.

Numerous and extensive free inns were established in different places by this performer of sacrifice. But here, this wise one, with a view to relieving the exhaustion of tired travelers, had a well excavated. To the east of the village Palamba and to the west of Kusumbhapura, he made a well which quenches thirst and removes fatigue.

May this well, like a lovely woman with rotund, heaving breasts, gorgeous with undulating necklaces, be the assuager of the thirst of many a lovesick swain and perfumed with the mass of petals from the flowery trees. This well, being very clear, laughs at the minds of good people taking it as turbid. Like the supreme knowledge of philosophers, it shines, causing restfulness to the self.

May this devout and noble Lord Uddhara, whose pleasure rests in the final salvation in Heaven, who is a devotee of Siva, accompanied by sons, wives, friends, and dependents, have the good fortune to enjoy all the worldly pleasures.

This praiseworthy eulogy has been composed by Pandit Yogisvara of eternal fame, to record the construction of this well of Uddhara, the sole receptacle of all blessings.

READING AND DISCUSSION QUESTIONS

1. The inscription provides an extensive genealogy of the householder who sponsored the digging of the well. What does this genealogy tell us about the role of the family in medieval India?

2. How does this document suggest that Indian society encouraged commercial activity and the development of trade routes during the medieval period?

3. What are some of the traits most admired in Indian society at the time?

DOCUMENT 11-3

MARCO POLO

From Travels: Description of the World

ca. 1298

Marco Polo (ca. 1253–1324) was an Italian merchant who traveled through Central Asia to China. He served as a government official for many years in the court of Khubilai Khan. Upon returning to Europe in 1295 — approximately twenty-five years after he began his journey — Polo wrote a popular book describing his adventures. Although historians have at times doubted the veracity of some of Polo's claims, his Travels nonetheless provide an important record of Central Asia during the time of the Mongols. In the following excerpt, Polo describes his journey along the Asian trade routes known as the Silk Road, including his crossing of the challenging Taklamakan Desert.

Let us turn next to the province of Yarkand [on the southwestern border of the Taklamakan Desert], five days' journey in extent. The inhabitants follow the law of Mahomet,[12] and there are also some Nestorian Christians. They are subject to the Great Khan's nephew, of whom I have already spoken. It is amply stocked with the means of life, especially cotton. But, since there is nothing here worth mentioning in our book, we shall pass on to Khotan,[13] which lies towards the east-north-east.

Khotan is a province eight days' journey in extent, which is subject to the Great Khan. The inhabitants all worship Mahomet. It has cities and towns in plenty, of which the most splendid, and the capital of the kingdom, bears the same name as the province, Khotan. It is amply stocked with the means of life. Cotton grows here in plenty. It has vineyards, estates, and orchards in plenty. The people live by trade and industry; they are not at all warlike.

Marco Polo, *Travels*, trans. Ronald Latham (London: Penguin, 1958), 82–85 and 87–88.

[12] **Mahomet:** Western Europeans mistakenly believed that Muslims worshipped a god named Mahomet, or Muhammad, who is in fact the founder of the Islamic religion and believed to be a prophet of God.

[13] **Khotan:** A city along a Silk Road trading route located on the southern border of the Taklamakan Desert.

Passing on from here we come to the province of Pem, five days' journey in extent, towards the east-north-east. Here too the inhabitants worship Mahomet and are subject to the Great Khan. It has villages and towns in plenty. The most splendid city and the capital of the province is called Pem. There are rivers here in which are found stones called jasper and chalcedony [both are quartz] in plenty. There is no lack of the means of life. Cotton is plentiful. The inhabitants live by trade and industry.

The following custom is prevalent among them. When a woman's husband leaves her to go on a journey of more than twenty days, then, as soon as he has left, she takes another husband, and this she is fully entitled to do by local usage. And the men, wherever they go, take wives in the same way.

You should know that all the provinces I have described, from Kashgar to Pem and some way beyond, are provinces of Turkestan [i.e., the area of Central Asia inhabited by Turks].

I will tell you next of another province of Turkestan, lying east-north-east, which is called Charchan. It used to be a splendid and fruitful country, but it has been much devastated by the Tartars [Mongols]. The inhabitants worship Mahomet. There are villages and towns in plenty, and the chief city of the kingdom is Charchan.[14] There are rivers producing jasper and chalcedony, which are exported for sale in Cathay and bring in a good profit; for they are plentiful and of good quality.

All this province is a tract of sand; and so is the country from Khotan to Pem and from Pem to here. There are many springs of bad and bitter water, though in some places the water is good and sweet. When it happens that an army passes through the country, if it is a hostile one, the people take flight with their wives and children and their beasts two or three days' journey into the sandy wastes to places where they know that there is water and they can live with their beasts. And I assure you that no one can tell which way they have gone, because the wind covers their tracks with sand, so that there is nothing to show where they have been, but the country looks as if it had never been traversed by man or beast. That is how they escape from their enemies. But, if it happens that a friendly army passes that way, they merely drive off their beasts, because they do not want to have them seized and eaten; for the armies never pay for what they take. And you should know that, when they harvest their grain, they store it far from any habitation, in certain caves among these wastes, for fear of the armies; and from these stores they bring home what they need month by month.

---

[14] **Charchan**: This was the next major city along the trade route.

After leaving Charchan, the road runs for fully five days through sandy wastes, where the water is bad and bitter, except in a few places where it is good and sweet; and there is nothing worth noting in our book. At the end of the five days' journey towards the east-north-east, is a city which stands on the verge of the Great Desert. It is here that men take in provisions for crossing the desert. Let us move on accordingly and proceed with our narrative.

The city I have mentioned, which stands at the point where the traveler enters the Great Desert, is a big city called Lop, and the desert is called the Desert of Lop. The city is subject to the Great Khan, and the inhabitants worship Mahomet. I can tell you that travelers who intend to cross the desert rest in this town for a week to refresh themselves and their beasts. At the end of the week they stock up with a month's provisions for themselves and their beasts. Then they leave the town and enter the desert.

This desert is reported to be so long that it would take a year to go from end to end; and at the narrowest point it takes a month to cross it. It consists entirely of mountains and sand and valleys. There is nothing at all to eat. But I can tell you that after traveling a day and a night you find drinking water [at an oasis] — not enough water to supply a large company, but enough for fifty or a hundred men with their beasts. And all the way through the desert you must go for a day and a night before you find water. And I can tell you that in three or four places you find the water bitter and brackish; but at all the other watering-places, that is, twenty-eight in all, the water is good. Beasts and birds there are none, because they find nothing to eat. But I assure you that one thing is found here, and that a very strange one, which I will relate to you.

The truth is this. When a man is riding by night through this desert and something happens to make him loiter and lose touch with his companions, by dropping asleep or for some other reason, and afterwards he wants to rejoin them, then he hears spirits talking in such a way that they seem to be his companions. Sometimes, indeed, they even hail him by name. Often these voices make him stray from the path, so that he never finds it again. And in this way many travelers have been lost and have perished. And sometimes in the night they are conscious of a noise like the clatter of a great cavalcade of riders away from the road; and, believing that these are some of their own company, they go where they hear the noise and, when day breaks, find they are victims of an illusion and in an awkward plight. And there are some who, in crossing this desert, have seen a host of men coming towards them and, suspecting that they were robbers, have taken flight; so, having left the beaten track and not knowing how to return to it, they have gone hopelessly astray. Yes, and even by daylight men hear these spirit voices, and often you fancy you are listening to the strains of many instruments, especially drums, and the clash of arms. For this reason bands of travelers make a point of keeping very close together. Before they go to sleep they set up a sign pointing in the direction in which they have to travel. And round the necks of all their beasts they fasten little bells, so that by listening to the sound they may prevent them from straying off the path.

That is how they cross the desert, with all the discomfort of which you have heard. . . .

Now I will tell you of some other cities, which lie towards the northwest near the edge of this desert.

The province of Kamul, which used to be a kingdom, contains towns and villages in plenty, the chief town being also called Kamul.[15] The province lies between two deserts, the Great Desert and a small one three days' journey in extent. The inhabitants are all idolaters [Buddhists] and speak a language of their own. They live on the produce of the soil; for they have a superfluity of foodstuffs and beverages, which they sell to travelers who pass that way. They are a very gay folk, who give no thought to anything but making music, singing and dancing, and reading and writing according to their own usage, and taking great delight in the pleasures of the body. I give you my word that if a stranger comes to a house here to seek hospitality he receives a very warm welcome. The host bids his wife do everything that the guest wishes. Then he leaves the house and goes about his own business and stays away two or three days. Meanwhile the guest stays with his wife in the house and does what he will with her, lying with her in one bed just as if she were his own wife; and they lead a gay life together. All the men of this city and province are thus cuckolded by their wives; but they are not the least ashamed of it. And the women are beautiful and vivacious and always ready to oblige.

Now it happened during the reign of Mongu Khan,[16] lord of the Tartars, that he was informed of this custom that prevailed among the men of Kamul of giving their wives in adultery to outsiders. Mongu thereupon commanded them under heavy penalties to desist from this form of hospitality. When they received this command, they were greatly distressed; but for three years they reluctantly obeyed. Then they held a council and

---

[15] **Kamul**: Known today as Hami, this city is located along the northern route, which Polo is apparently describing from secondhand accounts.

[16] **Mongu Khan**: Brother of Khubilai Khan, who was Great Khan from 1251 to 1259.

talked the matter over, and this is what they did. They took a rich gift and sent it to Mongu and entreated him to let them use their wives according to the traditions of their ancestors; for their ancestors had declared that by the pleasure they gave to guests with their wives and goods they won the favor of their idols and multiplied the yield of their crops and their tillage. When Mongu Khan heard this he said: "Since you desire your own shame, you may have it." So he let them have their way. And I can assure you that since then they have always upheld this tradition and uphold it still.

READING AND DISCUSSION QUESTIONS

1. What were some of the dangers of crossing the Silk Road?

2. Describe the role of the Mongols in the areas that Polo visits. What impact did the Mongol presence have in these territories?

3. Consider the story Polo tells regarding the wives of Kamul. What does the response of the Great Khan tell you about the political strength of the Mongol leader in his empire?

COMPARATIVE QUESTIONS

1. In *The Book of Routes and Realms* (Document 9-2), al-Bakri describes the introduction of Islam in western Africa. Similarly, Fa-hsien describes the introduction of Buddhism in Ceylon. Comparing these two sources, what impact did the introduction of these "foreign" religions have on western Africa and Ceylon? Are there ways in which older beliefs survived the introduction of new faiths?

2. Based on the sources in this chapter, how was trade encouraged in Central and Southern Asia? What were the cultural implications of the development of trade routes through the area?

3. Compare Polo's "Description of the World" with "To Commemorate Building a Well." What do the two readings suggest about the nature of political power in the areas that they describe? In what ways did local leaders circumvent or challenge the authority of kings?

CHAPTER 12

East Asia

ca. 800–1400

Throughout the medieval period, East Asia saw unprecedented economic growth, created sophisticated governments, and experienced a cultural boom. China drove this development and led in technological innovations such as mastering the printing press and perfecting the compass for overseas navigation. The Song Dynasty (960–1179) in particular advanced new forms of governance through the creation of an elite corps of educated civil servants and established thriving trade with its neighbors in Southeast Asia and beyond. China's vitality granted it tremendous influence over its neighbors, including Korea, Vietnam, and Japan. The sources in this chapter focus on the economic successes of China during the medieval period, as well as its cultural developments, and include accounts from Heian Japan (794–1185), a high point in the development of Japanese government and culture.

DOCUMENT 12-1

MURASAKI SHIKIBU

From The Tale of Genji

ca. 1021

Heian Japan (794–1185) developed a culturally vibrant aristocratic society — one in which women played remarkably important roles, especially in literary endeavors. During this period, the Japanese developed a phonetic writing system that appealed to women who often lacked the education needed to master the more complicated Chinese-based writing system. Court

From Murasaki Shikibu, *The Tale of Genji*, Edward Seidensticker, trans. (New York: Alfred A. Knopf, 1976).

society soon benefited from the entertainments of significant female writers such as Murasaki Shikibu, the author of the narrative masterpiece The Tale of Genji. *In the excerpts below, the characters of the story discuss how to pick a good wife and the role of women in marriage.*

They talked on, of the varieties of women.

"A man sees women, all manner of them, who seem beyond reproach," said the guards officer, "but when it comes to picking the wife who must be everything, matters are not simple. The emperor has trouble, after all, finding the minister who has all the qualifications. A man may be very wise, but no man can govern by himself. Superior is helped by subordinate, subordinate defers to superior, and so affairs proceed by agreement and concession. But when it comes to choosing the woman who is to be in charge of your house, the qualifications are altogether too many. A merit is balanced by a defect, there is this good point and that bad point, and even women who though not perfect can be made to do are not easy to find. I would not like to have you think me a profligate who has to try them all. But it is a question of the woman who must be everything, and it seems best, other things being equal, to find someone who does not require shaping and training, someone who has most of the qualifications from the start. The man who begins his search with all this in mind must be reconciled to searching for a very long time."

"There are those who display a womanly reticence to the world, as if they had never heard of complaining. They seem utterly calm. And then when their thoughts are too much for them they leave behind the most horrendous notes, the most flamboyant poems, the sort of keepsakes certain to call up dreadful memories, and off they go into the mountains or to some remote seashore. When I was a child I would hear the women reading romantic stories, and I would join them in their sniffling and think it all very sad, all very profound and moving. Now I am afraid that it suggests certain pretenses.

"It is very stupid, really, to run off and leave a perfectly kind and sympathetic man. He may have been guilty of some minor dereliction, but to run off with no understanding at all of his true feelings, with no purpose other than to attract attention and hope to upset him — it is an unpleasant sort of memory to have to live with. She gets drunk with admiration for herself and there she is, a nun. When she enters her convent she is sure that she has found enlightenment and has no regrets for the vulgar world.

"Her women come to see her. 'How very touching,' they say. 'How brave of you.'

"But she no longer feels quite as pleased with herself. The man, who has not lost his affection for her, hears of what has happened and weeps, and certain of her old attendants pass this intelligence on to her. 'He is a man of great feeling, you see. What a pity that it should have come to this.' The woman can only brush aside her newly cropped hair[1] to reveal a face on the edge of tears. She tries to hold them back and cannot, such are her regrets for the life she has left behind; and the Buddha is not likely to think her one who has cleansed her heart of passion. Probably she is in more danger of brimstone now in this fragile vocation than if she had stayed with us in our sullied world.

"The bond between husband and wife is a strong one. Suppose the man had hunted her out and brought her back. The memory of her acts would still be there, and inevitably, sooner or later, it would be cause for rancor. When there are crises, incidents, a woman should try to overlook them, for better or for worse, and make the bond into something durable. The wounds will remain, with the woman and with the man, when there are crises such as I have described. It is very foolish for a woman to let a little dalliance upset her so much that she shows her resentment openly. He has his adventures — but if he has fond memories of their early days together, his and hers, she may be sure that she matters. A commotion means the end of everything. She should be quiet and generous, and when something comes up that quite properly arouses her resentment she should make it known by delicate hints. The man will feel guilty and with tactful guidance he will mend his ways. Too much lenience can make a woman seem charmingly docile and trusting, but it can also make her seem somewhat wanting in substance. We have had instances enough of boats abandoned to the winds and waves. Do you not agree?"

Tô no Chûjô nodded. "It may be difficult when someone you are especially fond of, someone beautiful and charming, has been guilty of an indiscretion, but magnanimity produces wonders. They may not always work, but generosity and reasonableness and patience do on the whole seem best."

---

[1] **newly cropped hair**: Buddhist nuns were expected to cut off their hair upon entering the convent.

READING AND DISCUSSION QUESTIONS

1.   According to the characters, how is the selection of a wife similar to the emperor selecting a minister? Why is picking a wife more difficult?

2.   What do the characters believe is the proper reaction of a wife when she learns of a "little dalliance" by her husband? In what ways, if any, may she show her disapproval?

3.   Can the characters' views regarding the proper role of women in Japanese society be taken at face value? In what ways does the knowledge that the author of *The Tale of Genji* was a woman change its meaning?

4.   Given the lack of educational opportunities for Heian Japanese women, who do you suppose was Shikibu's audience?

DOCUMENT 12-2

From Okagami

ca. 1075–1125

Okagami (The Great Mirror) is a history of the Heian period (794–1185), when leaders looked less to China as an example and began developing distinctly Japanese approaches to governance. In Okagami, two elderly narrators describe the influence of the Fujiwara family, who ruled Japan on behalf of the imperial dynasty of the time. The narrators pay particular attention to Michinaga, who served as regent in the early eleventh century and was considered the model Fujiwara ruler. The excerpt below tells the story of Michinaga's rise to power and details the good luck that followed him in office.

"I have only one thing of importance on my mind," he went on, "and that is to describe Lord Michinaga's unprecedented successes to all of you here, clergy and laity of both sexes. It is a complicated subject, so I shall have to discuss a fair number of Emperors, Empresses, ministers of state, and senior nobles first. Then when I reach Michinaga himself, the most fortunate of all, you will understand just how everything came about. They

---

Helen Craig McCullough, trans., *Okagami* (Ann Arbor: University of Michigan Press, 1991), 68–69, 185, 190–191, 208–209.

tell us that the Buddha began by expounding other sutras when he wanted to explain the *Lotus*, which is why his sermons are called the teachings of the five periods.[2] That is how it is with me, too; I need to 'expound other sutras' in order to describe Michinaga's successes." . . .

"I suppose you youngsters nowadays think every Regent, minister of state, and senior noble in history has been very much like Michinaga. That is far from true. Of course, they have all been descendants of the same ancestor and members of the same family, but the family has produced many different kinds of people in the process of branching out. . . .

"Michinaga held the offices of Major Counselor and Master of the Empress's Household then. On the eleventh of the Fifth Month, at the age of thirty — a time when he was still very young and could look forward to a long career — he received the Imperial decree naming him Regent, and thereafter he began to prosper in earnest. The regency has never left his house, and we may assume that it never will." . . .

"Michinaga was named *kanpaku* [regent for an adult emperor] in his thirtieth year. After governing as he pleased during the reigns of Emperors Ichirō and Sanjō, he became the present Emperor's *sesshō* [regent for an emperor who has not attained adulthood] when His Majesty ascended the throne at the age of nine. He was then fifty-one. During that same year, he assumed the office of Chancellor,[3] ceding the regency to [his son] Yorimichi. He took Buddhist vows on the Twenty-First of the Third Month in the third year of Kannin [1019], when he was fifty-four. On the Eighth of the Fifth Month, the Court made him equivalent to the three Empresses in status, with annual ranks and offices, even though he was a monk. He is the grandfather of the Emperor and the Crown Prince, and the father of three Empresses, of the Regent Minister of the Left, of the Palace Minister, and of many Counselors; and he has governed the realm for approximately thirty-one years. Since this year is his sixtieth, people say there will be a celebration for him after the birth of Kishi's child. What a magnificent affair that will be, with so many great personages present!

"No other minister of state has ever been able to make three of his daughters Empresses at the same time. It must be counted a rare blessing that Michinaga's house has produced three Imperial ladies — Senior Grand Empress Shōshi, Grand Empress Kenshi, and Empress Ishi. Our

---

[2] **the teachings of the five periods**: A reference to the teachings of the Buddha, which are divided into five periods.

[3] **Chancellor**: A Fujiwara regent could continue to rule after the end of his regency by assuming the position of chancellor.

other Empress, Seishi, was the only one who belonged to a different house, but she was also descended from [Fuhiwara no] Tadahira, so we certainly can't think of her as an outsider. We may indeed call Michinaga the supreme ruler of the land, particularly since Empress Seishi's death this spring has left his three daughters as the sole surviving Empresses.

"The Chinese and Japanese poems Michinaga has composed on various occasions are so ingenious that I am sure not even Bo Zhuyi, Hito-maro, Mitsune, or Tsurayuki[4] could have thought of them. For example, there was the Imperial visit to Kasuga Shrine, a custom inaugurated in the reign of Emperor Ichijō. Since Emperor Ichijō's precedent was considered inviolable, our present sovereign made the journey in spite of his youth, with Senior Grand Empress Shōshi accompanying him in his litter. To call the spectacle brilliant would be trite. Above all, what can I say about the bearing and appearance of Michinaga, the Emperor's grand-father, as he rode in the Imperial train? It might have been disappointing if he had looked anything like an ordinary man. The crowds of country folk along the way must have been spellbound. Even sophisticated city dwellers, dazzled by a resplendence like that of the Wheel-Turning Sacred Monarchs,[5] found themselves, in perfectly natural confusion, raising their hands to their foreheads as though gazing on a buddha. . . .

"[Michinaga] is in a class by [himself]. He is a man who enjoys special protection from the gods of heaven and earth. Winds may rage and rains may fall day after day, but the skies will clear and the ground will dry out two or three days before he plans anything. Some people call him a rein-carnation of Shōtoku Taishi; others say he is Kōbō Daishi,[6] reborn to make Buddhism flourish. Even to the censorious eye of old age, he seems not an ordinary mortal but an awesome manifestation of a god or buddha.

"A nation is bound to be perfectly happy with a ruler like Michinaga. In the old days, cattle drivers and horse herders in the employ of noblemen and Princes were always dunning us for festivals and spirit services. They

---

[4] **Bo Zhnyi . . . or Tsurayuki**: All are Japanese poets; most date from the Heian period (794–1185).
[5] **Wheel-Turning Sacred Monarchs**: Wheel-turning monarchs were rulers acknowl-edged for closely following the principles of Buddhism during their reign.
[6] **Shōtoku Taishi . . . Kōbō Daishi**: Shōtoku Taishi (574–622) was a famous Japanese regent to the emperor. He is remembered for his Seventeen Article Constitution. Kōbō Daishi (774–835) was a Buddhist monk and scholar who founded the Shingon, or "True Word," school of Buddhism in Japan.

wouldn't even let anyone cut grass in the fields and hills. But now the minor functionaries of the great no longer seize a man's belongings, and there is no more talk of local headmen and village magistrates who pester people to defray the expenses of fire festivals and so forth. Can we ever hope to enjoy such safety and peace again?"

READING AND DISCUSSION QUESTIONS

1. According to the narrators of Michinaga's story, how were the Fujiwara able to rule Japan? What connections did the Fujiwara have to the imperial family? Why were members of the Fujiwara family needed to serve as regents?

2. What role did luck play in the successes of Michinaga? How did this good luck benefit not only Michinaga but all of Japan?

3. What advantages did the system of regents and chancellors have in terms of governing Japan? What were its limitations?

DOCUMENT 12-3

CHEN PU

On the Craft of Farming

1149

The Song Era (960–1179) marked a period of expansive growth in China's commercial economy, due in large part to the attention paid to agriculture. Rather than aiming for self-sufficiency, Chinese peasants often focused on farming cash crops, which gave them both reason and means for trading in the marketplace. Song officials aided the efforts of the peasants by publishing and distributing farming manuals such as the one excerpted below. Together, the government and the people of China were able to keep agricultural production in step with the rapidly growing Chinese population.

Chen Pu, "On Farming," trans. Clara Yu, in Patricia Buckley Ebrey, *Chinese Civilization and Society: A Sourcebook* (Simon & Schuster, 1981).

Finance and Labor

All those who engage in business should do so in accordance with their own capacity. They should refrain from careless investment and excessive greed, lest in the end they achieve nothing. . . . In the farming business, which is the most difficult business to manage, how can you afford not to calculate your financial and labor capacities carefully? Only when you are certain that you have sufficient funds and labor to assure success should you launch an enterprise. Anyone who covets more than he can manage is likely to fall into carelessness and irresponsibility. . . . Thus, to procure more land is to increase trouble, not profit.

On the other hand, anyone who plans carefully, begins with good methods, and continues in the same way can reasonably expect success and does not have to rely on luck. The proverb says, "Owning a great deal of emptiness is less desirable than reaping from a narrow patch of land." . . . For the farmer who is engaged in the management of fields, the secret lies not in expanding the farmland, but in balancing finance and labor. If the farmer can achieve that, he can expect prosperity and abundance. . . .

Plowing

Early and late plowing both have their advantages. For the early rice crop, as soon as the reaping is completed, immediately plow the fields and expose the stalks to glaring sunlight. Then add manure and bury the stalks to nourish the soil. Next, plant beans, wheat, and vegetables to ripen and fertilize the soil so as to minimize the next year's labor. In addition, when the harvest is good, these extra crops can add to the yearly income. For late crops, however, do not plow until spring. Because the rice stalks are soft but tough, it is necessary to wait until they have fully decayed to plow satisfactorily. . . .

The Six Kinds of Crops

There is an order to the planting of different crops. Anyone who knows the right timing and follows the order can cultivate one thing after another, and use one to assist the others. Then there will not be a day without planting, nor a month without harvest, and money will be coming in throughout the year. How can there then be any worry about cold, hunger, or lack of funds?

Plant the nettle-hemp in the first month. Apply manure in intervals of ten days and by the fifth or sixth month it will be time for reaping. The women should take charge of knotting and spinning cloth out of the hemp.

Plant millet in the second month. It is necessary to sow the seeds sparsely and then roll cart wheels over the soil to firm it up; this will make the millet grow luxuriantly, its stalks long and its grains full. In the seventh month the millet will be harvested, easing any temporary financial difficulties.

There are two crops of oil-hemp. The early crop is planted in the third month. Rake the field to spread out the seedlings. Repeat the raking process three times a month and the hemp will grow well. It can be harvested in the seventh or the eighth month.

In the fourth month plant beans. Rake as with hemp. They will be ripe by the seventh month.

In mid-fifth month plant the late oil-hemp. Proceed as with the early crop. The ninth month will be reaping time.

After the 7th day of the seventh month, plant radishes and cabbage.

In the eighth month, before the autumn sacrifice to the god of the Earth, wheat can be planted. It is advisable to apply manure and remove weeds frequently. When wheat grows from the autumn through the spring sacrifices to the god of the Earth, the harvest will double and the grains will be full and solid.

The *Book of Poetry*[7] says, "The tenth month is the time to harvest crops." You will have a large variety of crops, including millet, rice, beans, hemp, and wheat and will lack nothing needed through the year. Will you ever be concerned for want of resources? . . .

FERTILIZER

At the side of the farm house, erect a compost hut. Make the eaves low to prevent the wind and rain from entering it, for when the compost is exposed to the moon and the stars, it will lose its fertility. In this hut, dig a deep pit and line it with bricks to prevent leakage. Collect waste, ashes, chaff, broken stalks, and fallen leaves and burn them in the pit; then pour manure over them to make them fertile. In this way considerable quantities of compost are acquired over time. Then, whenever sowing is to be done, sieve and discard stones and tiles, mix the fine compost with the seeds, and plant them sparsely in pinches. When the seedlings have grown tall, again sprinkle the compost and bank it up against the roots. These methods will ensure a double yield.

---

[7] **Book of Poetry**: Known also as the *Book of Songs*, the *Book of Poetry* dates from 1700–700 B.C.E. and contains the earliest examples of Chinese poetry (see Document 3-2).

Some people say that when the soil is exhausted, grass and trees will not grow; that when the *qi* [the Neo-Confucian concept of energy or force] is weak, all living things will be stunted; and that after three to five years of continuous planting, the soil of any field will be exhausted. This theory is erroneous because it fails to recognize one factor: by adding new, fertile soil, enriched with compost, the land can be reinforced in strength. If this is so, where can the alleged exhaustion come from?

WEEDING

The *Book of Poetry* says, "Root out the weeds. Where the weeds decay, there the grains will grow luxuriantly." The author of the *Record of Ritual*[8] also remarks, "The months of mid-summer are advantageous for weeding. Weeds can fertilize the fields and improve the land." Modern farmers, ignorant of these principles, throw the weeds away. They do not know that, if mixed with soil and buried deep under the roots of rice seedlings, the weeds will eventually decay and the soil will be enriched; the harvest, as a result, will be abundant and of superior quality. . . .

CONCENTRATION

If something is thought out carefully, it will succeed; if not, it will fail; this is a universal truth. It is very rare that a person works and yet gains nothing. On the other hand, there is never any harm in trying too hard.

In farming it is especially appropriate to be concerned about what you are doing. Mencius[9] said, "Will a farmer discard his plow when he leaves his land?" Ordinary people will become idle if they have leisure and prosperity. Only those who love farming, who behave in harmony with it, who take pleasure in talking about it and think about it all the time will manage it without a moment's negligence. For these people a day's work results in a day's gain, a year's work in a year's gain. How can they escape affluence?

READING AND DISCUSSION QUESTIONS

1. Why does the author think that farmers should avoid acquiring too much land? What are his concerns regarding the amount of land farmed?

---

[8] *Record of Ritual*: A book detailing elite rituals or ceremonies that dated to the Qin era (221–206 B.C.E.).

[9] **Mencius**: Mencius (372–289 B.C.E.) was a follower of Confucius and prominent Confucian scholar.

2. In addition to providing practical advice for farmers, the author also draws heavily on Confucian and Neo-Confucian philosophy. Where are these philosophical influences visible in the manual? What does their inclusion tell you about the relationship between Confucianism and commercial life in Song China?

> DOCUMENT 12-4

ZHAU RUGUA

A Description of Foreign Peoples

ca. 1250

The commercial growth of Song China was not confined to its borders. China conducted extensive international trade through ongoing traffic along the Silk Road and the use of sea routes through Southeast Asia that connected China to the Islamic world. The following account describes China's trading partners through the eyes of Zhau Rugua (1170–1228), a customs inspector of the southern port city of Quanzhou. Although Zhau's knowledge was probably not firsthand, his descriptions hint at the important role that Arab merchants played in facilitating international trade.

THE LAND OF THE DASHI[10]

The Dashi are to the west and northwest of Quanzhou at a very great distance from it, so that foreign ships find it difficult to make a direct voyage there. After these ships have left Quanzhou they arrive in some forty days at Lanli [a Sumatran port city], where they trade. The following year they go to sea again, when with the aid of the regular wind, they take some sixty days to make the journey.

The products of the country [Arabia] are for the most part brought to Sanfozi [another Sumatran port], where they are sold to merchants who forward them to China.

The "Cotton Manuscript" of the British Museum, printed 1625, ch. 20, 30; adapted into modern English by A. J. Andrea.

[10] **Dashi**: Arabs.

This country of the Dashi is powerful and warlike. Its extent is very great, and its inhabitants are preeminent among all foreigners for their distinguished bearing. The climate throughout a large part of it is cold, snow falling to a depth of two or three feet; consequently rugs are much prized.

The capital of the country, called Maluoba [Merbat, in southwest Arabia], is an important center for the trade of foreign peoples. . . . The streets are more than fifty feet broad; in the middle is a roadway twenty feet broad and four feet high for use of camels, horses, and oxen carrying goods about. On either side, for the convenience of pedestrians' business, there are sidewalks paved with green and bluish black flagstones of surpassing beauty. . . .

Very rich persons use a measure instead of scales in business transactions of gold or silver. The markets are noisy and bustling, and are filled with a great store of gold and silver damasks, brocades, and similar wares. The artisans have the true artistic spirit.

The king, the officials, and all the people serve Heaven. They also have a Buddha by the name of Mahiawu [Muhammad]. Every seven days they cut their hair and clip their fingernails. At the New Year for a whole month they fast and chant prayers [during the holy month of Ramadan]. Daily they pray to Heaven five times.

The peasants work their fields without fear of floods or droughts; a sufficiency of water for irrigation is supplied by a river [the Nile] whose source is not known. During the season when no cultivation is in progress, the level of the river remains even with the banks; with the beginning of cultivation it rises day by day. Then it is that an official is appointed to watch the river and to await the highest water level, when he summons the people, who then plow and sow their fields. When they have had enough water, the river returns to its former level.

There is a great harbor in this country [probably Basra in modern-day Iraq], over two hundred feet deep, which opens to the southeast on the sea and has branches connecting with all quarters of the country. On either bank of the harbor the people have their dwellings and here daily are held fairs, where boats and wagons crowd in, all laden with hemp, wheat, millet, beans, sugar, meal, oil, . . . fowl, sheep, geese, ducks, fish, shrimp, date cakes, grapes, and other fruits.

The products of the country consist of pearls, ivory, rhinoceros horns, frankincense, ambergris, . . . cloves, nutmegs, benzoin, aloes, myrrh, dragon's blood, . . . borax, opaque and transparent glass, . . . coral, cat's eyes, gardenia flowers, rosewater, nutgalls, yellow wax, soft gold brocades, camel's-hair cloth, . . . and foreign satins.

The foreign traders who deal in these wares bring them to Sanfozi and to Foluoan [Beranang, on the Malay Peninsula] to barter. . . .

The country of Magia [Mecca] is reached by traveling eighty days westward by land from the country of Maluoba. This is where the Buddha Mahiawu was born. In the House of the Buddha [the Ka'ba] the walls are made of jade stone of every color. Every year, when the anniversary of the death of the Buddha comes around, people from all the countries of the Dashi assemble here, when they vie with each other in bringing presents of gold, silver, jewels, and precious stones. Then also is the House adorned anew with silk brocade.[11]

Farther off [in Medina] there is the tomb of the Buddha. Continually by day and night there is at this place such a brilliant radiance that no one can approach it; he who does is blinded. Whoever in the hour of his death rubs his breast with dirt taken from this tomb will, so they say, be restored to life again by the power of the Buddha.

MULANPI[12]

The country of Mulanpi is to the west of the Dashi country. There is a great sea, and to the west of this sea there are countless countries, but Mulanpi is the one country which is visited by the big ships of the Dashi. Putting to sea from Dobandi [Damietta, in Egypt] in the country of the Dashi, after sailing due west for a full hundred days, one reaches this country. A single one of these ships of theirs carries several thousand men [an exaggeration], and on board they have stores of wine and provisions, as well as weaving looms. If one speaks of big ships, there are none so big as those of Mulanpi.

The products of this country are extraordinary. The grains of wheat are three inches long, the melons six feet round, enough for a meal for twenty or thirty men. The pomegranates weigh five catties,[13] lemons over twenty catties, salad greens weigh over ten catties and have leaves three or four feet long. Rice and wheat are kept in silos for ten years without spoiling. Among the native products are foreign sheep that are several feet high and have tails as big as a fan. In the springtime they slit open their bellies and

---

[11] **Every year . . . brocade**: The author is describing the hajj, or Islamic pilgrimage to Mecca, when Muslims converge on the Ka'ba, the holy shrine at the center of that city. The author incorrectly connects the hajj to the anniversary of Muhammad's death.

[12] **Mulanpi**: An area of Southern Spain.

[13] **five catties**: A catty was equivalent to about one and one-third pounds.

take out some ten catties of fat, after which they sew them up again, and the sheep live on; if the fat were not removed, the animal would swell up and die.

If one travels by land [from Mulanpi] two hundred days' journey, the days are only six hours long.[14] In autumn if the west wind arises, men and beasts must at once drink to keep alive, and if they are not quick enough about it they die of thirst.

READING AND DISCUSSION QUESTIONS

1. What Islamic religious practices does Zhau describe? In what ways does Zhau's experience with Buddhism influence his understanding of Islam?

2. What are some of the goods traded along the routes that Zhau describes? How is trade encouraged along these routes?

DOCUMENT 12-5

Widows Loyal Unto Death

ca. 1754

The ordained and practical roles of women in medieval China present several contradictions. Surviving records suggest that women were active members of society — serving as midwives, living as Buddhist nuns, and helping their families run businesses — yet a number of popular practices existed that curtailed the lives of women, such as the right of husbands to take concubines and the custom of binding the feet of elite women. One of the more destructive traditions, described in the stories below, was the idea that widows should commit suicide after the deaths of their husbands in order to demonstrate their personal virtue.

From Patricia Buckley Ebrey, ed. and trans., *Chinese Civilization: A Sourcebook* (New York: Free Press, 1993), 253–255.

[14]**days . . . only six hours long**: The author describes the shortened winter days of northern Europe.

Xu Sungjie, daughter of Xu Yuanyan, married Chen Boshan at the age of seventeen. When her husband was gravely ill, he told her to remarry because she had no son. At his death, she embraced him and cried bitterly. After the coffin was closed, she hanged herself to die with her husband. The official Bai Bi was impressed with her fidelity and so arranged for her burial and had a banner with the inscription "filial piety and propriety" displayed at her door.

Lin Shunde, the daughter of the prefect Lin Jin, was engaged to Sun Mengbi. When Mengbi died, she was with her father at his post. Once the announcement of her fiance's death reached her, she put on mourning dress and wept to tell her parents that she wished to go to his home. Her parents packed for her and told her to behave properly. On arriving there, she performed the rituals for her first meeting with her parents-in-law, then she made an offering at her fiance's coffin. After he was buried, she served her mother-in-law for the rest of her life. The local official inscribed a placard with "She hurried to the funeral of a husband she had never seen. Suffering cold and frost, she swore not to remarry." . . .

Fu Xiajie was the wife of Chen Banghuai. Her husband was taken hostage by some bandits. She supported herself by making hemp cloth. After a long time someone told her that her husband had died. She was spinning at the time. She then immediately entered her bedroom and hanged herself.

Wu Jinshun was the wife of Sun Zhen. On the first anniversary of her husband's death, she was so forlorn that she died of grief.

Zhang Zhongyu was engaged to Chen Shunwei, who died prematurely when Zhongyu was eighteen. When she learned of his death, she decided to hurry to the Chen family. Her parents tried to stop her, but she cried and said, "Once you betrothed me to the Chen family, I became a daughter-in-law of the Chen family." So, she hurried to attend her fiance's funeral and bow to her mother-in-law. Then, she cut her hair and removed her ornaments. She lived a secluded life. In the first month of the xinsi year [1461], there was a fire in her neighborhood. She leaned herself against her husband's coffin, wanting to be burned up with her husband. Suddenly a wind came and extinguished the fire. Only her house survived. On the sixth day of the sixth month of the wuzi year [1468], a large army approached. People in the county fled helter-skelter. Zhongyu remained to guard the coffin, keeping a knife with her. When the army arrived the next day, she showed the banner and the tablet from the previous official. The soldiers recognized her righteousness, and general Bai attached his order on the door so that no other soldiers would enter her house. One day she became severely ill and told her mother-in-law, "Don't let any men put their hands on me when I am shrouded after I die. Use the money in the small box that I earned by splicing and spinning to bury me with my husband." Then she died.

Sun Yinxiao was the daughter of Sun Keren and married Lin Zengqing at the age of seventeen. Lin, who made his living fishing, drowned after they had been married for only two months. Sun was determined to kill herself. After the mourning period was over, she made a sacrifice with utmost grief. That night, she dressed carefully and bound a wide girdle round the beam to hang herself. When the magistrate Xu Jiadi heard of this, he paid a visit to offer a sacrifice to her soul.

Wang Yingjie was the wife of Qiu Bianyu. She was widowed at nineteen before bearing any children. As a consequence she decided to die. Her family had long been rich and her dowry was particularly ample. She gave it all to her husband's younger brother so that in the future he could arrange for an heir to succeed to her husband. Then she ceased eating. Her mother forced her to stop, so she had no alternative but to pretend to eat and drink as usual. When her mother relaxed her vigilance, she hanged herself.

Wang Jingjie, whose family had moved to Nantai, married Fu Yan, a candidate for the examinations. Yan studied so hard that he got ill and died. When Wang learned of this, she emptied out her savings and gave it to her father-in-law to pay for her husband's funeral, asking him to do it properly. The evening after he was buried, her brother came to console her and she asked how her parents were doing. Her brother slept in another room. At dawn, when the members of the family got up, they kept shouting to her, but she did not answer. When they pried open her door, she was already dead, having hanged herself. She was solemnly facing the inside, standing up straight. She was twenty-one.

Zhang Xiujie married He Liangpeng when she was eighteen. Before a year had passed, he became critically ill. He asked her what she would do, and she pointed to Heaven and swore to follow her husband in death. Since she wished to commit suicide, the other family members had to prevent her. After several months, their only son died of measles. Zhang wept and said, "It is my fate. I had been living for him." That night she hanged herself.

Huang Yijie was engaged to Chen Rujing from Changle who lived in Lianjiang. Before they were married, he died. When she was fifteen, she heard of it and was saddened by it. As she slowly understood what it meant, streams of tears rolled down her cheeks. Without her knowledge a matchmaker arranged a new engagement. In the fifth month of the bingyin year [1506], her first fiance's mother came to call. Huang followed the courtesies appropriate to a daughter-in-law when she went out to meet her, and they both expressed their grief, not holding back. After a while she asked her mother-in-law why she had come, and she told her that she had heard of the new engagement and so had come to get the brideprice back. The girl was startled and thought, "Could this be true? Only in extremely unfortunate circumstances is a dead man's wife sold." She told her mother-in-law, "Fortunately not much has been done with it. Let me make a plan." Disoriented, for a long time she sat, not saying a word. Then she asked her mother-in-law to stay for the night and told her everything she wanted to say. She gave her the hairpins and earrings she had received as betrothal gifts, saying, "Keep these to remember your son by." At dusk, her mother-in-law took her leave, and the girl, weeping, saw her to the gate. She then took a bath, combed her hair, and changed into new clothes. Those things done, she took a knife and cut her throat. The first cut did not sever it, so she had to cut it again before she died. In the morning when her family found her body, there were traces of three cuts.

READING AND DISCUSSION QUESTIONS

1. How did a widow demonstrate her virtue and integrity after the death of her husband? To whom was she obligated after the death of her husband?

2. How do you think accounts like this one perpetuated the practice of widows committing suicide?

COMPARATIVE QUESTIONS

1. Compare and contrast the reading "Widows Loyal Unto Death" with *The Tale of Genji*. In what ways did Chinese and Japanese societies have similar expectations for wives? In what ways did those expectations differ?

2. Both Marco Polo (Document 11-3) and Zhau Rugua describe the Islamic world and its people from the perspective of outsiders. What are their impressions of Islam? What do their accounts suggest about the role of religion in the development of commercial relationships?

3. The Song Dynasty was a period of economic expansion for China. According to Chen Pu's account and "A Description of Foreign Peoples," why was China so successful in growing its economy? What steps did the government and the Chinese people take to strengthen the economy?

4. Compare the extract from *Okagami* with "On the Craft of Farming." What philosophical or religious ideas influenced Japanese and Chinese understanding of good governance? How were these ideas similar or different?

CHAPTER 13

Europe in the Middle Ages

850–1400

After the division of Charlemagne's empire in 843, Europe entered a period known as the Middle Ages. Although later Renaissance schol-ars dismissively labeled this time the "Dark Ages" preceding their own cul-tural boom, in truth the Middle Ages witnessed a dynamic restructuring of Europe's political, social, and religious life. Europe's kings slowly consoli-dated their territories and their claim to power, while the introduction of feudalism and manorialism brought stability and order to European soci-ety. Although the medieval European experience was extremely diverse due to increased foreign encroachment, catastrophic outbreaks of disease, and civil and international warfare, the thriving Christian Church was a prominent and unifying element of society. Together, the Church, territo-rial leaders, and scholars guided society toward the development of a dis-tinct European way of life and identity.

DOCUMENT 13-1

NICETAS CHONIATES
From Annals
1118–1207

Nicetas Choniates (1155–1216) was a Byzantine government official who wrote a comprehensive history of the Byzantine Empire during the time of the Crusades. His firsthand account of the sacking of Constantinople by the Crusaders of Western Europe is the most extensive in existence. Poor plan-ning and financing of the Fourth Crusade (1202–1204) had prompted the

Harry J. Magoulias, trans., O City of Byzantium: Annals of Niketas Chronicles, 198, with the permission of Wayne State University Press (Detroit, 1984), 314–316.

Crusaders to set their sights on the wealthy Byzantine capital of Constan-
tinople. When the dust finally settled, the attack had devastated the once
mighty Byzantine Empire and irrevocably damaged the relationship be-
tween the Latin and Greek branches of Christianity.

The enemy, who had expected otherwise, found no one openly venturing
into battle or taking up arms to resist; they saw that the way was open
before them and everything there for the taking. The narrow streets were
clear and the crossroads unobstructed, safe from attack, and advantageous
to the enemy. The populace, moved by the hope of propitiating them, had
turned out to greet them with crosses and venerable icons of Christ as was
customary during festivals of solemn processions. But their disposition was
not at all affected by what they saw, nor did their lips break into the slightest smile, nor did the unexpected spectacle transform their grim and fren-
zied glance and fury into a semblance of cheerfulness. Instead, they
plundered with impunity and stripped their victims shamelessly, beginning with their carts. Not only did they rob them of their substance but also
the articles consecrated to God; the rest fortified themselves all around
with defensive weapons as their horses were roused at the sound of the war
trumpet.

What then should I recount first and what last of those things dared at
that time by these murderous men? O, the shameful dashing to earth of
the venerable icons and the flinging of the relics of the saints, who had suffered for Christ's sake, into defiled places! How horrible it was to see the
Divine Body and Blood of Christ [i.e., the consecrated bread and wine of
the Eucharist] poured out and thrown to the ground! These forerunners of
Antichrist,[1] chief agents and harbingers of his anticipated ungodly deeds,
seized as plunder the precious chalices and patens; some they smashed,
taking possession of the ornaments embellishing them, and they set the
remaining vessels on their tables to serve as bread dishes and wine goblets.
Just as happened long ago, Christ was now disrobed and mocked, his garments were parted, and lots were cast for them by this race; and although
his side was not pierced by the lance, yet once more streams of Divine
Blood poured to the earth.

---

[1] **Antichrist**: According to Christian belief, the Antichrist was a false Christ who would
appear in the guise of the true Christ before the second coming and cause chaos.

The report of the impious acts perpetrated in the Great Church [the Hagia Sophia] are unwelcome to the ears. The table of sacrifice, fashioned from every kind of precious material and fused by fire into one whole — blended together into a perfection of one multicolored thing of beauty, truly extraordinary and admired by all nations — was broken into pieces and divided among the despoilers, as was the lot of all the sacred church treasures, countless in number and unsurpassed in beauty. They found it fitting to bring out as so much booty the all-hallowed vessels and furnishings which had been wrought with incomparable elegance and craftsmanship from rare materials. In addition, in order to remove the pure silver which overlay the railing of the berna [where Mass is performed], the wondrous pulpit and the gates, as well as that which covered a great many other adornments, all of which were plated with gold, they led to the very sanctuary of the temple itself mules and asses with packsaddles; some of these, unable to keep their feet on the smoothly polished marble floors, slipped and were pierced by knives so that the excrement from the bowels and the spilled blood defiled the sacred floor. Moreover, a certain silly woman laden with sins . . . the handmaid of demons, the workshop of unspeakable spells and reprehensible charms, waxing wanton against Christ, sat upon the synthronon [throne for the head of the Greek church] and intoned a song, and then whirled about and kicked up her heels in dance.

It was not that these crimes were committed in this fashion while others were not, or that some acts were more heinous than others, but that the most wicked and impious deeds were perpetrated by all with one accord. Did these madmen, raging thus against the sacred, spare pious matrons and girls of marriageable age or those maidens who, having chosen a life of chastity, were consecrated to God? Above all, it was a difficult and arduous task to mollify the barbarians with entreaties and to dispose them kindly towards us, as they were highly irascible and bilious and unwilling to listen to anything. Everything incited their anger, and they were thought fools and became a laughingstock. He who spoke freely and openly was rebuked, and often the dagger would be drawn against him who expressed a small difference of opinion or who hesitated to carry out their wishes.

The whole head was in pain. There were lamentations and cries of woe and weeping in the narrow ways, wailing at the crossroads, moaning in the temples, outcries of men, screams of women, the taking of captives, and the dragging about, tearing in pieces, and raping of bodies heretofore sound and whole. They who were bashful of their sex were led about naked, they who were venerable in their old age uttered plaintive cries, and the wealthy were despoiled of their riches. Thus it was in the squares, thus it was on the corners, thus it was in the temples, thus it was in the hiding places; for there was no place that could escape detection or that could offer asylum to those who came streaming in.

O Christ our Emperor, what tribulation and distress of men at that time! The roaring of the sea, the darkening and dimming of the sun, the turning of the moon into blood, the displacement of the stars — did they not foretell in this way the last evils? Indeed, we have seen the abomination of desolation stand in the holy place, rounding off meretricious and petty speeches and other things which were moving definitely, if not altogether, contrariwise to those things deemed by Christians as holy and ennobling the word of faith.

Such then, to make a long story short, were the outrageous crimes committed by the Western armies against the inheritance of Christ. Without showing any feelings of humanity whatsoever, they exacted from all their money and chattel, dwellings and clothing, leaving to them nothing of all their goods. Thus behaved the brazen neck, the haughty spirit, the high brow, the evershaved and youthful cheek, the bloodthirsty right hand, the wrathful nostril, the disdainful eye, the insatiable jaw, the hateful heart, the piercing and running speech practically dancing over the lips. More to blame were the learned and wise among men, they who were faithful to their oaths, who loved the truth and hated evil, who were both more pious and just and scrupulous in keeping the commandments of Christ than we "Greeks." Even more culpable were those who had raised the cross to their shoulders, who had time and again sworn by it and the sayings of the Lord to cross over Christian lands without bloodletting, neither turning aside to the right nor inclining to the left, and to take up arms against the Saracens and to stain red their swords in their blood; they who had sacked Jerusalem, and had taken an oath not to marry or to have sexual intercourse with women as long as they carried the cross on their shoulders, and who were consecrated to God and commissioned to follow in his footsteps.

In truth, they were exposed as frauds. Seeking to avenge the Holy Sepulcher,[2] they raged openly against Christ and sinned by overturning the Cross with the cross they bore on their backs, not even shuddering

---

[2] **Holy Sepulcher**: The site in Jerusalem where Christians believe Jesus was crucified.

to trample on it for the sake of a little gold and silver. By grasping pearls, they rejected Christ, the pearl of great price, scattering among the most accursed of brutes the All-Hallowed One. The sons of Ismael [Muslims] did not behave in this way, for when the Latins overpowered Sion [Jerusalem] the Latins showed no compassion or kindness to their race. Neither did the Ismaelites neigh after Latin women, nor did they turn the cenotaph of Christ[3] into a common burial place of the fallen, nor did they transform the entranceway of the life-bringing tomb into a passageway leading down into Hades, nor did they replace the Resurrection with the Fall.

Rather, they allowed everyone to depart in exchange for the payment of a few gold coins; they took only the ransom money and left to the people all their possessions, even though these numbered more than the grains of sand. Thus the enemies of Christ dealt magnanimously with the Latin infidels, inflicting upon them neither sword, nor fire, nor hunger, nor persecution, nor nakedness, nor bruises, nor constraints. How differently, as we have briefly recounted, the Latins treated us who love Christ and are their fellow believers, guiltless of any wrong against them.

READING AND DISCUSSION QUESTIONS

1. According to Nicetas, what was the primary objective of the Crusaders?
2. Nicetas writes of the Crusaders, "In truth, they were exposed as frauds." What does he mean by this statement? How were the Crusaders frauds?
3. Nicetas compares the sacking of Constantinople by the Western Crusaders with earlier experiences with Muslim conquerors. How were the actions of the Crusaders different from those of the Muslims?

---

[3] **cenotaph of Christ**: The monument marking the site of the Holy Sepulcher.

DOCUMENT 13-2

KING JOHN OF ENGLAND

From Magna Carta: *The Great Charter of Liberties*

1215

In many ways, the Magna Carta is a traditional feudal document. A contract between King John of England (r. 1199–1216) and his barons, the Magna Carta represents an effort by England's rebellious nobility to ensure that the King could not make unfair demands of his vassals. However, the importance of the contract exceeds its feudal origins. It became the founding document for the development of justice and law in England and helped give rise to ideas such as the rule of law and due process.

John, by the grace of God, king of England, lord of Ireland, duke of Normandy and Aquitaine, and count of Anjou, to the archbishops, bishops, abbots, earls, barons . . . and faithful subjects, greeting. . . .

We have . . . granted to all free men of our kingdom, for ourselves and our heirs, for ever, all the liberties written below, to be had and held by them and their heirs of us and our heirs. . . .

No widow shall be forced to marry so long as she wishes to live without a husband, provided that she gives security not to marry without our consent if she holds [a fief] of us, or without the consent of her lord of whom she holds, if she holds of another.

No scutage [payment in lieu of performing military service] or aid shall be imposed in our kingdom unless by common counsel of our kingdom, except for ransoming our person, for making our eldest son a knight, and for once marrying our eldest daughter; and for these only a reasonable aid shall be levied. . . .

Neither we nor our bailiffs will take, for castles or other works of ours, timber which is not ours, except with the agreement of him whose timber it is.

David C. Douglas and Harry Rothwell, ed., *English Historical Documents*, vol. 3 (London: Eyre and Spottiswoode, 1975), 316–321.

We will not hold for more than a year and a day the lands of those convicted of felony, and then the lands shall be handed over to the lords of the fiefs.

No free man shall be arrested or imprisoned or disseised [dispossessed] or outlawed or exiled or in any way victimized, neither will we attack him or send anyone to attack him, except by the lawful judgment of his peers or by the law of the land.

To no one will we sell, to no one will we refuse or delay right or justice.

We will not make justices, constables, sheriffs, or bailiffs save of such as know the law of the kingdom and mean to observe it well.

READING AND DISCUSSION QUESTIONS

1. What practices of the king did the Magna Carta specifically prohibit? Under what conditions could the king engage in these practices?

2. What are some of the legal rights that the Magna Carta guarantees for individuals?

DOCUMENT 13-3

THOMAS AQUINAS

From Summa Theologica: *On Free Will*

1268

The development of the university was one of the most significant changes that occurred during the Middle Ages in Europe. Universities allowed for a flowering of European scholarship. Thomas Aquinas (ca. 1225–1274) was a Dominican priest and professor at the University of Paris. Aquinas practiced Scholasticism, using logic and reason to provide explanations for beliefs usually accepted on faith. In his massive Summa Theologica, *Aquinas assembled a compendium for all knowledge regarding theology. The excerpt below*

Thomas Aquinas, *Summa Theologica*, pt. 1, q. 83, art. 1, trans. Fathers of the English Dominican Province (London: Burns, Oates & Washbourne, 1912).

is a perfect example of the Scholastic method. In it, Aquinas poses an initial question regarding free will and then cites authorities in order to provide a reasoned solution to the query.

We proceed thus to the First Article: — Objection 1. It would seem that man has not free will. For whoever has free will does what he wills. But man does not what he wills; for it is written (Rom. vii. 19): *For the good which I will I do not, but the evil which I will not, that I do.* Therefore man has not free will.

Obj. 2. Further, whoever has free will has in his power to will or not to will, to do or not to do. But this is not in man's power: for it is written (Rom. ix. 16): *It is not of him that willeth* — namely, to will — *nor of him that runneth* — namely, to run. Therefore man has not free will.

Obj. 3. Further, what is *free is cause of itself,* as the Philosopher [Aristotle] says (*Metaph.* i. 2). Therefore what is moved by another is not free. But God moves the will, for it is written (Prov. xxi.1): *The heart of the king is in the hand of the Lord; whithersoever He will He shall turn it;* and (Phil. ii. 13): *It is God Who worketh in you both to will and to accomplish.* Therefore man has not free will.

Obj. 4. Further, whoever has free will is master of his own actions. But man is not master of his own actions: for it is written (Jer. x. 23): *The way of a man is not his: neither is it in a man to walk.* Therefore man has not free will.

Obj. 5. Further, the Philosopher says (Ethic. iii. 5): *According as each one is, such does the end seem to him.* But it is not in our power to be of one quality or another; for this comes to us from nature. Therefore it is natural to us to follow some particular end, and therefore we are not free in so doing.

On the contrary, It is written (Ecclus., xv. 14): *God made man from the beginning, and left him in the hand of his own counsel;* and the gloss adds: *That is of his free will.*

I answer that, Man has free will: otherwise counsels, exhortations, commands, prohibitions, rewards, and punishments would be in vain. In order to make this evident, we must observe that some things act without judgment; as a stone moves downwards; and in like manner all things which lack knowledge. And some act from judgment, but not a free judgment; as brute animals. For the sheep, seeing the wolf, judges it a thing to be shunned, from a natural and not a free judgment, because it judges, not from reason, but from natural instinct. And the same thing is to be said of any judgment of brute animals. But man acts from judgment, because by his apprehensive power he judges that something should be avoided or sought. But because this judgment, in the case of some particular act, is not from a natural instinct, but from some act of comparison in the reason, therefore he acts from free judgment and retains the power of being inclined to various things. For reason in contingent matters may follow opposite courses, as we see in dialectic syllogisms and rhetorical arguments. Now particular operations are contingent, and therefore in such matters the judgment of reason may follow opposite courses, and is not determinate to one. And forasmuch as man is rational is it necessary that man have a free will.

Reply Obj. 1. As we have said above, the sensitive appetite, though it obeys the reason, yet in a given case can resist by desiring what the reason forbids. This is therefore the good which man does not when he wishes — namely, *not to desire against reason*, as Augustine says (*ibid.*).

Reply Obj. 2. Those words of the Apostle [Paul] are not to be taken as though man does not wish or does not run of his free will, but because the free will is not sufficient thereto unless it be moved and helped by God.

Reply Obj. 3. Free will is the cause of its own movement, because by his free will man moves himself to act. But it does not of necessity belong to liberty that what is free should be the first cause of itself, as neither for one thing to be cause of another need it be the first cause. God, therefore, is the first cause, Who moves causes both natural and voluntary. And just as by moving natural causes He does not prevent their acts being natural, so by moving voluntary causes He does not deprive their actions of being voluntary: but rather is He the cause of this very thing in them; for He operates in each thing according to its own nature.

Reply Obj. 4. *Man's way* is said *not to be his* in the execution of his choice, wherein he may be impeded, whether he will or not. The choice itself, however, is in us, but presupposes the help of God.

Reply Obj. 5. Quality in man is of two kinds: natural and adventitious. Now the natural quality may be in the intellectual part, or in the body and its powers. From the very fact, therefore, that man is such by virtue of a natural quality which is in the intellectual part, he naturally desires his last end, which is happiness. Which desire, indeed, is a natural desire, and is not subject to free will, as is clear from what we have said above. But on the part of the body and its powers man may be such by virtue of a natural quality, inasmuch as he is of such a temperament or disposition due to any impression whatever produced by corporeal causes, which cannot affect the intellectual part, since it is not the act of a corporeal organ. And such as a man is by virtue of a corporeal quality, such also does his end seem to him, because from such a disposition a man is inclined to choose or reject something. But these inclinations are subject to the judgment of reason, which the lower appetite obeys, as we have said. Wherefore this is in no way prejudicial to free will.

The adventitious qualities are habits and passions, by virtue of which a man is inclined to one thing rather than to another. And yet even these inclinations are subject to the judgment of reason. Such qualities, too, are subject to reason, as it is in our power either to acquire them, whether by causing them or disposing ourselves to them, or to reject them. And so there is nothing in this that is repugnant to free will.

READING AND DISCUSSION QUESTIONS

1. In what ways does the *Summa Theologica* represent the medieval synthesis of Christian theology and classical philosophy? What authorities does Aquinas cite?

2. Does Aquinas believe in free will? What reasons does he give for his position?

COMPARATIVE QUESTIONS

1. Taking all of the documents into consideration, what role did Christianity play in medieval Europe? What, if any, signs are there that a secular society was developing?

2. What might Aquinas say about the actions of the Crusaders? On what grounds, if any, could they be held responsible for the events that Nicetas describes in his *Annals*?

3. How would Nicetas have responded to the Magna Carta? What might Nicetas have thought of European notions of justice?

CHAPTER **14**

Europe in the Renaissance and Reformation

1350–1600

The devastation of plague and warfare that marked the late Middle Ages stimulated Europe's economy by condensing wealth in the cities and creating an impetus for diversifying and revolutionizing business practices to adjust to a drastic labor shortage. Europeans were hopeful for a new beginning, a wish that came to fruition with the Renaissance, French for "rebirth." Originating in the commercial centers of Italy in the fourteenth century, the Renaissance was a cultural movement that spread throughout Europe. Renaissance writers and artists struck out in new directions and declared a definitive break from their medieval heritage. They looked to the classical past for inspiration and praised the abilities and achievements of human beings. In the fifteenth century, a second break came in the form of the Protestant Reformation (ca. 1517–1648), which splintered the Christian church in the West. The following documents reveal the vibrant cultures of the Renaissance and Reformation and address the new attitudes and ideas articulated by their leading thinkers.

DOCUMENT 14-1

FRANCESCO PEGOLOTTI

On the Practice of Commerce

ca. 1340

The Renaissance arose in the affluent city-states of northern Italy. From their coastal locations, cities such as Florence and Venice dominated the

Francesco Balducci Pegolotti, "Notices of the Land Route to Cathay," from *Cathay and the Way Thither: Being a Collection of Medieval Notices of China*, trans. Henry Yule (London: Hakluyt Society, 1866), 291–294.

Mediterranean trade routes as well as access to points beyond. The elite of these cities, having amassed great commercial fortunes, thought it fashionable to act as patrons of the artists of the Renaissance. In the following reading, one such Florentine merchant, Francesco Pegolotti (1310–1347), describes a trading expedition to China (Cathay), highlighting both the opportunities and dangers that awaited Europe's willing traders.

THINGS NEEDFUL FOR MERCHANTS WHO DESIRE TO MAKE THE JOURNEY TO CATHAY

In the first place, you must let your beard grow long and not shave. And at Tana [modern-day Azov, near the Black Sea] you should furnish yourself with a dragoman [an interpreter, usually of Persian, Turkish, or Arabic]. And you must not try to save money in the matter of dragomen by taking [a] bad one instead of a good one. For the additional wages of the good one will not cost you so much as you will save by having him. And besides the dragoman it will be well to take at least two good menservants, who are acquainted with the Cumanian[1] tongue. And if the merchant likes to take a woman with him from Tana, he can do so; if he does not like to take one there is no obligation, only if he does take one he will be kept much more comfortably than if he does not take one. Howbeit, if he does take one, it will be well that she be acquainted with the Cumanian tongue as well as the men.

And from Tana traveling to Gittarchan [modern-day Astrakhan, on the Volga] you should take with you twenty-five days' provisions, that is to say, flour and salt fish, for as to meat you will find enough of it at all the places along the road. And so also at all the chief stations noted in going from one country to another in the route, according to the number of days set down above, you should furnish yourself with flour and salt fish; other things you will find in sufficiency, and especially meat.

The road you travel from Tana to Cathay is perfectly safe, whether by day or by night, according to what merchants say who have used it. Only if the merchant, in going or coming, should die upon the road, everything belonging to him will become the perquisite of the lord of the country in which he dies, and the officers of the lord will take possession of all. And in like manner if he die in Cathay. But if his brother be with him, or an intimate friend and comrade calling himself his brother, then to

---

[1] **Cumanian**: A Turkic people. Like many of areas discussed by Pegolotti, the Cumanian occupied an area near the Volga River.

such a one they will surrender the property of the deceased, and so it will be rescued.

And there is another danger: this is when the lord of the country dies, and before the new lord who is to have the lordship is proclaimed; during such intervals there have sometimes been irregularities practiced on the Franks, and other foreigners. (They call "Franks" all the Christians of these parts from Romania [i.e., the Byzantine Empire] westward.) And neither will the roads be safe to travel until the other lord be proclaimed who is to reign in place of him who is deceased.

Cathay is a province which contains a multitude of cities and towns. Among others there is one in particular, that is to say the capital city, to which merchants flock, and in which there is a vast amount of trade; and this city is called Cambalec.[2] And the said city has a circuit of one hundred miles, and is all full of people and houses and of dwellers in the said city. . . .

You may reckon also that from Tana to Sara [Sarai, on the Volga] the road is less safe than on any other part of the journey; and yet even when this part of the road is at its worst, if you are some sixty men in the company you will go as safely as if you were in your own house.

Anyone from Genoa or from Venice, wishing to go to the places above-named, and to make the journey to Cathay, should carry linens with him, and if he visit Organci [Urgench, in Central Asia] he will dispose of these well. In Organci he should purchase *sommi* [units] of silver, and with these he should proceed without making any further investment, unless it be some bales of the very finest stuffs which go in small bulk, and cost no more for carriage than coarser stuffs would do.

Merchants who travel this road can ride on horseback or on asses, or mounted in any way that they choose to be mounted.

Whatever silver the merchants may carry with them as far as Cathay the lord of Cathay will take from them and put into his treasury. And to merchants who thus bring silver they give that paper money of theirs in exchange. This is of yellow paper, stamped with the seal of the lord aforesaid. And this money is called *balishi*; and with this money you can readily buy silk and all other merchandise that you have a desire to buy. And all the people of the country are bound to receive it. And yet you shall not pay a higher price for your goods because your money is of paper. And of the said paper money there are three kinds, one being worth more than another, according to the value which has been established for each by that lord.

---

[2] **Cambalec**: Khanbalik, a city in Mongol China. Modern-day Beijing is built on the same site.

READING AND DISCUSSION QUESTIONS

1. For whom has Pegolotti written this account?

2. How does Pegolotti describe the trade routes to China? According to Pegolotti, what difficulties might merchants face in their travels to China?

3. According to Pegolotti, how should European merchants prepare for their journey? What supplies and support staff does he suggest they bring?

4. In the absence of a common currency, how did merchants among the disparate civilizations exchange goods?

DOCUMENT 14-2

NICCOLÒ MACHIAVELLI

From The Prince: *Power Politics During the Italian Renaissance*

1513

The writings of Niccolò Machiavelli (1469–1527) represent the culmination of Renaissance humanism, a school of thought that emphasized classical models and the importance of human endeavor. Humanists looked to classical and historical examples to direct political reform in their own times, but Machiavelli, a Florentine diplomat, was less of an idealist and more of a pragmatist. In The Prince, *which was circulated privately until after his death, the author advised rulers to think of governance as a process that demanded practical responses to the often fluctuating circumstances created by human frailties.*

Every one understands how praiseworthy it is in a prince to keep faith, and to live uprightly and not craftily. Nevertheless we see, from what has taken place in our own days, that princes who have set little store by their word,

Niccolò Machiavelli, *The Prince*, trans. N. H. Thomson, in James Harvey Robinson, ed., *Readings in European History* (Boston: Ginn, 1904), 2:10–13.

but have known how to overreach men by their cunning, have accomplished great things, and in the end got the better of those who trusted to honest dealing.

Be it known, then, that there are two ways of contending, — one in accordance with the laws, the other by force; the first of which is proper to men, the second to beasts. But since the first method is often ineffectual, it becomes necessary to resort to the second. A prince should, therefore, understand how to use well both the man and the beast. . . . But inasmuch as a prince should know how to use the beast's nature wisely, he ought of beasts to choose both the lion and the fox; for the lion cannot guard himself from the toils, nor the fox from wolves. He must therefore be a fox to discern toils, and a lion to drive off wolves.

To rely wholly on the lion is unwise; and for this reason a prudent prince neither can nor ought to keep his word when to keep it is hurtful to him and the causes which led him to pledge it are removed. If all men were good, this would not be good advice, but since they are dishonest and do not keep faith with you, you in return need not keep faith with them; and no prince was ever at a loss for plausible reasons to cloak a breach of faith. Of this numberless recent instances could be given, and it might be shown how many solemn treaties and engagements have been rendered inoperative and idle through want of faith among princes, and that he who has best known how to play the fox has had the best success.

It is necessary, indeed, to put a good color on this nature, and to be skilled in simulating and dissembling. But men are so simple, and governed so absolutely by their present needs, that he who wishes to deceive will never fail in finding willing dupes. One recent example I will not omit. Pope Alexander VI had no care or thought but how to deceive, and always found material to work on. No man ever had a more effective manner or asseverating, or made promises with more solemn protestations, or observed them less. And yet, because he understood this side of human nature, his frauds always succeeded. . . .

In his efforts to aggrandize his son the duke [Caesar Borgia], Alexander VI had to face many difficulties, both immediate and remote. In the first place, he saw no way to make him ruler of any state which did not belong to the Church. Yet, if he sought to take for him a state of the Church, he knew that the duke of Milan and the Venetians would withhold their consent, Faenza and Rimini [towns in the province of Romagna] being already under the protection of the latter. Further, he saw that the forces of Italy, and those more especially of which he might have availed himself, were in the hands of men who had reason to fear his aggrandizement, — that is, of the Orsini, the Colonnesi [Roman noble families] and their followers. These, therefore, he could not trust. . . .

And since this part of his [Caesar Borgia's] conduct merits both attention and imitation, I shall not pass it over in silence. After the duke had taken Romagna, finding that it had been ruled by feeble lords, who thought more of plundering than of governing their subjects, — which gave them more cause for division than for union, so that the country was overrun with robbery, tumult, and every kind of outrage, — he judged it necessary, with a view to rendering it peaceful, and obedient to his authority, to provide it with a good government. Accordingly he set over it Messer Remiro d'Orco, a stern and prompt ruler, who, being intrusted with the fullest powers, in a very short time, and with much credit to himself, restored it to tranquillity and order. But afterwards the duke, apprehending that such unlimited authority might become odious, decided that it was no longer needed, and established [at] the center of the province a civil tribunal, with an excellent president, in which every town was represented by its advocate. And knowing that past severities had generated ill feeling against himself, in order to purge the minds of the people and gain their good will, he sought to show them that any cruelty which had been done had not originated with him, but in the harsh disposition of this minister. Availing himself of the pretext which this afforded, he one morning caused Remiro to be beheaded, and exposed in the market place of Cesena with a block and bloody ax by his side. The barbarity of this spectacle at once astounded and satisfied the populace.

READING AND DISCUSSION QUESTIONS

1. Why does Machiavelli say that a good ruler must "be skilled in simulating and dissembling"? What advantages does the ability to deceive give to the ruler?

2. How does Machiavelli view human nature? How does this idea of human nature affect his ideas regarding governance?

3. Like other humanists, Machiavelli often looked to history for guidance. What examples from the past does he reference? What lessons does Machiavelli draw from these examples?

DOCUMENT 14-3

MARTIN LUTHER
On Salvation
ca. 1566

Martin Luther (1483–1546) was an Augustinian monk from eastern Germany whose translation of the Bible contributed to the development of the modern German language. In penning his Ninety-five Theses *(1517) criticizing the Catholic Church's sale of indulgences, which allowed for the remission of sins without penance, Luther became the father of the Protestant Reformation. Some scholars argue that the theses, which Luther enclosed in a letter to a German archbishop, were posed in a format traditionally used as an invitation to debate and that their author could not have foreseen the consequences of his dissension. In the following reading, taken from a collection of his teachings published posthumously by his students, Luther addresses his understanding of salvation and the role of the Church.*

Salvation and Damnation

Because as the everlasting, merciful God, through his Word and Sacraments, talks and deals with us, all other creatures excluded, not of temporal things which pertain to this vanishing life . . . but as to where we shall go when we depart from here, and gives unto us his Son for a Savior, delivering us from sin and death, and purchasing for us everlasting righteousness, life, and salvation, therefore it is most certain, that we do not die away like the beasts that have no understanding; but so many of us . . . shall through him be raised again to life everlasting at the last day, and the ungodly to everlasting destruction.

* * *

Faith versus Good Works

He that goes from the gospel to the law [i.e., religious rules and mandates], thinking to be saved by good works, falls as uneasily as he who falls from the true service of God to idolatry; for, without Christ, all is idolatry and fictitious imaginings of God, whether of the Turkish Quran, of the pope's

William Hazlitt, ed. and trans., *The Table Talk of Martin Luther* (London: H. G. Bohn, 1857), 25–27, 117, 198, 205–206, 219, 294, 298, 300, 357, 359.

decrees, or Moses' laws; if a man think thereby to be justified and saved before God, he is undone.

* * *

The gospel preaches nothing of the merit of works; he that says the gospel requires works for salvation, I say, flat and plain, is a liar.

Nothing that is properly good proceeds out of the works of the law, unless grace be present; for what we are forced to do, goes not from the heart, nor is acceptable.

* * *

A Capuchin says: wear a grey coat and a hood, a rope round thy body, and sandals on thy feet. A Cordelier says: put on a black hood; an ordinary papist [member of the Roman Catholic Church] says: do this or that work, hear mass, pray, fast, give alms, etc.[3] But a true Christian says: I am justified and saved only by faith in Christ, without any works or merits of my own; compare these together, and judge which is the true righteousness.

* * *

I have often been resolved to live uprightly, and to lead a true godly life, and to set everything aside that would hinder this, but it was far from being put in execution; even as it was with Peter [the martyred disciple], when he swore he would lay down his life for Christ.

I will not lie or dissemble before my God, but will freely confess, I am not able to effect that good which I intend, but await the happy hour when God shall be pleased to meet me with his grace.

* * *

A Christian's worshiping is not the external, hypocritical mask that our friars wear, when they chastise their bodies, torment and make themselves faint, with ostentatious fasting, watching, singing, wearing hair shirts, scourging themselves, etc. Such worshiping God does not desire.

The Bible

Great is the strength of the divine Word. In the epistle to the Hebrews, it is called "a two-edged sword." But we have neglected and scorned the pure and clear Word, and have drunk not of the fresh and cool spring; we are gone from the clear fountain to the foul puddle, and drunk its filthy water; that is, we have sedulously read old writers and teachers, who went about with speculative reasonings, like the monks and friars.

* * *

---

[3] **A Capuchin . . . etc.**: Capuchins and Cordeliers were two Franciscan orders, each with its own set of requirements for salvation.

The ungodly papists prefer the authority of the church far above God's Word; a blasphemy abominable and not to be endured; void of all shame and piety, they spit in God's face. Truly, God's patience is exceeding great, in that they are not destroyed; but so it always has been.

THE PAPACY AND THE MONASTIC ORDERS

How does it happen that the popes pretend that they form the Church, when, all the while, they are bitter enemies of the Church, and have no knowledge, certainly no comprehension, of the holy gospel? Pope, cardinals, bishops, not a soul of them has read the Bible; it is a book unknown to them. They are a pack of guzzling, gluttonous wretches, rich, wallowing in wealth and laziness, resting secure in their power, and never, for a moment, thinking of accomplishing God's will.

＊　＊　＊

Kings and princes coin money only out of metals, but the pope coins money out of everything — indulgences, ceremonies, dispensations, pardons; all fish come to his net. . . .

A gentleman being at the point of death, a monk from the next convent came to see what he could pick up, and said to the gentleman: Sir, will you give so and so to our monastery? The dying man, unable to speak, replied by a nod of the head, whereupon the monk, turning to the gentleman's son, said: You see, your father makes us this bequest. The son said to the father: Sir, is it your pleasure that I kick this monk down the stairs? The dying man nodded as before, and the son immediately drove the monk out of doors.

＊　＊　＊

The papists took the invocation of saints from the pagans, who divided God into numberless images and idols, and ordained to each its particular office and work. . . .

The invocation of saints is a most abominable blindness and heresy; yet the papists will not give it up. The pope's greatest profit arises from the dead; for the calling on dead saints brings him infinite sums of money and riches, far more than he gets from the living. . . .

＊　＊　＊

In Italy, the monasteries are very wealthy. There are but three or four monks to each; the surplus of their revenues goes to the pope and his cardinals.

＊　＊　＊

The fasting of the friars is more easy to them than our eating to us. For one day of fasting there are three of feasting. Every friar for his supper has two quarts of beer, a quart of wine, and spice-cakes, or bread prepared with spice and salt, the better to relish their drink. Thus go on these poor fasting brethren; getting so pale and wan, they are like the fiery angels.

* * *

In Popedom they make priests, not to preach and teach God's Word, but only to celebrate mass, and to roam about with the sacrament. For, when a bishop ordains a man, he says: Take the power to celebrate mass, and to offer it for the living and the dead. But we ordain priests according to the command of Christ and St. Paul, namely, to preach the pure gospel and God's Word. The papists in their ordinations make no mention of preaching and teaching God's Word, therefore their consecrating and ordaining is false and wrong, for all worshiping which is not ordained of God, or erected by God's Word and command, is worthless, yea, mere idolatry.

The Reform of the Church

The pope and his crew can in no way endure the idea of reformation; the mere word creates more alarm at Rome than thunderbolts from heaven or the day of judgment. A cardinal said the other day: Let them eat, and drink, and do what they will; but as to reforming us, we think that is a vain idea; we will not endure it. Neither will we Protestants be satisfied, though they administer the sacrament in both kinds,[4] and permit priests to marry; we will also have the doctrine of the faith pure and unfalsified, and the righteousness that justifies and saves before God, and which expels and drives away all idolatry and false-worshiping; with these gone and banished, the foundation on which Popedom is built also falls.

* * *

The chief cause that I fell out with the pope was this: the pope boasted that he was the head of the church, and condemned all that would not be under his power and authority; . . . Further, he took upon him power, rule, and authority over the Christian church, and over the Holy Scriptures, the Word of God; no man must presume to expound the Scriptures, but only he, and according to his ridiculous conceits; this was not to be endured. They who, against God's word, boast of the church's authority, are mere idiots.

---

[4] **administer the sacrament in both kinds**: Protestants partake of both the bread and wine of the Eucharist; in Catholic practice, only the priest received the wine.

READING AND DISCUSSION QUESTIONS

1. Why did Luther believe that humans could not earn their salvation? How are humans saved, according to Luther?

2. The teachings of Luther are often associated with the phrase "Scripture alone." Based on this excerpt, what might this phrase mean? What authorities for religious guidance does Luther reject?

3. What are Luther's criticisms of the clergy?

4. How does the tone of this passage reflect the time at which it was written?

COMPARATIVE QUESTIONS

1. Compare Luther's argument to Thomas Aquinas's discussion of free will in *Summa Theologica* (Document 13-3). How might Luther respond to Aquinas's assertion that humans have free will?

2. Compare Machiavelli's understanding of human nature with that of Luther. How are they similar? Where do they diverge?

3. In his "Description of the World" (Document 11-3), Marco Polo detailed a journey to the far east. Compare his work with that of Pegolotti. How do Pegolotti and Polo encourage others to make such a journey? How do they discourage such trips?

4. How might Luther respond to the humanist notion — as presented in *The Prince* — that the past can serve as a model for the present?

CHAPTER 15

The Acceleration of Global Contact

A lthough long-standing trade routes meant that many of the world's civilizations were in contact with one another before 1500, this interaction accelerated drastically in the sixteenth century when Europe became a much larger player in world trade. Europe began establishing trade routes to the newly discovered Americas and sent Christian missionaries to all corners of the globe. The sources in this chapter examine the impact of Europe's entrance into the global community and address the continued importance of the civilizations that had established earlier trade routes in the Indian Ocean.

DOCUMENT 15-1

BARTOLOMÉ DE LAS CASAS

From Brief Account of the Devastation of the Indies

1542

Bartolomé de Las Casas (1484–1566) was one of the most vocal opponents of the Spaniards' treatment of the native people of the West Indies. In particular, the Dominican missionary criticized the encomienda *system, which allowed Spanish colonists to force local peoples to work the colonists' land or mines — often under deplorable conditions. In his* Brief Account, Las Casas *discusses the detrimental impact that the arrival of the Europeans had on the West Indies. He pays significant attention to the steep depopulation of*

Bartolomé de Las Casas, *The Devastation of the Indies: A Brief Account,* translated by Herma Briffault (New York: A Continuum Book from Seabury Press, 1974), 37–44, 51–52.

the islands of the Caribbean, one of the most dramatic events associated with the colonization of the West Indies.

The [West] Indies were discovered in the year one thousand four hundred and ninety-two. In the following year a great many Spaniards went there with the intention of settling the land. Thus, forty-nine years have passed since the first settlers penetrated the land, the first so-claimed being the large and most happy isle called Hispaniola, which is six hundred leagues in circumference. Around it in all directions are many other islands, some very big, others very small, and all of them were, as we saw with our own eyes, densely populated with native peoples called Indians. This large island was perhaps the most densely populated place in the world. There must be close to two hundred leagues of land on this island, and the sea-coast has been explored for more than ten thousand leagues, and each day more of it is being explored. And all the land so far discovered is a beehive of people; it is as though God had crowded into these lands the great majority of mankind.

And of all the infinite universe of humanity, these people are the most guileless, the most devoid of wickedness and duplicity, the most obedient and faithful to their native masters and to the Spanish Christians whom they serve. They are by nature the most humble, patient, and peaceable, holding no grudges, free from embroilments, neither excitable nor quarrelsome. These people are the most devoid of rancors, hatreds, or desire for vengeance of any people in the world. And because they are so weak and complaisant, they are less able to endure heavy labor and soon die of no matter what malady. The sons of nobles among us, brought up in the enjoyments of life's refinements, are no more delicate than are these Indians, even those among them who are of the lowest rank of laborers. They are also poor people, for they not only possess little but have no desire to possess worldly goods. For this reason they are not arrogant, embittered, or greedy. Their repasts are such that the food of the holy fathers in the desert can scarcely be more parsimonious, scanty, and poor. As to their dress, they are generally naked, with only their pudenda covered somewhat. And when they cover their shoulders it is with a square cloth no more than two varas [approximately 33 inches] in size. They have no beds, but sleep on a kind of matting or else in a kind of suspended net called hamacas. They are very clean in their persons, with alert, intelligent minds, docile and open to doctrine, very apt to receive our holy Catholic faith, to be endowed with virtuous customs, and to behave in a godly fashion. And once they begin to hear the tidings of the Faith, they are so insistent on knowing more and on taking the sacraments of the Church and on observing the divine cult that, truly, the missionaries who are here need to be endowed by God with great patience in order to cope with such eagerness. Some of the secular Spaniards who have been here for many years say that the goodness of the Indians is undeniable and that if this gifted people could be brought to know the one true God they would be the most fortunate people in the world.

Yet into this sheepfold, into this land of meek outcasts there came some Spaniards who immediately behaved like ravening wild beasts, wolves, tigers, or lions that had been starved for many days. And Spaniards have behaved in no other way during the past forty years, down to the present time, for they are still acting like ravening beasts, killing, terrorizing, afflicting, torturing, and destroying the native peoples, doing all this with the strangest and most varied new methods of cruelty, never seen or heard of before, and to such a degree that this Island of Hispaniola once so populous (having a population that I estimated to be more than three millions), has now a population of barely two hundred persons.

The island of Cuba is nearly as long as the distance between Valladolid and Rome; it is now almost completely depopulated. San Juan [Puerto Rico] and Jamaica are two of the largest, most productive and attractive islands; both are now deserted and devastated. On the northern side of Cuba and Hispaniola lie the neighboring Lucayos comprising more than sixty islands including those called Gigantes, beside numerous other islands, some small some large. The least felicitous of them were more fertile and beautiful than the gardens of the King of Seville. They have the healthiest lands in the world, where lived more than five hundred thousand souls; they are now deserted, inhabited by not a single living creature. All the people were slain or died after being taken into captivity and brought to the Island of Hispaniola to be sold as slaves. When the Spaniards saw that some of these had escaped, they sent a ship to find them, and it voyaged for three years among the islands searching for those who had escaped being slaughtered, for a good Christian had helped them escape, taking pity on them and had won them over to Christ; of these there were eleven persons and these I saw. . . .

As for the vast mainland, which is ten times larger than all Spain, even including Aragon and Portugal, containing more land than the distance between Seville and Jerusalem, or more than two thousand leagues, we are sure that our Spaniards, with their cruel and abominable acts, have devastated the land and exterminated the rational people who fully inhabited it.

We can estimate very surely and truthfully that in the forty years that have passed, with the infernal actions of the Christians, there have been unjustly slain more than twelve million men, women, and children. In truth, I believe without trying to deceive myself that the number of the slain is more like fifteen million.

The common ways mainly employed by the Spaniards who call themselves Christian and who have gone there to extirpate those pitiful nations and wipe them off the earth is by unjustly waging cruel and bloody wars. Then, when they have slain all those who fought for their lives or to escape the tortures they would have to endure, that is to say, when they have slain all the native rulers and young men (since the Spaniards usually spare only the women and children, who are subjected to the hardest and bitterest servitude ever suffered by man or beast), they enslave any survivors. With these infernal methods of tyranny they debase and weaken countless numbers of those pitiful Indian nations.

Their reason for killing and destroying such an infinite number of souls is that the Christians have an ultimate aim, which is to acquire gold, and to swell themselves with riches in a very brief time and thus rise to a high estate disproportionate to their merits. It should be kept in mind that their insatiable greed and ambition, the greatest ever seen in the world, is the cause of their villainies. And also, those lands are so rich and felicitous, the native peoples so meek and patient, so easy to subject, that our Spaniards have no more consideration for them than beasts. And I say this from my own knowledge of the acts I witnessed. But I should not say "than beasts" for, thanks be to God, they have treated beasts with some respect; I should say instead like excrement on the public squares. And thus they have deprived the Indians of their lives and souls, for the millions I mentioned have died without the Faith and without the benefit of the sacraments. This is a well known and proven fact which even the tyrant Governors, themselves killers, know and admit. And never have the Indians in all the Indies committed any act against the Spanish Christians, until those Christians have first and many times committed countless cruel aggressions against them or against neighboring nations. For in the beginning the Indians regarded the Spaniards as angels from Heaven. Only after the Spaniards had used violence against them, killing, robbing, torturing, did the Indians ever rise up against them. On the Island Hispaniola was where the Spaniards first landed, as I have said. Here those Christians perpetrated their first ravages and oppressions against the native peoples. This was the first land in the New World to be destroyed and depopulated by the Christians, and here they began their subjection of the women and children, taking them away from the Indians to use them and ill use them, eating the food they provided with their sweat and toil. The Spaniards did not content themselves with what the Indians gave them of their own free will, according to their ability, which was always too little to satisfy enormous appetites, for a Christian eats and consumes in one day an amount of food that would suffice to feed three houses inhabited by ten Indians for one month. And they committed other acts of force and violence and oppression which made the Indians realize that these men had not come from Heaven. And some of the Indians concealed their foods while others concealed their wives and children and still others fled to the mountains to avoid the terrible transactions of the Christians.

And the Christians attacked them with buffets and beatings, until finally they laid hands on the nobles of the villages. Then they behaved with such temerity and shamelessness that the most powerful ruler of the islands had to see his own wife raped by a Christian officer.

From that time onward the Indians began to seek ways to throw the Christians out of their lands. They took up arms, but their weapons were very weak and of little service in offense and still less in defense. (Because of this, the wars of the Indians against each other are little more than games played by children.) And the Christians, with their horses and swords and pikes began to carry out massacres and strange cruelties against them. They attacked the towns and spared neither the children nor the aged nor pregnant women nor women in childbed, not only stabbing them and dismembering them but cutting them to pieces as if dealing with sheep in the slaughter house. They laid bets as to who, with one stroke of the sword, could split a man in two or could cut off his head or spill out his entrails with a single stroke of the pike. They took infants from their mothers' breasts, snatching them by the legs and pitching them head-first against the crags or snatched them by the arms and threw them into the rivers, roaring with laughter and saying as the babies fell into the water, "Boil there, you offspring of the devil!" Other infants they put to the sword along with their mothers and anyone else who happened to be nearby. They made some low wide gallows on which the hanged victim's feet almost touched the ground, stringing up their victims in lots of thirteen, in memory of Our Redeemer and His twelve Apostles, then set burning wood at their feet and thus burned them alive. To others they attached straw or wrapped their whole bodies in straw and set them afire. With still others, all those they wanted to capture alive, they cut off their hands and hung them round the victim's neck, saying, "Go now, carry the message," meaning, Take the news to the Indians who have fled to the mountains. They usually dealt with the chieftains and nobles in the following way: they made a grid of rods which they placed on forked sticks, then lashed the victims to the grid and lighted a smoldering fire underneath, so that little by little, as those captives screamed in despair and torment, their souls would leave them. . . .

After the wars and the killings had ended, when usually there survived only some boys, some women, and children, these survivors were distributed among the Christians to be slaves. The repartimiento or distribution was made according to the rank and importance of the Christian to whom the Indians were allocated, one of them being given thirty, another forty, still another, one or two hundred, and besides the rank of the Christian there was also to be considered in what favor he stood with the tyrant they called Governor. The pretext was that these allocated Indians were to be instructed in the articles of the Christian Faith. As if those Christians who were as a rule foolish and cruel and greedy and vicious could be caretakers of souls! And the care they took was to send the men to the mines to dig for gold, which is intolerable labor, and to send the women into the fields of the big ranches to hoe and till the land, work suitable for strong men. Nor to either the men or the women did they give any food except herbs and legumes, things of little substance. The milk in the breasts of the women with infants dried up and thus in a short while the infants perished. And since men and women were separated, there could be no marital relations. And the men died in the mines and the women died on the ranches from the same causes, exhaustion and hunger. And thus was depopulated that island which had been densely populated.

READING AND DISCUSSION QUESTIONS

1. According to Las Casas, what motivated the Spaniards to settle the West Indies? What did they hope to gain?

2. Why did the West Indies experience a rapid depopulation when the Europeans arrived? According to Las Casas, how was this depopulation avoidable?

3. How does Las Casas suggest that the Christian mission to the New World had failed?

DOCUMENT 15-2

ZHENG HE

Stele Inscription

1431

Before the Europeans crossed the Atlantic and began exploring the New World, the Indian Ocean was the center of the world's sea trading routes and China dominated much of the trading activity. Zheng He (1371–1433) was an admiral during the Ming Dynasty who led seven naval expeditions to locations such as the Arabian peninsula, East Africa, India, and Southeast Asia. Compared to the three ships comprising Columbus's initial expedition, Zheng He's earlier fleet was massive, somewhere between 200 and 300 ships carrying around 28,000 men. Zheng He's inscription is a stele, or large rock monument, that describes his expeditions.

Record of the miraculous answer (to prayer) of the goddess the Celestial Spouse.[1]

The Imperial Ming Dynasty unifying seas and continents, surpassing the three dynasties even goes beyond the Han and Tang dynasties. The countries beyond the horizon and from the ends of the earth have all become subjects and to the most western of the western or the most northern of the northern countries, however far they may be, the distance and the routes may be calculated. Thus the barbarians from beyond the seas, though their countries are truly distant, "with double translation" have come to audience bearing precious objects and presents.

The Emperor, approving of their loyalty and sincerity, has ordered us (Zheng) He and others at the head of several tens of thousands of officers and flag-troops to ascend more than one hundred large ships to go and confer presents on them in order to make manifest the transforming power

Teobaldo Filesi, *China and Africa in the Middle Ages*, trans. David Morison (London: Frank Cass, 1972), 57–61.

[1] **the goddess the Celestial Spouse:** While in human form during the Song Dynasty, the goddess Tian Fei, or Mazu, was believed to have miraculously saved her merchant brothers during a storm at sea. As such, she was a natural choice for the explorer Zheng He to direct his prayers.

of the (imperial) virtue and to treat distant people with kindness. From the third year of Yongle[2] (1405) till now we have seven times received the commission of ambassadors to countries of the western ocean. The barbarian countries which we have visited are: by way of Zhancheng, Zhaowa, Sanfoqi, and Xianlo crossing straight over to Xilanshan in South India, Guli, and Kezhi, we have gone to the western regions Hulumosi, Adan, Mugudushu, altogether more than thirty countries large and small.[3] We have traversed more than one hundred thousand li[4] of immense water spaces and have beheld in the ocean huge waves like mountains rising sky-high, and we have set eyes on barbarian regions far away hidden in a blue transparency of light vapors, while our sails loftily unfurled like clouds day and night continued their course (rapid like that) of a star, traversing those savage waves as if we were treading a public thoroughfare. Truly this was due to the majesty and the good fortune of the Court and moreover we owe it to the protecting virtue of the divine Celestial Spouse.

The power of the goddess having indeed been manifested in previous times has been abundantly revealed in the present generation. In the midst of the rushing waters it happened that, when there was a hurricane, suddenly there was a divine lantern shining in the mast, and as soon as this miraculous light appeared the danger was appeased, so that even in the danger of capsizing one felt reassured that there was no cause for fear. When we arrived in the distant countries we captured alive those of the native kings who were not respectful and exterminated those barbarian robbers who were engaged in piracy, so that consequently the sea route was cleansed and pacified and the natives put their trust in it. All this is due to the favors of the goddess.

It is not easy to enumerate completely all the cases where the goddess has answered (prayers). Previously in a memorial to the Court we have requested that her virtue be registered in the Court of Sacrificial Worship and a temple be built at Nanking on the bank of the dragon river where regular sacrifices should be transmitted for ever. We have respectfully received an Imperial commemorative composition exalting the miraculous favors, which is the highest recompense and praise indeed. However, the miraculous power of the goddess resides wherever one goes. As for the

---

[2] **Yongle**: He was Emperor during most of Zheng He's expeditions.

[3] **by way of Zhancheng . . . small**: The journey that Zheng He describes routes around present-day Indonesia, south below India, and into the eastern coast of Africa.

[4] **one hundred thousand li**: One li is roughly a third of a mile, so they have sailed over 33,000 miles.

temporary palace on the southern mountain at Changle, I have, at the head of the fleet, frequently resided there awaiting the [favorable] wind to set sail for the ocean.

We, Zheng He and others, on the one hand have received the high favor of a gracious commission of our Sacred Lord, and on the other hand carry to the distant barbarians the benefits of respect and good faith (on their part). Commanding the multitudes on the fleet and (being responsible for) a quantity of money and valuables in the face of the violence of the winds and the nights our one fear is not to be able to succeed; how should we then dare not to serve our dynasty with exertion of all our loyalty and the gods with the utmost sincerity? How would it be possible not to realize what is the source of the tranquillity of the fleet and the troops and the salvation on the voyage both going and returning? Therefore we have made manifest the virtue of the goddess on stone and have moreover recorded the years and months of the voyages to the barbarian countries and the return in order to leave (the memory) for ever.

I. In the third year of Yongle (1405) commanding the fleet we went to Guli and other countries. At that time the pirate Chen Zuyi had gathered his followers in the country of Sanfoqi, where he plundered the native merchants. When he also advanced to resist our fleet, supernatural soldiers secretly came to the rescue so that after one beating of the drum he was annihilated. In the fifth year (1407) we returned.

II. In the fifth year of Yongle (1407) commanding the fleet we went to Zhaowa, Guli, Kezhi, and Xianle. The kings of these countries all sent as tribute precious objects, precious birds and rare animals. In the seventh year (1409) we returned.

III. In the seventh year of Yongle (1409) commanding the fleet we went to the countries (visited) before and took our route by the country of Xilanshan. Its king Yaliekunaier [King of Sri Lanka] was guilty of a gross lack of respect and plotted against the fleet. Owing to the manifest answer to prayer of the goddess (the plot) was discovered and thereupon that king was captured alive. In the ninth year (1411) on our return the king was presented (to the throne) (as a prisoner); subsequently he received the Imperial favor of returning to his own country.

IV. In the eleventh year of Yongle (1413) commanding the fleet we went to Hulumosi [Ormuz] and other countries. In the country of

Sumendala [Samudra] there was a false king Suganla[5] who was marauding and invading his country. Its king Cainu-liabiding had sent an envoy to the Palace Gates in order to lodge a complaint. We went thither with the official troups [troops] under our command and exterminated some and arrested (other rebels), and owing to the silent aid of the goddess we captured the false king alive. In the thirteenth year (1415) on our return he was presented (to the Emperor as a prisoner). In that year the king of the country of Manlajia [Malacca] came in person with his wife and son to present tribute.

V. In the fifteenth year of Yongle (1417) commanding the fleet we visited the western regions. The country of Hulumosi presented lions, leopards with gold spots, and large western horses. The country of Adan presented qilin of which the native name is culafa [a giraffe] as well as the long-horned animal maha [oryx antelope]. The country of Mugudushu presented huafu lu [zebras] as well as lions. The country of Bulawa [Brava] presented camels which run one thousand li as well as camel-birds [ostriches]. The countries of Zhaowa and Guli presented the animal miligao. They all vied in presenting the marvellous objects preserved in the mountains or hidden in the seas and the beautiful treasures buried in the sand or deposited on the shores. Some sent a maternal uncle of the king, others a paternal uncle or a younger brother of the king in order to present a letter of homage written on gold leaf as well as tribute.

VI. In the nineteenth year of Yongle (1421) commanding the fleet we conducted the ambassadors from Hulumosi and the other countries who had been in attendance at the capital for a long time back to their countries. The kings of all these countries prepared even more tribute than previously.

VII. In the sixth year of Xuande (1431) once more commanding the fleet we have left for the barbarian countries in order to read to them (an Imperial edict) and to confer presents.

We have anchored in this port awaiting a north wind to take the sea, and recalling how previously we have on several occasions received the benefits of the protection of the divine intelligence we have thus recorded an inscription in stone.

---

[5] **false king Suganla**: Sekandar, who usurped the throne from the rightful ruler Zain Al'-Abidin. He is referred to as Cainu-liabiding in the next sentence.

READING AND DISCUSSION QUESTIONS

1. What does the inscription suggest about the importance of overseas exploration to the Ming Dynasty?

2. Describe the relationship between the Chinese explorers and the local populations that they encountered. How did the Chinese treat these populations? How did these people respond to the Chinese presence?

DOCUMENT 15-3

KING FERDINAND AND QUEEN ISABELLA
Agreements with Columbus
1492

An Italian of modest birth, Christopher Columbus (1451–1506) was an experienced seafarer when he approached King Ferdinand and Queen Isabella of Spain. He sought their funding for an expedition across the Atlantic, which Columbus mistakenly believed was a shorter route to Asia than the journey east that Europeans typically made. In the end, Columbus did not reach Asia, but rather discovered two continents previously unknown to medieval Europeans. As his initial agreements with the Spanish monarchs made clear, the trip westward was a dangerous but potentially profitable one for the Italian explorer.

AGREEMENT OF APRIL 17, 1492

The things supplicated and which your Highnesses give and declare to Christopher Columbus in some satisfaction . . . for the voyage which now, with the aid of God, he is about to make therein, in the service of your Highnesses, are as follows:

King Ferdinand and Queen Isabella, "Agreements with Columbus of April 17 and April 30, 1492," in J. B. Thatcher, *Christopher Columbus, His Life and Work*, 3 vols. (New York and London: Putnam's Sons, 1903), 2:442–451.

Firstly, that your Highnesses as Lords that are of the said oceans, make from this time the said Don Christopher Columbus your Admiral in all those islands and mainlands which by his hand and industry shall be discovered or acquired in the said oceans, during his life, and after his death, his heirs and successors, from one to another perpetually, with all the preeminences and prerogatives belonging to the said office. . . .

Likewise, that your Highnesses make the said Don Christopher your Viceroy and Governor General in all the said islands and mainlands and islands which as has been said, he may discover or acquire in the said seas; and that for the government of each one and of any one of them, he may make selection of three persons for each office, and that your Highnesses may choose and select the one who shall be most serviceable to you, and thus the lands which our Lord shall permit him to discover and acquire will be better governed, in the service of your Highnesses. . . .

Item, that all and whatever merchandise, whether it be pearls, precious stones, gold, silver, spices, and other things whatsoever, and merchandise of whatever kind, name, and manner it may be, which may be bought, bartered, discovered, acquired, or obtained within the limits of the said Admiralty, your Highnesses grant henceforth to the said Don Christopher, and will that he may have and take for himself, the tenth part of all of them, deducting all the expenses which may be incurred therein; so that of what shall remain free and clear, he may have and take the tenth part for himself, and do with it as he wills, the other nine parts remaining for your Highnesses. . . .

Item, that in all the vessels which may be equipped for the said traffic and negotiation each time and whenever and as often as they may be equipped, the said Admiral Don Christopher Columbus may, if he wishes, contribute and pay the eighth part of all that may be expended in the equipment. And also that he may have and take of the profit, the eighth part of all which may result from such equipment. . . .

These are executed and despatched with the responses of your Highnesses at the end of each article in the town of Santa Fe de la Vega de Granada, on the seventeenth day of April in the year of the nativity of our Savior Jesus Christ one thousand four hundred and ninety-two.

AGREEMENT OF APRIL 30, 1492

Forasmuch as you, Christopher Columbus, are going by our command, with some of our ships and with our subjects, to discover and acquire certain islands and mainland in the ocean, and it is hoped that, by the help of

God, some of the said islands and mainland in the said ocean will be discovered and acquired by your pains and industry; and therefore it is a just and reasonable thing that since you incur the said danger for our service you should be rewarded for it . . . it is our will and pleasure that you, the said Christopher Columbus, after you have discovered and acquired the said islands and mainland in the said ocean, or any of them whatsoever, shall be our Admiral of the said islands and mainland and Viceroy and Governor therein, and shall be empowered from that time forward to call and entitle yourself Don Christopher Columbus, and that your sons and successors in the said office and charge may likewise entitle and call themselves Don, and Admiral and Viceroy and Governor thereof; and that you may have power to use and exercise the said office of Admiral, together with the said office of Viceroy and Governor of the said islands and mainland . . . and to hear and determine all the suits and causes civil and criminal appertaining to the said office of Admiralty, Viceroy, and Governor according as you shall find by law, . . . and may have power to punish and chastise delinquents, and exercise the said offices . . . in all that concerns and appertains to the said offices . . . and that you shall have and levy the fees and salaries annexed, belonging and appertaining to the said offices and to each of them, according as our High Admiral in the Admiralty of our kingdoms levies and is accustomed to levy them.

READING AND DISCUSSION QUESTIONS

1. According to the agreements, what rewards could Columbus expect if his venture was successful? What reason is given for offering these rewards to Columbus?

2. What motivated King Ferdinand and Queen Isabella to fund Columbus's expedition?

BERNARDINO DE SAHAGÚN
From General History of the Things of New Spain
ca. 1545–1578

A member of the Franciscan order, the Spaniard Bernardino de Sahagún (1499–1590) was one of the earliest missionaries to arrive in Mexico. Although committed to converting the native population of Mexico to Christianity, Sahagún learned the Aztec language of Nahuatl and wrote an extensive study of Aztec culture and religious beliefs. This study raised concern among Sahagún's superiors for its sympathetic portrayal of the Aztec people. The controversial General History of the Things of New Spain *remained in manuscript form in a Spanish convent until its eventual publication in the nineteenth century. In the excerpt below, Sahagún describes the Spanish conquest of Mexico, led by Hernando Cortés (1485–1547).*

And after the dying in Cholula, the Spaniards set off on their way to Mexico,[6] coming gathered and bunched, raising dust. . . .

Thereupon Moteucçoma[7] named and sent noblemen and a great many other agents of his . . . to go meet [Cortés] . . . at Quauhtechcac. They gave [the Spaniards] golden banners of precious feathers, and golden necklaces.

And when they had given the things to them, they seemed to smile, to rejoice and to be very happy. Like monkeys they grabbed the gold. It was as though their hearts were put to rest, brightened, freshened. For gold was what they greatly thirsted for; they were gluttonous for it, starved for it, piggishly wanting it. They came lifting up the golden banners, waving them

---

James Lockhart, ed. and trans., *We People Here: Nahuatl Accounts of the Conquest of Mexico* (Berkeley: University of California Press, 1993), 96, 98, 100, 106, 108, 110, 112, 132, 134, 136, 180, 182, 186, 188, 210, 216, 218, 238, 240, 242.

[6] **Mexico**: Sahagún uses the term *Mexico* to refer to Tenochtitlán, the capital of the Aztec Empire. *Mexica* refers to the people living in Tenochtitlán and its suburbs.

[7] **Moteucçoma**: Sometimes spelled Montezuma, Moteucçoma (1466–1520) was the Aztec emperor at the time of the Spanish conquest.

from side to side, showing them to each other. They seemed to babble; what they said to each other was in a babbling tongue. . . .

(Cortés and his entourage continue their march.)

Then they set out in this direction, about to enter Mexico here. Then they all dressed and equipped themselves for war. They girded themselves, tying their battle gear tightly on themselves and then on their horses. Then they arranged themselves in rows, files, ranks.

Four horsemen came ahead going first, staying ahead, leading. . . .

Also the dogs, their dogs [bred for combat], came ahead, sniffing at things and constantly panting.

By himself came marching ahead, all alone, the one who bore the standard on his shoulder. He came waving it about, making it spin, tossing it here and there. . . .

Following him came those with iron swords. Their iron swords came bare and gleaming. On their shoulders they bore their shields, of wood or leather.

The second contingent and file were horses carrying people, each with his cotton cuirass [chest armor], his leather shield, his iron lance, and his iron sword hanging down from the horse's neck. They came with bells on, jingling or rattling. The horses, the deer [horses], neighed, there was much neighing, and they would sweat a great deal; water seemed to fall from them. And their flecks of foam splatted on the ground, like soapsuds splatting. . . .

The third file were those with iron crossbows, the crossbowmen. Their quivers went hanging at their sides, passed under their armpits, well filled, packed with arrows, with iron bolts. . . .

The fourth file were likewise horsemen; their outfits were the same as has been said.

The fifth group were those with harquebuses,[8] the harquebusiers, shouldering their harquebuses; some held them [level]. And when they went into the great palace, the residence of the ruler, they repeatedly shot off their harquebuses. They exploded, sputtered, discharged, thundered, disgorged. Smoke spread, it grew dark with smoke, everyplace filled with smoke. The fetid smell made people dizzy and faint.

Then all those from the various altepetl [sovereign territories] on the other side of the mountains, the Tlaxcalans, the people of Tliliuhquitepec, of Huexotzinco, came following behind. They came outfitted for war with their cotton upper armor, shields, and bows, their quivers full and packed

---

[8] **harquebuses**: The guns of the Spanish conquerors.

with feathered arrows, some barbed, some blunted, some with obsidian [glass] points. They went crouching, hitting their mouths with their hands yelling, singing, . . . whistling, shaking their heads. . . .

(Cortés and his army entered Tenochtitlán in November 1519 and were amicably received by Moctezuma, who was nonetheless taken captive by the Spaniards. Cortés's army was allowed to remain in a palace compound, but tensions grew the following spring. Pedro de Alvarado, in command while Cortés left to deal with a threat to his authority from the governor of Cuba, became increasingly concerned for the Spaniards' safety as the people of Tenochtitlán prepared to celebrate the annual festival in honor of Huitzilopochtli, the warrior god of the sun.)

And when it had dawned and was already the day of his festivity, very early in the morning those who had made vows to him [i.e., Huitzilopochtli, the sun god] unveiled his face. Forming a single row before him they offered him incense; each in his place laid down before him offerings of food for fasting and rolled amaranth dough. And it was as though all the youthful warriors had gathered together and had hit on the idea of holding and observing the festivity in order to show the Spaniards something, to make them marvel and instruct them. . . .

When it was time, when the moment had come for the Spaniards to do the killing, they came out equipped for battle. They came and closed off each of the places where people went in and out. . . . And when they had closed these exits, they stationed themselves in each, and no one could come out any more. . . . Then they surrounded those who were dancing, going among the cylindrical drums. They struck a drummer's arms; both of his hands were severed. Then they struck his neck; his head landed far away. Then they stabbed everyone with iron lances and struck them with iron swords. They struck some in the belly, and then their entrails came spilling out. They split open the heads of some, they really cut their skulls to pieces, their skulls were cut up into little bits. And if someone still tried to run it was useless; he just dragged his intestines along. There was a stench as if of sulfur. Those who tried to escape could go nowhere. When anyone tried to go out, at the entryways they struck and stabbed him.

And when it became known what was happening, everyone cried out, "Mexica warriors, come running, get outfitted with devices, shields, and arrows, hurry, come running, the warriors are dying; they have died, perished, been annihilated, O Mexica warriors!" Thereupon there were war cries, shouting, and beating of hands against lips. The warriors quickly came outfitted, bunched together, carrying arrows and shields. Then the fighting began; they shot at them with barbed darts, spears, and tridents, and they hurled darts with broad obsidian points at them. . . .

The fighting that ensued drove the Spaniards and their allies back to the palace enclave. Without a reliable supply of food and water, in July 1520, Cortés, who had returned with his power intact, led his followers on a desperate nocturnal escape from the city, but they were discovered and suffered heavy losses as they fled. They retreated to the other side of the lake, and the Aztecs believed the Spanish threat had passed.

Before the Spanish appeared to us, first an epidemic broke out, a sickness of pustules [smallpox]. . . . Large bumps spread on people; some were entirely covered. They spread everywhere, on the face, the head, the chest, etc. The disease brought great desolation; a great many died of it. They could no longer walk about, but lay in their dwellings and sleeping places, no longer able to move or stir. They were unable to change position, to stretch out on their sides or face down, or raise their heads. And when they made a motion, they called out loudly. The pustules that covered people caused great desolation; very many people died of them, and many just starved to death; starvation reigned, and no one took care of others any longer. . . .

This disease of pustules lasted a full sixty days; after sixty days it abated and ended. When people were convalescing and reviving, the pustules disease began to move in the direction of Chalco. And many were disabled or paralyzed by it, but they were not disabled forever. . . . The Mexica warriors were greatly weakened by it.

And when things were in this state, the Spaniards came, moving toward us from Tetzcoco. . . .

(Having resupplied his Spanish/Tlaxcalan army and having constructed a dozen cannon-carrying brigantines for use on the lake, Cortés resumed his offensive late in 1520. In April 1521 he reached Tenochtitlán and placed the city under a blockade.)

When their twelve boats had come from Tetzcoco, at first they were all assembled at Acachinanco, and then the Marqués [Cortés] moved to Acachinanco. He went about searching where the boats could enter, where the canals were straight, whether they were deep or not, so that they would not be grounded somewhere. But the canals were winding and bent back and forth, and they could not get them in. They did get two boats in; they forced them down the road coming straight from Xoloco. . . .

And the two boats came gradually, keeping on one side. On the other side no boats came, because there were houses there. They came ahead, fighting as they came; there were deaths on both sides, and on both sides captives were taken. When the Tenochca who lived in Çoquipan saw this, they fled, fled in fear. . . . They took nothing at all with them, they just left all their poor property in fear, they just scattered everything in their haste. And our enemies[9] went snatching things up, taking whatever they came upon. Whatever they hit on they carried away, whether cloaks, lengths of cotton cloth, warrior's devices, log drums, or cylindrical drums.

The Tlatelolca fought in Çoquipan, in war boats. And in Xoloco the Spaniards came to a place where there was a wall in the middle of the road, blocking it. They fired the big guns at it.

At the first shot it did not give way, but the second time it began to crumble. The third time, at last parts of it fell to the ground, and the fourth time finally the wall went to the ground once and for all. . . .

Once they got two of their boats into the canal at Xocotitlan. When they had beached them, then they went looking into the house sites of the people of Xocotitlan. But Tzilacatzin and some other warriors who saw the Spaniards immediately came out to face them; they came running after them, throwing stones at them, and they scattered the Spaniards into the water. . . .

When they got to Tlilhuacan, the warriors crouched far down and hid themselves, hugging the ground, waiting for the war cry, when there would be shouting and cries of encouragement. When the cry went up, "O Mexica, up and at them!" the Tlappanecatl Ecatzin, a warrior of Otomi rank,[10] faced the Spaniards and threw himself at them, saying, "O Tlatelolca warriors, up and at them, who are these barbarians? Come running!" Then he went and threw a Spaniard down, knocking him to the ground; the one he threw down was the one who came first, who came leading them. And when he had thrown him down, he dragged the Spaniard off.

And at this point they let loose with all the warriors who had been crouching there; they came out and chased the Spaniards in the passage-ways, and when the Spaniards saw it they, the Mexica, seemed to be in-toxicated. Then captives were taken. Many Tlaxcalans, and people of Acolhuacan, Chalco, Xochimilco, etc. [i.e., allies of the Spaniards], were captured. A great abundance were captured and killed. . . .

Then they took the captives to Yacacolco, hurrying them along, going along herding their captives together. Some went weeping, some singing, some went shouting while hitting their hands against their mouths. When

---

[9] **our enemies**: The American Indian tribes that were allies of the Spaniards.

[10] **warrior of Otomi rank**: Warriors who swore an oath never to retreat.

they got them to Yacacolco, they lined them all up. Each one went to the altar platform where the sacrifice was performed. The Spaniards went first, going in the lead; the people of the different altepetl just followed, coming last. And when the sacrifice was over, they strung the Spaniards' heads on poles on skull racks; they also strung up the horses' heads. They placed them below, and the Spaniards' heads were above them, strung up facing east. . . .

(Despite this victory, the Aztecs could not overcome the problems of shortages of food, water, and warriors. In mid July 1521 the Spaniards and their allies resumed their assault, and in early August the Aztecs decided to send into battle a quetzal-owl [sacred bird] warrior, whose success or failure, it was believed, would reveal if the gods wished the Aztecs to continue the war.)

And all the common people suffered greatly. There was famine; many died of hunger. They no longer drank good, pure water, but the water they drank was salty. Many people died of it, and because of it many got dysentery and died. Everything was eaten: lizards, swallows, maize straw, grass that grows on salt flats. And they chewed at . . . wood, glue flowers, plaster, leather, and deerskin, which they roasted, baked, and toasted so that they could eat them, and they ground up medicinal herbs and adobe bricks. There had never been the like of such suffering. The siege was frightening, and great numbers died of hunger. And bit by bit they came pressing us back against the wall, herding us together. . . . There was no place to go; people shoved, pressed and trampled one another; many died in the press. But one woman came to very close quarters with our enemies, throwing water at them, throwing water in their faces, making it stream down their faces.

And when the ruler Quauhtemoctzin[11] and the warriors Coyohue-huetzin, Temilotzin, Topantemoctzin, the Mixcoatlailotlac Ahuelitoctzin, Tlacotzin, and Petlauhtzin took a great warrior named Tlapaltecatl opochtzin . . . and outfitted him, dressing him in a quetzal-owl costume. . . . "Let him wear it, let him die in it. Let him dazzle people with it, let him show them something; let our enemies see and admire it." When they put it on him he looked very frightening and splendid. And they ordered four [others] to come helping him, to accompany him. They gave him the darts of the devil,[12] darts of wooden rods with flint tips. And the

---

[11] **Quauhtemoctzin**: The Aztec emperor after Moteucçoma died while in Spanish captivity.

[12] **darts of the devil**: The battle darts of the god Huitzilopochtli.

reason they did this was that it was as though the fate of the rulers of the Mexica were being determined.

When our enemies saw him, it was as though a mountain had fallen. Every one of the Spaniards was frightened; he intimidated them, they seemed to respect him a great deal. Then the quetzal-owl climbed up on the roof. But when some of our enemies had taken a good look at him they rose and turned him back, pursuing him. Then the quetzal-owl turned them again and pursued them. Then he snatched up the precious feathers and gold and dropped down off the roof. He did not die, and our enemies did not carry him off. Also three of our enemies were captured. At that the war stopped for good. There was silence, nothing more happened. Then our enemies went away. It was silent and nothing more happened until it got dark.

And the next day nothing more happened at all, no one made a sound. The common people just lay collapsed. The Spaniards did nothing more either, but lay still, looking at the people. Nothing was going on, they just lay still. . . .

(Two weeks passed before the Aztecs surrendered on August 13, 1521, after a siege of over three months' duration.)

READING AND DISCUSSION QUESTIONS

1. What hardships did the Aztecs experience with the arrival of the Spaniards?

2. What were Cortés and his men seeking?

3. What different strategies of attack did the Spanish use against the Aztecs? How, ultimately, were they able to defeat the Aztecs?

4. What is Sahagún's attitude toward the Spaniards? What is his attitude toward the Aztecs? With whom does he identify?

DOCUMENT 15-5

MATTEO RICCI

From China in the Sixteenth Century

ca. 1607

Matteo Ricci (1552–1610) was an Italian Jesuit missionary to China. An exceptional scientist and mathematician, Ricci impressed China's scholars and eventually received an invitation from the emperor to visit the palace in Beijing. Ricci was an admirer of Chinese culture, who learned the language and studied Confucian texts as part of his missionary work. He hoped to convert the Chinese by demonstrating the ultimate compatibility between the Christian and Chinese traditions. This reading comes from the journal that he wrote in for twenty-seven years. Published after his death, Ricci's journals were a major source of information about China for Europeans.

During 1606 and the year following, the progress of Christianity in Nancian[13] was in no wise retarded. . . . The number of neophytes [converts] increased by more than two hundred, all of whom manifested an extraordinary piety in their religious devotions. As a result, the reputation of the Christian religion became known throughout the length and breadth of this metropolitan city. . . .

Through the efforts of Father Emanuele Dias another and a larger house was purchased, in August of 1607, at a price of a thousand gold pieces. This change was necessary, because the house he had was too small for his needs and was situated in a flood area. Just as the community was about to change from one house to the other, a sudden uprising broke out against them. . . .

At the beginning of each month, the Magistrates hold a public assembly . . . in the temple of their great Philosopher [Confucius]. When the rites of the new-moon were completed in the temple, and these are civil

---

From Matthew Ricci, *China in the Sixteenth Century*, trans. Louis J. Gallagher, S. J., copyright 1942, 1953, and renewed 1970 by Louis J. Gallagher, S. J. (New York: Random House, 1970).

[13] **Nancian**: Nanchang; a city in southeastern China founded during the Han Dynasty.

rather than religious rites,[14] one of those present took advantage of the occasion to speak on behalf of the others, and to address the highest Magistrate present. . . . "We wish to warn you," he said, "that there are certain foreign priests in this royal city, who are preaching a law, hitherto unheard of in this kingdom, and who are holding large gatherings of people in their house." Having said this, he referred them to their local Magistrate, . . . and he in turn ordered the plaintiffs to present their case in writing, assuring them that he would support it with all his authority, in an effort to have the foreign priests expelled. The complaint was written out that same day and signed with twenty-seven signatures. . . . The content of the document was somewhat as follows.

Matthew Ricci, Giovanni Soerio, Emanuele Dias, and certain other foreigners from western kingdoms, men who are guilty of high treason against the throne, are scattered amongst us, in five different provinces. They are continually communicating with each other and are here and there practicing brigandage on the rivers, collecting money, and then distributing it to the people, in order to curry favor with the multitudes. They are frequently visited by the Magistrates, by the high nobility and by the Military Prefects, with whom they have entered into a secret pact, binding unto death.

These men teach that we should pay no respect to the images of our ancestors, a doctrine which is destined to extinguish the love of future generations for their forebears. Some of them break up the idols, leaving the temples empty and the gods to be pitied, without any patronage. In the beginning they lived in small houses, but by this time they have bought up large and magnificent residences. The doctrine they teach is something infernal. It attracts the ignorant into its fraudulent meshes, and great crowds of this class are continually assembled at their houses. Their doctrine gets beyond the city walls and spreads itself through the neighboring towns and villages and into the open country, and the people become so wrapt up in its falsity, that students are not following their course, laborers are neglecting their work, farmers are not cultivating their acres, and even the women have no interest in their housework. The whole city has become disturbed, and, whereas in the beginning there were only a hundred or so professing their faith, now there are more than twenty thousand. These priests distribute pictures of some Tartar or Saracen,[15] who they say

---

[14] **civil rather than religious rites**: The Jesuits maintained that Confucian ceremonies were purely civil rather than religious in nature.

[15] **some Tartar or Saracen**: A reference to Jesus Christ.

is God, who came down from Heaven to redeem and to instruct all of humanity, and who alone, according to their doctrine, can give wealth and happiness; a doctrine by which the simple people are very easily deceived. These men are an abomination on the face of the Earth, and there is just ground for fear that once they have erected their own temples, they will start a rebellion. . . . Wherefore, moved by their interest in the maintenance of the public good, in the conservation of the realm, and in the preservation, whole and entire, of their ancient laws, the petitioners are presenting this complaint and demanding, in the name of the entire province, that a rescript of it be forwarded to the King, asking that these foreigners be sentenced to death, or banished from the realm, to some deserted island in the sea. . . .

Each of the Magistrates to whom the indictment was presented asserted that the spread of Christianity should be prohibited, and that the foreign priests should be expelled from the city, if the Mayor saw fit, after hearing the case, and notifying the foreigners. . . . But the Fathers [Jesuit priests], themselves, were not too greatly disturbed, placing their confidence in Divine Providence, which had always been present to assist them on other such dangerous occasions.

[Father Emanuele is summoned before the Chief Justice.]

Father Emanuele, in his own defense, . . . gave a brief outline of the Christian doctrine. Then he showed that according to the divine law, the first to be honored, after God, were a man's parents. But the judge had no mind to hear or to accept any of this and he made it known that he thought it was all false. After that repulse, with things going from bad to worse, it looked as if they were on the verge of desperation, so much so, indeed, that they increased their prayers, their sacrifices, and their bodily penances, in petition for a favorable solution of their difficulty. Their adversaries appeared to be triumphantly victorious. They were already wrangling about the division of the furniture of the Mission residences, and to make results doubly certain, they stirred up the flames anew with added accusations and indictments. . . .

The Mayor, who was somewhat friendly with the Fathers, realizing that there was much in the accusation that was patently false, asked the Magistrate Director of the Schools,[16] if he knew whether or not this man Emanuele was a companion of Matthew Ricci, who was so highly respected at the royal court, and who was granted a subsidy from the royal treasury, because of the gifts he had presented to the King. Did he realize

---

[16] **Magistrate Director of the Schools**: The local Confucian academy. In this case, the director of the local academy was opposed to the Jesuit presence.

that the Fathers had lived in Nankin [Nanjing] for twelve years, and that no true complaint had ever been entered against them for having violated the laws. Then he asked him if he had really given full consideration as to what was to be proven in the present indictment. To this the Director of the Schools replied that he wished the Mayor to make a detailed investigation of the case and then to confer with him. The Chief Justice then ordered the same thing to be done. Fortunately, it was this same Justice who was in charge of city affairs when Father Ricci first arrived in Nancian. It was he who first gave the Fathers permission, with the authority of the Viceroy, to open a house there. . . .

After the Mayor had examined the charges of the plaintiffs and the reply of the defendants, he subjected the quasi-literati[17] to an examination in open court, and taking the Fathers under his patronage, he took it upon himself to refute the calumnies of their accusers. He said he was fully convinced that these strangers were honest men, and that he knew that there were only two of them in their local residence and not twenty, as had been asserted. To this they replied that the Chinese were becoming their disciples. To which the Justice in turn replied: "What of it? Why should we be afraid of our own people? Perhaps you are unaware of the fact that Matthew Ricci's company is cultivated by everyone in Pekin [Beijing], and that he is being subsidized by the royal treasury. How dare the Magistrates who are living outside of the royal city expel men who have permission to live at the royal court? These men here have lived peacefully in Nankin for twelve years. I command," he added, "that they buy no more large houses, and that the people are not to follow their law." . . .

A few days later, the court decision was pronounced and written out . . . and was then posted at the city gates as a public edict. The following is a summary of their declaration. Having examined the cause of Father Emanuele and his companions, it was found that these men had come here from the West because they had heard so much about the fame of the great Chinese Empire, and that they had already been living in the realm for some years, without any display of ill-will. Father Emanuele should be permitted to practice his own religion, but it was not considered to be the right thing for the common people, who are attracted by novelties, to adore the God of Heaven. For them to go over to the religion of foreigners would indeed be most unbecoming. . . . It would therefore seem to be . . . [in] . . . the best interests of the Kingdom, to . . . [warn] . . . everyone in a public edict not to abandon the sacrifices of their ancient religion

---

[17] **quasi-literati**: The local scholars who criticized Ricci and the Jesuits. Most of these scholars had only passed the first of the three Confucian civil service exams.

by accepting the cult of foreigners. Such a movement might, indeed, result in calling together certain gatherings, detrimental to the public welfare, and harmful also to the foreigner, himself. Wherefore, the Governor of this district, by order of the high Magistrates, admonishes the said Father Emanuele to refrain from perverting the people, by inducing them to accept a foreign religion. The man who sold him the larger house is to restore his money and Emanuele is to buy a smaller place, sufficient for his needs, and to live there peaceably, as he has done, up to the present. Emanuele, himself, has agreed to these terms and the Military Prefects of the district have been ordered to make a search of the houses there and to confiscate the pictures of the God they speak of, wherever they find them. It is not permitted for any of the native people to go over to the religion of the foreigners, nor is it permitted to gather together for prayer meetings. Whoever does contrary to these prescriptions will be severely punished, and if the Military Prefects are remiss in enforcing them, they will be held to be guilty of the same crimes. To his part of the edict, the Director of the Schools added, that the common people were forbidden to accept the law of the foreigners, and that a sign should be posted above the door of the Father's residence, notifying the public that these men were forbidden to have frequent contact with the people.

The Fathers were not too disturbed by this pronouncement, because they were afraid that it was going to be much worse. In fact, everyone thought it was rather favorable, and that the injunction launched against the spread of the faith was a perfunctory order to make it appear that the literati were not wholly overlooked, since the Fathers were not banished from the city, as the literati had demanded. Moreover it was not considered a grave misdemeanor for the Chinese to change their religion, and it was not customary to inflict a serious punishment on those violating such an order. The neophytes, themselves, proved this when they continued, as formerly, to attend Mass.

READING AND DISCUSSION QUESTIONS

1. What were the concerns of the officials in Nanchang regarding the Jesuit missionaries?

2. How did Father Emanuele try to convince the Chinese authorities that Christianity and the Jesuits did not pose a threat? What reasons did he give for the continued work of the missionaries?

3. Aside from their roles as missionaries, what other roles did the Jesuits play in China, as implied by this account?

COMPARATIVE QUESTIONS

1. Compare Zheng He's inscription and Columbus's agreements with the Spanish rulers. What do these sources suggest about the role that exploration played in strengthening the Spanish and Chinese governments?

2. According to Las Casas and Sahagún, how did the Spaniards treat the native populations that they encountered? According to Zheng He's inscription, how did the Chinese treat local populations?

3. Compare Zheng He's inscription and the journals of Matteo Ricci. In what ways did the explorers and missionaries of this time feel that their actions were divinely compelled? What proof did they provide of divine favor?

4. Taking all the documents into consideration, what motivated the explorers of both the Western and Eastern worlds? What impact did this exploration have on the areas that they visited?

CHAPTER 16

Absolutism and Constitutionalism in Europe

ca. 1589–1725

The seventeenth century was a time of deep crisis for Europe. The commercial and agricultural sectors suffered from prolonged economic stagnation, and many nations found themselves locked in expensive and devastating internal and external wars. Despite these difficulties, as the century came to a close, Europe's governments experienced significant growth with increased control over taxation, the military, and the state bureaucracy. The following documents reveal the reactions of European governments to the difficulties of the seventeenth century. As the sources illustrate, Europe was divided in its response. Some countries, such as England, took the path of constitutionalism, while others — including France and Eastern European states — chose absolutism. Regardless of these differing paths, each country answered the challenges of the century by establishing centralized states that asserted sovereignty over their people.

> DOCUMENT 16-1

LOUIS XIV
From Mémoires for the Instruction of the Dauphin
ca. 1666–1670

Louis XIV (r. 1643–1715) was a few months shy of his fifth birthday when he ascended to the French throne. At the time, France faced daunting challenges,

---

Louis XIV, *Mémoires for the Instruction of the Dauphin*, trans. and ed. Paul Sonnino (New York: Free Press, 1970), 21–26, 28–33, 35, 37–38, 40–44, 53–58, 68, 78.

including an increasingly disgruntled nobility and involvement in the Thirty Years' War. During the course of his seventy-two-year reign, Louis worked tirelessly to neutralize threats to his authority, claiming ultimately to have absolute power over his kingdom and its subjects. To ensure his legacy, Louis wrote the following instructions for his son to offer guidance to his heir. As it turned out, Louis outlived his son, as well as his grandsons. At his death in 1715, his five-year-old great-grandson inherited the throne and France's tradition of absolutism.

My son, many excellent reasons have prompted me to go to a considerable effort in the midst of my greatest occupations in order to leave you these memoirs of my reign and of my principal actions. I have never believed that kings, feeling as they do all the paternal affections and attachments in themselves, were dispensed from the common and natural obligation of fathers to instruct their children by example and by counsel. . . .

I have considered, moreover, what I have so often experienced myself: the crowd of people who will press around you, each with his own design; the difficulty that you will have in obtaining sincere advice from them; the entire assurance that you will be able to take in that of a father who will have had no interest but your own, nor any passion except for your greatness. . . .

Disorder reigned everywhere. My court, in general, was still quite far removed from the sentiments in which I hope that you will find it. People of quality accustomed to continual bargaining with a minister who did not mind it, and who had sometimes found it necessary, were always inventing an imaginary right to whatever was to their fancy; no governor of a stronghold who was not difficult to govern; no request that was not mingled with some reproach over the past, or with some veiled threat of future dissatisfaction. Graces [favors] exacted and torn rather than awaited, and extorted in consequence of each other, no longer really obligated anyone, merely serving to offend those to whom they were refused.

The finances, which move and activate the whole great body of the monarchy, were so exhausted that there hardly seemed to be any recourse left. Many of the most necessary and imperative expenses for my household and for my own person were either shamefully postponed or were supported solely through credit, to be made up for later. Affluence prevailed, meanwhile, among the financiers who, on the one hand, covered their irregularities by all kinds of artifices while they uncovered them, on the other, by insolent and brazen luxury, as if they were afraid to leave me ignorant of them.

The Church aside from its usual troubles, after long disputes over scholastic matters that were admittedly unnecessary for salvation — differences mounting each day with the excitement and the obstinacy of tempers and even mingling constantly with new human interest — was finally threatened openly with a schism [Jansenism] by people all the more dangerous since they could have been very useful, of great merit had they been less convinced of it. It was no longer merely a question of some individual theologians in hiding, but of bishops established in their see, capable of drawing the populace after them, of high reputation, of piety indeed worthy of reverence as long as it were accompanied by submission to the opinions of the Church, by mildness, by moderation, and by charity. . . .

The least of the defects in the order of the nobility was the infinite number of usurpers in its midst, without any title or having a title acquired by purchase rather than by service. The tyranny that it exercised over its vassals and over its neighbors in some of my provinces could neither be tolerated nor could it be suppressed without examples of severity and of rigor. The fury of duels, somewhat mitigated since my strict and inflexible enforcement of the latest regulations, already showed through the well-advanced recovery from such a deep-rooted evil that none was beyond remedy.

Justice, which was responsible for reforming all the rest, seemed itself to me as the most difficult to reform. An infinite number of things contributed to this: offices filled by chance and by money rather than by choice and by merit; lack of experience among the judges, even less learning; the ordinances of my predecessors on age and on service circumvented almost everywhere. . . . Even my council, instead of regulating the other jurisdictions, all too often confused them through an incredible number of conflicting decisions all given in my name as if coming from me, which made the disorder even more shameful.

All these evils, or rather, their consequences and their effects, fell primarily upon the lower class, burdened, moreover, with taxes and pressed by extreme poverty in many areas, disturbed in others by their own idleness since the peace, and especially in need of relief and of employment. . . .

All was calm everywhere. Not the slightest hint of any movement within the kingdom that could interrupt or oppose my plans. There was peace with my neighbors, apparently for as long as I would want it myself, owing to the circumstances in which they found themselves. . . .

It would undoubtedly have been a waste of such perfect and such rare tranquillity not to put it to good use, although my youth and the pleasure of leading my armies would have made me wish for a few more external affairs. . . .

Two things were necessary for me, undoubtedly: a great deal of work on my part; a careful choice of the persons who were to support me and relieve me in it.

As to work, my son, it may be that you will begin to read these memoirs at an age when it is far more customary to fear it than to enjoy it, delighted to have escaped from subjection to teachers and to masters, and to have no more set hours nor long and fixed concentration.

Here I shall not merely tell you that this is nonetheless how one reigns, why one reigns, and that there is ingratitude and temerity toward God as well as injustice and tyranny toward men in wanting one without the other, that these demands of royalty which may sometimes seem harsh and unpleasant to you from such a lofty post would appear delightful and pleasant to you if it were a question of attaining them! . . .

I made it a rule to work regularly twice a day for two to three hours at a time with various persons, aside from the hours that I worked alone or that I might devote extraordinarily to extraordinary affairs if any arose, there being no moment when it was not permitted to discuss with me anything that was pressing, except for foreign envoys, who sometimes use the familiarity that they are permitted in order to obtain something or to pry, and who must not be heard without preparation.

I cannot tell you what fruits I immediately gathered from this decision. I could almost feel my spirits and my courage rising. I was a different person. I discovered something new about myself and joyfully wondered how I could have ignored it for so long. That first shyness, which always comes with good sense and which was especially disturbing when I had to speak at some length in public, vanished in less than no time. I knew then that I was king, and born for it. I experienced, finally, an indescribable delight that you will simply have to discover for yourself. . . . The function of kings consists primarily of using good sense, which always comes naturally and easily. . . . Everything that is most necessary to this effort is at the same time pleasant. For it consists, in short, my son, of keeping an eye on the whole earth, of constantly learning the news of all the provinces and of all the nations, the secret of all the courts, the dispositions and the weaknesses of all the foreign princes and of all their ministers; of being informed of an infinite number of things that we are presumed to ignore; of seeing around us what is hidden from us with the greatest care; of discovering the most remote ideas and the most hidden interests of our courtiers coming to us through conflicting interests; and I don't know, finally, what other pleasures we would not abandon for this one, for the sake of curiosity alone. . . .

I commanded the four secretaries of state not to sign anything at all any longer without discussing it with me, the superintendent likewise, and for nothing to be transacted at the finances without being registered in a little book that was to remain with me, where I could always see at a glance, briefly summarized, the current balance and the expenditures made or pending. . . .

I announced that all requests for graces [favors] of any type had to be made directly to me, and I granted to all my subjects without distinction the privilege of appealing to me at any time, in person or by petitions. The petitions were initially very numerous, which did not discourage me, however. The disorder into which my affairs had fallen produced many of them; the idle or unjustified hopes which were raised by this novelty hardly stimulated a lesser number. I was given a great many [petitions] about lawsuits, which I saw no reason for withdrawing arbitrarily from the ordinary jurisdictions for trial before me. But even in these apparently useless things I discovered much that was useful. I learned thereby many details about the condition of my people. They saw that I was concerned about them, and nothing did so much to win me their hearts. . . .

As to the persons who were to support me in my work, I resolved above all not to have a prime minister, and if you and all your successors take my advice, my son, the name will forever be abolished in France, there being nothing more shameful than to see on the one hand all the functions and on the other the mere title of king.

For this purpose, it was absolutely necessary to divide my confidence and the execution of my orders without entirely entrusting it to anyone, assigning these various persons to various functions in keeping with their various talents, which is perhaps the first and foremost talent of princes. . . .

And as for this art of knowing men, which will be so important to you not merely on this but also on every other occasion of your life, I shall tell you, my son, that it can be learned but that it cannot be taught.

Indeed, it is only reasonable to attribute a great deal to a general and established reputation, because the public is impartial and is difficult to deceive over a long period. It is wise to listen to everyone, and not to believe entirely those around us, except for the good that they are compelled to admit in their enemies and for the bad that they try to excuse in their friends; still wiser is it to test of oneself in little things those whom one wants to employ in greater ones. But the summary of these precepts for properly identifying the talents, the inclinations, and the potential of each one is to work at it and to take pleasure in it. For, in general, from the smallest things to the greatest, you will never master a single one unless you derive pleasure and enjoyment from them. . . .

But to be perfectly honest with you, it was not in my interest to select individuals of greater eminence. It was above all necessary to establish my own reputation and to make the public realize by the very rank of those whom I selected, that it was not my intention to share my authority with them. It was important for they themselves not to conceive any greater hopes than I would please to give them, which is difficult for persons of high birth: and even with all these precautions, it took the world a rather long time to get to know me.

Many were convinced that before long some one around me would gain control over my mind and over my affairs. Most regarded my diligence as enthusiasm that must soon slacken, and those who wanted to judge it more favorably waited to decide later. . . .

I have believed it necessary to indicate this [seizure of personal power] to you, my son, lest from excessively good intentions in your early youth and from the very ardor that these mémoires will perhaps inspire in you, you might confuse two entirely different things; I mean ruling personally and not listening to any counsel, which would be an extreme as dangerous as that of being governed.

The most able private individuals procure the advice of other able persons about their petty interests. What then of kings who hold the public interest in their hands and whose decisions make for the misery or well-being of the whole earth? None [no decisions] should ever be reached of such importance without [our] having summoned, if it were possible, all the enlightenment, wisdom, and good sense of our subjects. . . .

But when, on important occasions, they have reported to us on all the sides and on all the conflicting arguments, on all that is done elsewhere in such and such a case, it is for us, my son, to decide what must actually be done. And as to this decision, I shall venture to tell you that if few lack neither sense nor courage, another never makes it as well as we. For decision requires the spirit of a master, and it is infinitely easier to be oneself than to imitate someone else. . . .

It was necessary for a thousand reasons, including the urgently needed reform of justice, to diminish the excessive authority of the principal courts, which, under the pretext that their judgments were without appeal, or as they say, sovereign and of the last instance, had gradually assumed the name of sovereign courts and considered themselves as so many separate and independent sovereignties. I announced that I would not tolerate their schemes any longer and to set an example, the Court of Excises of Paris having been the first to depart slightly from its duty, I exiled some of its officials, believing that a strong dose of this remedy initially would dispense me from having to use it often later, which has succeeded for me. . . .

I prohibited them all in general, by this decision, from ever rendering any [decisions] contrary to those of my council under any pretext whatsoever, whether of their jurisdiction or of the right of private individuals, and I ordered them, whenever they might believe that either one of them had been disturbed, to complain about it to me and to have recourse to my authority, that which I had entrusted to them being only for rendering justice to my subjects and not for procuring it for themselves, which is a part of sovereignty so essentially royal and so proper to the king alone that it cannot be transmitted to anyone else. . . .

In all these things, my son, and in some others that you will see subsequently which have undoubtedly humiliated my judicial officials, I don't want you to attribute to me, as those who know me less well may have done, motives of fear, hatred, and vengeance for what had transpired during the Fronde, when it cannot be denied that these courts often forgot themselves to the point of amazing excesses.

But in the first place, this resentment which appears initially so just might not perhaps fare so well on closer scrutiny. They have returned by themselves and without constraint to their duty. The good servants have recalled the bad. Why impute to the entire body the faults of a few, rather than the services which have prevailed in the end? . . .

It is usual for mature minds, which have received their first disposition for piety at an early age, to turn directly toward God in the midst of good fortune, although, as a major consequence of our weakness, a long sequence of successes, which we then regard as being naturally and properly due us, will customarily make us forget Him. I confess that in these beginnings, seeing my reputation growing each day, everything succeeding for me and becoming easy for me, I was as deeply struck as I have ever been by the desire to serve Him and to please Him. . . .

I revived, by a new ordinance, the rigor of the old edicts against swearing and blasphemy and wanted some examples to be made immediately; and I can say in this regard that my cares and the aversion that I have displayed toward this scandalous disorder have not been useless, my court being, God be thanked, more exempt from it than it long has been under the kings my predecessors. . . .

I dedicated myself to destroying Jansenism and to breaking up the communities where this spirit of novelty was developing, well-intentioned, perhaps, but which seemed to want to ignore the dangerous consequences that it could have. . . .

And as to my great number of subjects of the supposedly reformed religion [Huguenots], which was an evil that I had always regarded, and still regard, with sorrow, I devised at that time the plan of my entire policy toward them, which I have no grounds for regretting, since God has blessed it and still blesses it every day with a great number of conversions.

It seemed to me, my son, that those who wanted to employ violent remedies did not know the nature of this disease, caused in part by the excitement of tempers: which must be allowed to pass and to die gradually instead of rekindling it with equally strong contradictions, always useless, moreover, when the corruption is not limited to a clearly defined number, but spread throughout the state.

As far as I have been able to understand, the ignorance of the clergy in previous centuries, their luxury, their debaucheries, the bad examples that they set, those that they were obliged to tolerate for that very reason, the excesses, finally, that they condoned in the conduct of individuals contrary to the public rules and sentiments of the Church gave rise, more than anything else, to those grave wounds that it has received from schism and from heresy [the Protestant Reformation]. The new reformers obviously spoke the truth on many matters of fact and of this nature, which they decried with both justice and bitterness. They were presumptuous in regard to belief, and people cannot possibly distinguish a well-disguised error when it lies hidden, moreover, among many evident truths. It all began with some minor differences which I have learned that the Protestants of Germany and the Huguenots of France hardly consider any more today. These produced greater ones, primarily because too much pressure was put upon a violent and bold man [Martin Luther] who, seeing no other honorable retreat for himself, pushed ahead into the fray and, abandoning himself to his own reasoning, took the liberty of examining everything that he had accepted, promised the world an easy and shortened path to salvation, a means very suitable for flattering human reasoning and for drawing the populace. Love of novelty seduced many of them. The interests of various princes mingled in this quarrel. . . .

From this general knowledge, I believed, my son, that the best means to reduce gradually the number of Huguenots in my kingdom was, in the first place, not to press them at all by any new rigor against them, to implement what they had obtained from my predecessors but to grant them nothing further, and even to restrict its execution within the narrowest limits that justice and propriety would permit. . . .

But as to the graces [favors] that depended solely on me, I resolved, and I have rather scrupulously observed it since, not to grant them any, and this out of kindness rather than out of bitterness, so as to oblige them thereby to consider from time to time, by themselves and without constraint, if they had some good reason for depriving themselves voluntarily of the advantages that they could share with all my other subjects.

However, to profit from their greater willingness to be disabused of their errors, I also resolved to attract, even to reward, those who might be receptive; to do all I could to inspire the bishops to work at their instruction and to eliminate the scandals that sometimes separated them from us; to place, finally, in these highest posts and in all those to which I appoint for any reason whatsoever, only persons of piety, of dedication, of learning, capable of repairing, by an entirely different conduct, the disorders that their predecessors had primarily produced in the Church. . . .

[Louis warns against the practice of religion for purely selfish reasons.]

For indeed, my son, we must consider the good of our subjects far more than our own. They are almost a part of ourselves, since we are the head of a body and they are its members. It is only for their own advantage that we must give them laws, and our power over them must only be used by us in order to work more effectively for their happiness. It is wonderful to deserve from them the name of father along with that of master, and if the one belongs to us by right of birth, the other must be the sweetest object of our ambition. I am well aware that such a wonderful title is not obtained without a great deal of effort, but in praiseworthy undertakings one must not be stopped by the idea of difficulty. Work only dismays weak souls, and when a plan is advantageous and just, it is weakness not to execute it. . . .

I hope that I shall leave you with still more power and more greatness than I possess, and I want to believe that you will make still better use of it than I. But when everything that will surround you will conspire to fill you with nothing but yourself, don't compare yourself, my son, to lesser princes than you or to those who have borne or who may still unworthily bear the title of king. It is no great advantage to be a little better; think rather about all those who have furnished the greatest cause for esteem in past times, who from a private station or with very limited power have managed by the sole force of their merit to found great empires, have passed like comets from one part of the world to another, charmed the whole earth by their great qualities, and left, after so many centuries, a long and lasting memory of themselves that seems, instead of fading, to intensify and to gain strength with every passing day. If this does not suffice, be still more fair to yourself and consider for how many things you will be praised that you will perhaps owe entirely to fortune or to those whom it has itself placed in your service. Get down to some serious consideration of your own weaknesses, for even though you may imagine that all men, and even the greatest, have similar ones, nevertheless since you would find this harder to imagine and to believe of them than of yourself, it would undoubtedly diminish your conceit, which is the usual pitfall of brilliance and of fame.

Thereby, my son, and in this respect you will be humble. But when it will be a question, as on the occasion that I have just described to you, of your rank in the world, of the rights of your crown, of the king, finally, and not of the private individual, boldly assume as much loftiness of heart and of spirit as you can, and do not betray the glory of your predecessors nor the interest of your successors, whose trustee you are. . . .

READING AND DISCUSSION QUESTIONS

1. Two of the biggest threats to Louis' authority were the strength of the nobility and the dissension of French Protestants. How did Louis address these threats?

2. How would you summarize Louis' approach to governing?

3. What advice does Louis give to his son regarding his personal relationship with God? How does it differ from the advice he gives him regarding the church?

4. What, if any, missteps does Louis admit to making during his reign to this point?

DOCUMENT 16-2

JACQUES-BENIGNE BOSSUET

On Divine Right

ca. 1675–1680

French Absolutism developed in the seventeenth-century as a response to a number of crises, including the French Wars of Religion (ca. 1562–1598) and a civil war known as the Fronde (1648–1653). A bishop in the French Catholic church and tutor to the son of Louis XIV, Jacques-Benigne Bossuet (1627–1704) was an important architect of French absolutism. Drawing from biblical sources, Bossuet argued in his treatises that the monarch received his authority directly from God. This concept of the divine right of kings implied that any challenge to the authority of the king was tantamount to questioning God's divine plan.

We have already seen that all power is of God. The ruler, adds St. Paul, "is the minister of God to thee for good. But if thou do that which is evil, be afraid; for he beareth not the sword in vain: for he is the minister of God, a revenger to execute wrath upon him that doeth evil" [Rom. 13:1–7]. Rulers then act as the ministers of God and as his lieutenants on earth. It is through them that God exercises his empire. Think ye "to withstand the kingdom of the Lord in the hand of the sons of David" [Chron. 13:8]? Consequently, as we have seen, the royal throne is not the throne of a man, but the throne of God himself. . . .

Moreover, that no one may assume that the Israelites were peculiar in having kings over them who were established by God, note what is said in Ecclesiasticus: "God has given to every people its ruler, and Israel is manifestly reserved to him" [Eccl. 17:14–15]. He therefore governs all peoples and gives them their kings, although he governed Israel in a more intimate and obvious manner.

It appears from all this that the person of the king is sacred, and that to attack him in any way is sacrilege. God has the kings anointed by his prophets with the holy unction in like manner as he has bishops and altars anointed. But even without the external application in thus being anointed,

J. H. Robinson, ed., *Readings in European History*, 2 vols. (Boston: Ginn, 1906), 2:273–277.

they are by their very office the representatives of the divine majesty deputed by Providence for the execution of his purposes. . . . Kings should be guarded as holy things, and whosoever neglects to protect them is worthy of death. . . .

But kings, although their power comes from on high, as has been said, should not regard themselves as masters of that power to use it at their pleasure; . . . they must employ it with fear and self-restraint, as a thing coming from God and of which God will demand an account. "Hear, O kings, and take heed, understand, judges of the earth, lend your ears, ye who hold the peoples under your sway, and delight to see the multitude that surround you. It is God who gives you the power. Your strength comes from the Most High, who will question your works and penetrate the depths of your thoughts, for, being ministers of his kingdom, ye have not given righteous judgments nor have ye walked according to his will. He will straightway appear to you in a terrible manner, for to those who command is the heaviest punishment reserved. The humble and the weak shall receive mercy, but the mighty shall be mightily tormented. For God fears not the power of any one, because he made both great and small and he has care for both" [Ws 6:2]. . . .

Kings should tremble then as they use the power God has granted them; and let them think how horrible is the sacrilege if they use for evil a power which comes from God. We behold kings seated upon the throne of the Lord, bearing in their hand the sword which God himself has given them. What profanation, what arrogance, for the unjust king to sit on God's throne to render decrees contrary to his laws and to use the sword which God has put in his hand for deeds of violence and to slay his children! . . .

The royal power is absolute. With the aim of making this truth hateful and insufferable, many writers have tried to confound absolute government with arbitrary government. But no two things could be more unlike, as we shall show when we come to speak of justice.

The prince need render account of his acts to no one. "I counsel thee to keep the king's commandment, and that in regard of the oath of God. Be not hasty to go out of his sight: stand not on an evil thing for he doeth whatsoever pleaseth him. Where the word of a king is, there is power: and who may say unto him, What doest thou? Whoso keepeth the commandment shall feel no evil thing" [Eccles. 8:2–5]. Without this absolute authority the king could neither do good nor repress evil. It is necessary that his power be such that no one can hope to escape him, and, finally, the only protection of individuals against the public authority should be their innocence. This conforms with the teaching of St. Paul: "Wilt thou then not be afraid of the power? do that which is good" [Rom. 13:3].

I do not call majesty that pomp which surrounds kings or that exterior magnificence which dazzles the vulgar. That is but the reflection of majesty and not majesty itself. Majesty is the image of the grandeur of God in the prince.

God is infinite, God is all. The prince, as prince, is not regarded as a private person: he is a public personage, all the state is in him; the will of all the people is included in his. As all perfection and all strength are united in God, so all the power of individuals is united in the person of the prince. What grandeur that a single man should embody so much!

The power of God makes itself felt in a moment from one extremity of the earth to another. Royal power works at the same time throughout all the realm. It holds all the realm in position, as God holds the earth. Should God withdraw his hand, the earth would fall to pieces; should the king's authority cease in the realm, all would be in confusion.

Look at the prince in his cabinet. Thence go out the orders which cause the magistrates and the captains, the citizens and the soldiers, the provinces and the armies on land and on sea, to work in concert. He is the image of God, who, seated on his throne high in the heavens, makes all nature move. . . .

Finally, let us put together the things so great and so august which we have said about royal authority. Behold an immense people united in a single person; behold this holy power, paternal and absolute; behold the secret cause which governs the whole body of the state, contained in a single head: you see the image of God in the king, and you have the idea of royal majesty. God is holiness itself, goodness itself, and power itself. In these things lies the majesty of God. In the image of these things lies the majesty of the prince.

So great is this majesty that it cannot reside in the prince as in its source; it is borrowed from God, who gives it to him for the good of the people, for whom it is good to be checked by a superior force. Something of divinity itself is attached to princes and inspires fear in the people. The king should not forget this. "I have said," — it is God who speaks, — "I have said, Ye are gods; and all of you are children of the Most High. But ye shall die like men, and fall like one of the princes" [Ps. 82:6–7]. "I have said, Ye are gods"; that is to say, you have in your authority, and you bear on your forehead, a divine imprint. "You are the children of the Most High"; it is he who has established your power for the good of mankind. But, O gods of flesh and blood, gods of clay and dust, "ye shall die like men, and fall like princes." Grandeur separates men for a little time, but a common fall makes them all equal at the end.

O kings, exercise your power then boldly, for it is divine and salutary for human kind, but exercise it with humility. You are endowed with it from without. At bottom it leaves you feeble, it leaves you mortal, it leaves you sinners, and charges you before God with a very heavy account.

READING AND DISCUSSION QUESTIONS

1. According to Bossuet, what is the nature of monarchical authority? What are its sources and purposes?

2. Why must a prince wield his absolute power carefully?

3. To whom does the author seem to be addressing this treatise? What gives you that impression?

DOCUMENT 16-3

JOHN LOCKE

From Two Treatises of Government: *"Of the Ends of Political Society and Government"*

1690

John Locke (1632–1704) provided a theoretical foundation for the development of constitutionalism in England. Locke was a physician, philosopher, and teacher who had ties to the pro-parliamentary faction of the English government. While in exile in the Dutch Republic during the early 1680s, Locke worked on his Two Treatises of Government. *The second of these documents, excerpted below, helped to justify the Glorious Revolution of 1688. Locke began the treatise by imagining the time before the establishment of government when humans lived in a state of nature. He then speculated on*

John Locke, *Two Treatises of Government*, A. Millnar et al. (London, 1764).

the circumstances surrounding the formation of government in an effort to determine the origins and nature of political power.

Sec. 123. If man in the state of nature be so free, as has been said; if he be absolute lord of his own person and possessions, equal to the greatest, and subject to no body, why will he part with his freedom? Why will he give up this empire, and subject himself to the dominion and control of any other power? To which it is obvious to answer, that though in the state of nature he hath such a right, yet the enjoyment of it is very uncertain, and constantly exposed to the invasion of others: for all being kings as much as he, every man his equal, and the greater part no strict observers of equity and justice, the enjoyment of the property he has in this state is very unsafe, very unsecure. This makes him willing to quit a condition, which, however free, is full of fears and continual dangers: and it is not without reason, that he seeks out, and is willing to join in society with others, who are already united, or have a mind to unite, for the mutual preservation of their lives, liberties, and estates, which I call by the general name, property.

Sec. 124. The great and chief end, therefore, of men's uniting into commonwealths, and putting themselves under government, is the preservation of their property. To which in the state of nature there are many things wanting.

First, There wants an established, settled, known law, received and allowed by common consent to be the standard of right and wrong, and the common measure to decide all controversies between them: for though the law of nature be plain and intelligible to all rational creatures; yet men being biassed by their interest, as well as ignorant for want of study of it, are not apt to allow of it as a law binding to them in the application of it to their particular cases.

Sec. 125. Secondly, In the state of nature there wants a known and indifferent judge, with authority to determine all differences according to the established law: for every one in that state being both judge and executioner of the law of nature, men being partial to themselves, passion and revenge is very apt to carry them too far, and with too much heat, in their own cases; as well as negligence, and unconcernedness, to make them too remiss in other men's.

Sec. 126. Thirdly, In the state of nature there often wants power to back and support the sentence when right, and to give it due execution, They who by any injustice offended, will seldom fail, where they are able, by force to make good their injustice; such resistance many times makes the punishment dangerous, and frequently destructive, to those who attempt it.

Sec. 127. Thus mankind, notwithstanding all the privileges of the state of nature, being but in an ill condition, while they remain in it, are quickly driven into society. Hence it comes to pass, that we seldom find any number of men live any time together in this state. The inconveniencies that they are therein exposed to, by the irregular and uncertain exercise of the power every man has of punishing the transgressions of others, make them take sanctuary under the established laws of government, and therein seek the preservation of their property. It is this makes them so willingly give up every one his single power of punishing, to be exercised by such alone, as shall be appointed to it amongst them; and by such rules as the community, or those authorized by them to that purpose, shall agree on. And in this we have the original right and rise of both the legislative and executive power, as well as of the governments and societies themselves.

Sec. 128. For in the state of nature, to omit the liberty he has of innocent delights, a man has two powers.

The first is to do whatsoever he thinks fit for the preservation of himself, and others within the permission of the law of nature: by which law, common to them all, he and all the rest of mankind are one community, make up one society, distinct from all other creatures. And were it not for the corruption and vitiousness of degenerate men, there would be no need of any other; no necessity that men should separate from this great and natural community, and by positive agreements combine into smaller and divided associations.

The other power a man has in the state of nature, is the power to punish the crimes committed against that law. Both these he gives up, when he joins in a private, if I may so call it, or particular politic society, and incorporates into any commonwealth, separate from the rest of mankind.

Sec. 129. The first power, viz. of doing whatsoever he thought for the preservation of himself, and the rest of mankind, he gives up to be regulated by laws made by the society, so far forth as the preservation of himself, and the rest of that society shall require; which laws of the society in many things confine the liberty he had by the law of nature.

Sec. 130. Secondly, The power of punishing he wholly gives up, and engages his natural force, (which he might before employ in the execution of the law of nature, by his own single authority, as he thought fit) to assist the executive power of the society, as the law thereof shall require: for being now in a new state, wherein he is to enjoy many conveniencies, from the labor, assistance, and society of others in the same community, as well as protection from its whole strength; he is to part also with as much of his natural liberty, in providing for himself, as the good, prosperity, and safety of the society shall require; which is not only necessary, but just, since the other members of the society do the like.

Sec. 131. But though men, when they enter into society, give up the equality, liberty, and executive power they had in the state of nature, into the hands of the society, to be so far disposed of by the legislative, as the good of the society shall require; yet it being only with an intention in every one the better to preserve himself, his liberty and property; (for no rational creature can be supposed to change his condition with an intention to be worse) the power of the society, or legislative constituted by them, can never be supposed to extend farther, than the common good; but is obliged to secure every one's property, by providing against those three defects above mentioned, that made the state of nature so unsafe and uneasy. And so whoever has the legislative or supreme power of any commonwealth, is bound to govern by established standing laws, promulgated and known to the people, and not by extemporary decrees; by indifferent and upright judges, who are to decide controversies by those laws; and to employ the force of the community at home, only in the execution of such laws, or abroad to prevent or redress foreign injuries, and secure the community from inroads and invasion. And all this to be directed to no other end, but the peace, safety, and public good of the people.

READING AND DISCUSSION QUESTIONS

1. According to Locke, what powers do individuals have in the state of nature? What are some of the inevitable difficulties that arise when living in the state of nature?

2. Once individuals agree to form a government, what powers does the government have? What are its primary obligations?

3. In what ways does the treatise challenge the absolutist tendencies of seventeenth-century English monarchs?

PETER THE GREAT

Edicts and Decrees: Imposing Western Style on the Russians

ca. 1699–1723

While all of seventeenth-century Europe struggled, Russia had unique eco-
nomic and political challenges to address as a result of two hundred years
of Mongol rule. When the tsar Peter the Great (r. 1682–1725) came to power,
his predecessors had already broken free from the so-called Mongol Yoke and
had significantly strengthened the Russian monarchy. To destroy any re-
maining cultural legacy of the Mongols, Peter turned to Western Europe as
a model for reforming the customs of the Russian people. He also looked to
the West for guidance on his extensive economic reforms.

DECREE ON THE NEW CALENDAR, 1699

It is known to His Majesty that not only many European Christian lands,
but also Slavic nations which are in total accord with our Eastern Orthodox Church . . . agree to count their years from the eighth day after the
birth of Christ, that is from the first day of January, and not from the creation of the world,[1] because of the many difficulties and discrepancies of
this reckoning. It is now the year 1699 from the birth of Christ, and from
the first of January will begin both the new year 1700 and a new century;
and so His Majesty has ordered, as a good and useful measure, that from
now on time will be reckoned in government offices and dates be noted on
documents and property deeds, starting from the first of January 1700. And
to celebrate this good undertaking and the new century . . . in the sovereign city of Moscow . . . let the reputable citizens arrange decorations of
pine, fir, and juniper trees and boughs along the busiest main streets and
by the houses of eminent church and lay persons of rank. . . . Poorer per-

---

L. Jay Oliva, *Peter the Great* (Englewood Cliffs, NJ: Prentice-Hall, 1970).

[1] **agree to count their years . . . world**: Before January 1, 1700, Russians began the
year on September 1, which they believed corresponded to the creation of the world.

sons should place at least one shrub or bough on their gates or on their house. . . . Also . . . as a sign of rejoicing, wishes for the new year and century will be exchanged, and the following will be organized: when fireworks are lit and guns fired on the great Red Square, let the boyars [nobility], the Lords of the Palace, of the Chamber, and the Council, and the eminent personages of Court, Army, and Merchant ranks, each in his own grounds, fire three times from small guns, if they have any, or from muskets and other small arms, and shoot some rockets into the air.

DECREE ON THE INVITATION OF FOREIGNERS, 1702

Since our accession to the throne all our efforts and intentions have tended to govern this realm in such a way that all of our subjects should, through our care for the general good, become more and more prosperous. For this end we have always tried to maintain internal order, to defend the state against invasion, and in every possible way to improve and to extend trade. With this purpose we have been compelled to make some necessary and salutary changes in the administration, in order that our subjects might more easily gain a knowledge of matters of which they were before ignorant, and become more skillful in their commercial relations. We have therefore given orders, made dispositions, and founded institutions indispensable for increasing our trade with foreigners, and shall do the same in the future. Nevertheless we fear that matters are not in such a good condition as we desire, and that our subjects cannot in perfect quietness enjoy the fruits of our labors, and we have therefore considered still other means to protect our frontier from the invasion of the enemy, and to preserve the rights and privileges of our State, and the general peace of all Christians. . . .

To attain these worthy aims, we have endeavored to improve our military forces, which are the protection of our State, so that our troops may consist of well-drilled men, maintained in perfect order and discipline. In order to obtain greater improvement in this respect, and to encourage foreigners, who are able to assist us in this way, as well as artisans profitable to the State, to come in numbers to our country, we have issued this manifesto, and have ordered printed copies of it to be sent throughout Europe. . . . And as in our residence of Moscow, the free exercise of religion of all other sects, although not agreeing with our church, is already allowed, so shall this be hereby confirmed anew in such manner that we, by the power granted to us by the Almighty, shall exercise no compulsion over the consciences of men, and shall gladly allow every Christian to care for his own salvation at his own risk.

An Instruction to Russian Students Abroad Studying Navigation, 1714

1. Learn how to draw plans and charts and how to use the compass and other naval indicators.

2. Learn how to navigate a vessel in battle as well as in a simple maneuver, and learn how to use all appropriate tools and instruments; namely, sails, ropes, and oars, and the like matters, on row boats and other vessels.

3. Discover . . . how to put ships to sea during a naval battle. . . . Obtain from foreign naval officers written statements, bearing their signatures and seals, of how adequately you are prepared for naval duties.

4. If, upon his return, anyone wishes to receive from the Tsar greater favors, he should learn, in addition to the above enumerated instructions, how to construct those vessels [aboard] which he would like to demonstrate his skills.

5. Upon his return to Moscow, every foreign-trained Russian should bring with him at his own expense, for which he will later be reimbursed, at least two experienced masters of naval science. They the returnees will be assigned soldiers, one soldier per returnee, to teach them what they have learned abroad. . . .

Decree on Western Dress, 1701

Western dress shall be worn by all the boyars, members of our councils and of our court . . . gentry of Moscow, secretaries, . . . provincial gentry, gosti,[2] government officials, streltsy,[3] members of the guilds purveying for our household, citizens of Moscow of all ranks, and residents of provincial cities . . . excepting the clergy and peasant tillers of the soil. The upper dress shall be of French or Saxon cut, and the lower dress . . . — waistcoat, trousers, boots, shoes, and hats — shall be of the German type. They shall also ride German saddles. Likewise the womenfolk of all ranks, including the priests', deacons', and church attendants' wives, the wives of the dragoons, the soldiers, and the streltsy, and their children, shall wear Western dresses, hats, jackets, and underwear — undervests and petticoats — and shoes. From now on no one of the abovementioned is to wear Russian dress or Circassian[4] coats, sheepskin coats, or Russian peasant coats,

---

[2] **gosti**: Merchants in the employ of the tsar.

[3] **streltsy**: The imperial guard in Moscow.

[4] **Circassian**: The Russian territory Circassia was located between the Caspian and Black Seas.

trousers, boots, and shoes. It is also forbidden to ride Russian saddles, and the craftsmen shall not manufacture them or sell them at the market-places.

DECREE ON SHAVING, 1705

Henceforth, in accordance with this, His Majesty's decree, all court attendants . . . provincial service men, government officials of all ranks, military men, all the gosti, members of the wholesale merchants' guild, and members of the guilds purveying for our household must shave their beards and moustaches. But, if it happens that some of them do not wish to shave their beards and moustaches, let a yearly tax be collected from such persons; from court attendants. . . . Special badges shall be issued to them from the Administrator of Land Affairs of Public Order . . . which they must wear. . . . As for the peasants, let a toll of two half-copecks[5] per beard be collected at the town gates each time they enter or leave a town; and do not let the peasants pass the town gates, into or out of town, without paying this toll.

DECREE ON PROMOTION TO OFFICER'S RANK, 1714

Since there are many who promote to officer rank their relatives and friends — young men who do not know the fundamentals of soldiering, not having served in the lower ranks — and since even those who serve [in the ranks] do so for a few weeks or months only, as a formality; therefore . . . let a decree be promulgated that henceforth there shall be no promotion [to officer rank] of men of noble extraction or of any others who have not first served as privates in the Guards. This decree does not apply to soldiers of lowly origin who, after long service in the ranks, have received their commissions through honest service or to those who are promoted on the basis of merit, now or in the future. . . .

STATUTE FOR THE COLLEGE OF MANUFACTURES, 1723

His Imperial Majesty is diligently striving to establish and develop in the Russian Empire such manufacturing plants and factories as are found in other states, for the general welfare and prosperity of his subjects. He [therefore] most graciously charges the College of Manufactures to exert itself in devising the means to introduce, with the least expense, and to

---

[5] **half-copecks**: A half-copeck was equivalent to one-twentieth of a ruble, the basic currency unit of Russia.

spread in the Russian Empire these and other ingenious arts, and especially those for which materials can be found within the empire. . . .

His Imperial Majesty gives permission to everyone, without distinction of rank or condition, to open factories wherever he may find suitable. . . .

Factory owners must be closely supervised, in order that they have at their plants good and experienced [foreign] master craftsmen, who are able to train Russians in such a way that these, in turn, may themselves become masters, so that their produce may bring glory to the Russian manufactures. . . .

By the former decrees of His Majesty commercial people were forbidden to buy villages [i.e., to own serfs], the reason being that they were not engaged in any other activity beneficial for the state save commerce; but since it is now clear to all that many of them have started to found manufacturing establishments and build plants, . . . which tend to increase the welfare of the state . . . therefore permission is granted both to the gentry and to men of commerce to acquire villages for these factories without hindrance. . . .

In order to stimulate voluntary immigration of various craftsmen from other countries into the Russian Empire, and to encourage them to establish factories and manufacturing plants freely and at their own expense, the College of Manufactures must send appropriate announcements to the Russian envoys accredited at foreign courts. The envoys should then, in an appropriate way, bring these announcements to the attention of men of various professions, urge them to come to settle in Russia, and help them to move.

READING AND DISCUSSION QUESTIONS

1. Peter the Great looked westward for models for reforming and improving Russia. What specific policies did he institute to increase contact between Russia and Western Europe?

2. What reforms did Peter introduce to stimulate the Russian economy and encourage commercial growth?

3. How did Peter address the lingering Mongol traditions in Russian society? How did he expect the social groups within his kingdom to respond to his reform of Russian customs?

COMPARATIVE QUESTIONS

1. Locke's treatise on constitutionalism in England and Louis XIV's letter to his son extolling French absolutism both address the nature of political authority. According to these two theories, what is the source of political authority? What are the obligations of the institutions or people who exercise political authority? What are the limits to political authority?

2. How might Locke have interpreted Bossuet's political treatise on divine right? Is there room for religion in Locke's state of nature?

3. Before the seventeenth century, the nobility wielded a significant amount of power in Europe. In what ways did the absolutist monarchs Louis XIV and Peter the Great attempt to weaken the nobility? How did these monarchs work with the nobility in order to secure sovereignty over their respective territories?

4. Both Locke's treatise and the earlier Magna Carta (Document 13-2) were critical to the development of constitutionalism in England. How did each document contribute to the ideas behind constitutionalism?

Acknowledgments *(continued from p. iv)*

CHAPTER 1
1-1. "The Epic of Gilgamesh," Anonymous. From *The Epic of Gilgamesh*, translated by N. K. Sandars (Penguin Classics 1960, Third edition 1972). Copyright © 1960, 1964, 1972 N. K. Sanders, 1960, 1964, 1972. Reprinted by permission of Penguin Books Ltd.

1-2. The Egyptian Book of the Dead's "Declaration of Innocence," Anonymous. Reprinted in *Ancient Egyptian Literature: A Book of Readings*, translated and edited by Miriam Lichtheim, Vol. II: *The New Kingdom*. Copyright © 2006 by the Regents of the University of California. Reprinted with the permission of University of California Press via Copyright Clearance Center in the format Textbook. All rights reserved.

1-3. Hammurabi's Code: "The State Regulates Health Care." Adapted from *Ancient Near Eastern Texts Relating to the Old Testament*, Third Edition with Supplement, edited by F. A. Speiser and James B. Prichard. Copyright © 1950, 1955, 1969, renewed 1978 by Princeton University Press. Reprinted by permission of Princeton University Press.

1-4. "Advice to Ambitious Young Egyptians from a Royal Scribe: Rise Above the Masses, Become a Scribe!" Nebmare-nakht. Reprinted in *Ancient Egyptian Literature: A Book of Readings: The Old and Middle Kingdoms*, translated and edited by Miriam Lichtheim. Copyright © 2006 by the Regents of the University of California. Reprinted with the permission of University of California Press via Copyright Clearance Center in the format Textbook. All rights reserved.

1-5. "Hymn to the Nile," Anonymous. From *Ancient Near Eastern Texts Relating to the Old Testament*, Third Edition with Supplement, edited by F. A. Speiser and James B. Pritchard. Copyright © 1950, 1955, 1969, renewed 1978 by Princeton University Press. Reprinted by permission of Princeton University Press.

1-7. Ashur-Nasir-Pal II, "An Assyrian Emperor's Resume (Year 4: A Third Campaign Against Zamua)." From *Ancient Records of Assyria and Babylonia*, edited by D. D. Luckenbill (University of Chicago Press, 1926): 151–154. Reprinted with the permission of The Oriental Institute of The University of Chicago.

CHAPTER 2
2-1. "Rigveda," Anonymous. From *The Rig Veda*, by Wendy Doniger O'Flaherty, editor, translator, contributor (Penguin Classics 1981): 160–162. Copyright © 1981 by Wendy Doniger O'Flaherty. Reprinted by permission of Penguin Books Ltd.

2-3. "An Account of the Gods and the Creation of the World." Excerpt from *The Mahabharata*, Volume 1, translated by J. A. B. van Buitenen. Copyright © 1973 by The University of Chicago Press. Reprinted by permission.

CHAPTER 3
3-2. From *Book of Songs*. Translated by Arthur Waley. Copyright © 1937 by Arthur Waley. Reprinted by permission of the Estate of Arthur Waley and Grove/Atlantic, Inc.

3-3. Lao Tzu, from *Dao De Jing*: "Administering the Empire." "The Book of the Way" from *Tao Te Jing*, translated by D. C. Lau. Copyright © 1963 by Penguin Books. Reprinted with the permission of Penguin Books, Ltd.

3-4. "Anecdotes from the Warring States Period," extracts from *Hawaii Reader in Traditional Chinese Culture*, edited by Victor H. Mair, Nancy Steinhardt, and Paul R. Goldin (University of Hawaii Press, 2005): 143–146. Copyright © 2005. Reprinted by permission of the publisher.

CHAPTER 4

4-2. Sappho, "A Lyric Poem Laments as Absent Lover." From *Ancient and Modern Images of Sappho*, translated by Jeffrey M. Duban. Copyright © 1983 by Jeffrey M. Duban. Reprinted with the permission of University Press of America.

4-3. Plato, from *Apologia*. From *The Trial and Death of Socrates*, translated by F. J. Church (London: Macmillan, 1880), with emendations from the Greek text by A. J. Andrea. Reprinted with the permission of Alfred J. Andrea.

CHAPTER 6

6-1. Ban Zhao, from *Lessons for Woman*. From *Pan Chao: Foremost Woman Scholar of China*, translated by Nancy Lee Swann (New York: Century Co., 1932): 111–114. Reprinted by permission of the Gest Oriental Library, Princeton University.

6-4. Han Yu, *Memorial on Buddhism*. From *Ennin's Travels in T'ang China* by Edwin O. Reischauer (John Wiley & Sons, Inc. 1955): 221–224. Copyright © 1955. Reprinted with the permission of John Wiley & Sons, Inc.

CHAPTER 7

7-1. Tertullian, from *Apologia*. Translated from the Latin by A. J. Andrea. Reprinted with permission of Alfred J. Andrea.

7-5. Liudprand of Cremona, "A report on the Embassy to Constantinople." From *The Works of Liudprand of Cremoma*, translated by F. A. Wright (E. P. Dutton & Co., 1930): 243–245. Originally published by George Routledge, London, 1930. Reprinted with the permission of Routledge.

CHAPTER 8

8-2. Muhammad, "The Consititution of Medina: Muslims and Jews at the Dawn of Islam." From *Themes in Islamic Culture*, by J. A. Williams (Berkeley and Los Angeles: University of California Press, 1971). Reprinted with the permission of John Alden Williams.

8-4. Zakariya al-Qazwini, "Frank-land: An Islamic View of the West." From *Athar al-bilad* in Bernard Lewis's *Islam: From the Prophet Muhammad to the Capture of Constantinople*. Copyright © 1974 by Bernard Lewis. Reprinted with the permission of Oxford University Press, Ltd.

CHAPTER 9

9-2. Abu Ubaydallah al-Bakri, from *The Book of Routes and Realms*. From *Corpus of Early Arabic Sources for West African History*, by N. Levtzion and J. F. P. Hopkins. Translated by J. F. P. Hopkins. Copyright © 1981 by Cambridge University Press. Reprinted with the permission of Cambridge University Press.

9-3. Ibn Battuta, excerpt from *Travels in Asia and Africa*. Translated and edited by H. A. R. Gibb. Reprinted with the permission of David Higham Associates, Ltd.

CHAPTER 10

10-1. Pedro de Cieza de León, excerpts from *Chronicles: The Incas of Pedro de Cieza de Leon*, by Pedro de Cieza de Leon, translated by Harriet de Onis, edited by Victor Wolfgang Von Hagen, pp. 165–167, 169–174, 177–178. Copyright © 1959. Reprinted with the permission of the University of Oklahoma Press.

10-2. Diego Durán, excerpts from *Book of the Gods and Rites and the Ancient Calendar*, translated by Fernando Horcasitas and Doris Heyden. Copyright © 1971 by Fernando Horcasitas and Doris Heyden. Reprinted with the permission of the University of Oklahoma Press.

CHAPTER 11

11-2. *To Commemorate Building a Well*, Anonymous. Adapted from *Sanskrit Inscriptions of Delhi Sultanate, 1191–1526*, edited by Pushpa Prasad, pp. 12–15. Copyright © 1990. Reprinted by permission of Oxford University Press India, New Delhi.

11-3. Marco Polo, "Description of the World." Excerpt from *The Travels of Marco Polo* by Marco Polo, translated by Ronald Latham. Copyright © 1958 by Ronald Latham. Reprinted with the permission of Penguin Books, Ltd.

CHAPTER 12

12-1. Murasaki Shikibu, excerpt from *The Tale of Genji*, Vol. I & Vol. II by Lady Murasaki Shikibu, translated by Edward G. Seidensticker. Translation copyright © 1976, copyright renewed 2004 by Edward G. Seidensticker. Used by permission of Alfred A. Knopf, a division of Random House, Inc.

12-2. From *Okagami, The Great Mirror*, translated by Helen Craig McCullough. Copyright © 1980 by Princeton University Press. Reprinted by permission of Princeton University Press.

12-3. Chen Pu, "On the Craft of Farming," excerpt from *Chinese Civilization and Society: A Sourcebook* by Patricia Buckley Ebrey. Copyright © 1981 by The Free Press. Reprinted with the permission of The Free Press, a division of Simon & Schuster, Inc. All rights reserved.

12-4. Zhau Rugua, "A Description of Foreign Peoples." Friederich Hirth and W. W. Rockhill, *Chau Ju-kau: His Work on the Chinese and the Arab Trade in the 12th and 13th Centuries*, entitled Chu-fan-chi (St. Petersburg, Imperial Academy of Science, 1911): 111–116, 124–125, 142–143, revised by A. J. Andrea. John Manderville, Cotton MS (British Museum, 1625), chapters 20 and 30. Modernized by A. J. Andrea. Reprinted with the permission of Alfred J. Andrea.

12-5. "Widows Loyal Unto Death," excerpt from *Chinese Civilization: A Sourcebook*, Second Edition by Patricia Buckley Ebrey. Copyright © 1993 by Patricia Buckley Ebrey. Reprinted with the permission of The Free Press, a division of Simon & Schuster, Inc. All rights reserved.

CHAPTER 13

13-1. Nicetas Choniates, *Annals*. Excerpt from *O City of Byzantium: Annals of Niketas Chronicles*, translated by Harry J. Magoulias. Copyright © 1984 by Wayne State University Press. Reprinted with the permission of Wayne State University Press.

CHAPTER 15

15-1. Bartolomé de Las Casas, excerpt from *Brief Account of the Devastation of the Indies* (1542), *The Devastation of the Indies: A Brief Account,* translated by Herma Briffault (New York: A Continuum Book, Seabury Press 1974): 37–44, 51–52. Copyright © 1974 by Seabury Press. Reprinted by permission.

15-2. Zheng He, *Stele Inscription.* From *China and Africa in the Middle Ages,* translated by David Morison. Copyright © 1972. Reprinted with the permission of Taylor & Francis Ltd.

15-4. Bernardino de Sahagún, excerpt from *General History of the Things of New Spain* in *We People Here: Nahuatl Accounts of the Conquest of Mexico,* edited and translated by James Lockhart. Copyright © 1993. Reprinted with the permission of James Lockhart.

15-5. Matteo Ricci, excerpt from *China in the Sixteenth Century,* translated by Louis J. Gallagher, S. J. Copyright © 1942, 1953. Renewed © 1970 by Louis J. Gallagher, S. J. Used by permission of Random House, Inc.

CHAPTER 16

16-1. Louis XIV, from *Mémoires for the Instruction of the Dauphin,* translated and edited by Paul Sonnino. Copyright © 1970 by The Free Press. Reprinted with the permission of The Free Press, a Division of Simon & Schuster, Inc. All rights reserved.

16-2. Jacques-Benigne Bossuet, "On Divine Right." Excerpt from *Politics Drawn from the Very Words of Holy Scripture,* translated and edited by Patrick Riley. Copyright © 1990 by Cambridge University Press. Reprinted with the permission of Cambridge University Press.

16-4. Peter the Great, "Edicts and Decrees: Imposing Western Style on the Russians." Excerpts from *Peter the Great,* by Jay Oliva, p. 50. Prentice-Hall, 1970. *Peter the Great,* vol. 2, pp. 176–177. "Decree on the New Calendar (1699), from *Life and Thought in Old Russia,* translated by Marthe Blinoff, pp. 49–50. Copyright © 1961 by The Pennsylvania State University. Reprinted with the permission of Penn State Press. Excerpts from *A Source Book for Russian History from Early Times to 1917,* vol. 2, by George Vernadsky et al., pp. 347, 329, 357. Copyright © 1972. Reprinted by permission of Yale University Press.